IPv6

IPv6

The Next Generation Internet Protocol

Stewart S. Miller

DIGITAL PRESS
Boston Oxford Johannesburg Melbourne New Delhi Singapore

Butterworth–Heinemann supports the efforts of American Forests and the Global ReLeaf program in its campaign for the betterment of trees, forests, and our environment.

Library of Congress Cataloging-in-Publication Data

Miller, Stewart S.
 IPV6 : the next generation internet protocol / Stewart S. Miller.
  p.   cm.
 Includes index.
 ISBN 1-55558-188-9 (alk. paper)
 1. TCP/IP (Computer network protocol)   2. Internet (Computer network)   I. Title.
TK5105.585.M565   1997
004.6'2—DC21   97-37940
                                                                        CIP

British Library Cataloguing-in-Publication Data
A catalogue record for this book is available from the British Library.

The publisher offers special discounts on bulk orders of this book.
For information, please contact:

 Manager of Special Sales
 Butterworth–Heinemann
 225 Wildwood Avenue
 Woburn, MA 01801
 Tel: 781-904-2500
 Fax: 781-904-2620

For information on all Digital Press publications available, contact our World Wide Web home page at: http://www.bh.com/digitalpress

Order number: EY–W909E–DP

10 9 8 7 6 5 4 3 2 1

Printed in the United States of America

To my family whom I love most dearly

Contents

13 **Routing Issues   217**

14 **Security Management   235**

15 **IPv6 Architectural Specifics   253**

Preface

The Internet is one of the fastest growing mediums in history. The Information Age is expanding exponentially each day, it therefore becomes extremely important to be able to look as far forward to the future as possible to keep up with the pace. The Internet was an excellent idea and was perfect for original purpose of serving the educational and scientific community. However, the Internet was such a good idea that it quickly expanded to every client or workstation in the business community. Usage of the Internet has increased to support a world-wide community. Traffic patterns have produced a conglomerate of interactivity in many forms. As this activity increased, the amount of addressing space has become more and more sparse with time. A new protocol must be adopted to account for this growth.

IPv6 or Internet Protocol version 6 is the replacement for the current version 4. Its capacity can account for the tremendous growth of the Internet and take the global online community into the twenty-first century. As time is limited for version 4, it is very important to produce a guide to IPv6 that will both inform and educate IS managers, network managers, and virtually anyone who must be conversant with the addressing scheme of the Internet about the future of this medium.

At this point in time more and more trade magazines are starting to refer to IPv6, but for the online community to adapt to this new standard a reference must be established in this text. This text is meant to guide you through the transition the Internet is about to undergo. Adoption of version 6 is without a doubt a necessary and important step in the evolution of the Internet, but for this migration to occur you must have as much knowledge as possible.

This guide will serve as the foundation for your knowledge about the most important aspects that IPv6 will offer you. As a reference tool it explains what IPv6 is all about, and help you guide your systems to take advantage of this new Internet protocol.

Being prepared for future technologies is a very important aspect to me. It is my hope that this text serves as an invaluable tool that will help you prepare for this new protocol and give you an advantage in knowing about this technology now.

Introduction

IPv6 will become the cornerstone of the Internet in the next few years. This text dissects IPv6 into its various structural components to give you a clear picture of exactly what makes version 6 and how it will meet the needs of a growing Internet community.

We start by looking at the components of IPv6, specifically dealing with the header format and looking at the ways in which this new version handles both addressing and routing issues along your network. While looking at these factors we examine the transition from the current version 4 to version 6. This migration does take into account the issues of security, which is paramount to any secure network implementation. Our next step is to take a typical implementation that deals explicitly with your host operating systems and implicitly with your router implementations involving your networked systems.

Knowing the basics of implementation provides a good background into what exactly IPv6 does for you, next this text takes a look into the actual specifications of IPv6 itself. We see the actual format of IPv6 and the new features that it offers the Internet community. Those features are primarily based upon its new method of addressing. Its addressing and address allocation methods are key to the way in which IPv6 works. We look into various addressing formats, point out specifics in what they involve, and then provide sound methods whereby these allocations can be tested. Then we look into specific address types in an effort to determine interfaces for IPv6 address types and examine different addressing schemes on a comparative basis. This allows you to see each method side by side and determine how IPv6 applies to each one.

Once you determine your addressing needs, you can look into specific IPv6 services which take advantage of the addressing structures outlined in the early sections of this text and looks for alternative architectures that my also prove useful to your needs. Those needs may also require messaging protocols that deal with the Internet Control Messaging Protocol for IPv6 and Path MTU discovery. These issues lead to a discussion regarding both header compression techniques and packet tunneling.

With all of the information presented here about IPv6, it is understood that we are still in a transitionary state from version 4, therefore it is important to point out aspects of IPv4's compatibility with IPv6. This involves encapsulated IPv4 addresses within IPv6 as well as restricting the actual role that IPv4 addresses will have within an IPv6 implementation. At these early stages of implementation, IPv6 is living in a world dominated by version 4. It is then important to examine how IPv6 packets are transmitted over IPv4 networks and look into RIP, IDRP, and OSPF for both IPv4 and IPv6. Knowing how each of these protocols will co-exist will guide you through this transition, but it is important to take into account routing issues that involve multi-homing support and routing table size issues pertinent to both Internet protocol versions.

A key component to the goal of this text is to incorporate a detailed discussion on security management. We look into the architecture and determine aspects such as the IP authentication header, encapsulating security payload, and MD5 authentication methods. These security issues are then tied into the actual specific of IPv6. Security is also maintained through careful monitoring of this protocol's configuration. To function, configuration must involve a discussion with the dynamic host configuration protocol as well as the stateless autoconfiguration aspects of IPv6.

This text then ties all of these issues together by discussing aspects of IPv6's mobility, mapping, and packet transmission over various media types. The discussion then specifically deals with Ethernet, FDDI, Token Ring,

ARCnet, and PPP networks that are involved integrally in most every business organization transmission method. Finally, all of these transmission discussions conclude with a look into network management issues that deal specifically with NBMA, transient neighbors, and Neighbor Discovery issues over ATM.

In essence, this text gives you a wealth of management and technical information which are key to understanding what IPv6 represents to both the Internet and your company. Having a firm grasp of tomorrow's technology today will give you the competitive edge to know exactly what IPv6 means to you today and will mean for your organization in the future. I am very interested in keeping my clients up-to-date with respect to this evolving medium, and I encourage you to contact me at Telephone# 1-800-IT-MAVEN or by e-mail at: Miller@ITMaven.com

Stewart S. Miller
President and CEO
Executive Information Services

Components of a Protocol

1

1.1. IPV6 OVERVIEW

IP version 6 (IPv6) is the newest version of Internet Protocol that is the replacement for IP version 4 (Ipv4). To look at the newest enhancements that IPv6 offers, we shall begin by looking at the changes from IPv4 to IPv6.

This chapter looks at the header format that IPv6 uses and then adds dimension to its extensions, addressing, and routing capabilities. That functionality is further expanded upon by looking at the quality of service capabilities, security, and finally the transition mechanisms.

IPv4 is a fine protocol, but with the overwhelming expansion of the Internet, it is insufficient to keep up with the demand for addresses. This deficiency needed to be resolved; otherwise there would not be enough room for all of the various domain structures which exist on the Internet. IPv6 is the next generation protocol to alleviate the congestion that version 4 encounters.

The resolution is achieved by having more addressable nodes. IPv6 has 128 bits over its predecessor that has 32 bits. The expansion of this new protocol has an exponential advantage over the old one.

Expanded Addressing Capabilities

IPv6 increases the IP address size from 32 bits to 128 bits, which allows it to:

- Handle additional addressing levels
- Have more addressable nodes
- Use easier auto-configuration of addresses (now uses MAC addresses).

Multicast Routing

IPv4 is best used for unicast addressing: a single address bit pattern corresponds to a single host. Some other types of addressing are not supported as well. This is mainly because the address size is restricted to 32 bits and partly because no provision is made for specific addressing modes. IPv6 incorporates the idea of an anycast address, in which a packet is delivered to just one of a set of nodes.

The scalability of multicast routing is enhanced through the addition of a scope field applied to multicast addresses. In addition, another type of address designated as an anycast address is utilized to transmit a packet to any one of a group of nodes.

Enhancements

The IPv4 Network Address is based on the current IPv4 routable address for the subscriber for which the interface is connected. It is established by taking the high order 24 bits of the IPv4 address.

Simplified header format is achieved through a few of the IPv4 header fields have been eliminated in order to reduce the common case processing cost of packet handling besides restricting the bandwidth expense of the IPv6 header, as illustrated in Figure 1.1.

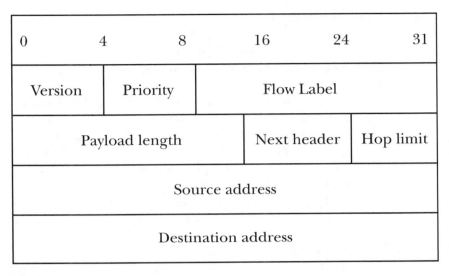

0	4	8	16	24	31
Version	Priority	Flow Label			
Payload length			Next header	Hop limit	
Source address					
Destination address					

Figure 1.1. IPv6 Header

There is also improved support for both extensions and options. There are changes in the way in which the IP header options are encoded. This permits a more effective forwarding method. There are also fewer restrictions on the option length, as well as increased versatility for introducing new options at a later time are also available for version 6.

There is a new Flow Labeling Capability which has been added to label packets which is a part of a specific traffic patterns in which the sender asks for special handling which may include either a real-time service or non-default quality of service.

The 24-bit Flow Label field in the IPv6 header can be utilized by a source to label those packets for which it requests special handling by the IPv6 routers. This includes non-default *quality of service* or "real-time" service. Hosts or routers which do not support the functions of the Flow Label field must set the field to zero when originating a packet, pass the field on unchanged when forwarding a packet, and ignore the field when receiving a packet.

IPv6 also specifies capabilities that range into using both authentication and privacy. There are several extensions which support authentication and data integrity. This can possibly include even data confidentiality.

1.2. HEADER FORMAT

In the case where greater than one extension header is employed within the same packet, those headers should be listed in the following sequence: IPv6 header, Hop-by-Hop Options header, Destination Options header, Routing header, Fragment header, Authentication header, Encapsulating, Security Payload header, Destination Options header, and the Upper-Layer header.

It is important to note that each extension header needs to appear only one time, with the exception that the Destination Options header needs to appear no more than two times — the first time prior to a Routing header and one time prior to the Upper-Layer header.

Under the condition that the Upper-Layer header is an additional IPv6 header (e.g., IPv6 being tunneled over or encapsulated within IPv6) it can be succeeded by its own extension headers. The same ordering methods must approve each header.

IPv6 nodes need both to accept and try to operate on extension headers in any given order which occurs any number of times within the same packet. However, there is the exception of the Hop-by-Hop Options header that is restrained from materializing just after an IPv6 header.

1.3. EXTENSION HEADERS

When working with IPv6, optional Internet layer information is encoded within individual headers that can be inserted between the IPv6 header and the Upper-Layer header in the packet. In addition, there are only a small number of such extension headers. Each of these headers are distinguished by a single Next Header value. The IPv6 packet may have zero, one, or more extension headers, each is distinguished by the Next Header field of the header preceding header.

Any node does not usually process extension headers on a packet's delivery path until that packet has reached the node designated in the Destination Address field of the IPv6 header. Under these circumstances, demultiplexing the Next Header field of the IPv6 header asks the module to operate on the first extension header. However, there is no extension header there, so it must work on the Upper-Layer header. Both contents and semantics of each specific extension header determine when and if the next header is operated upon.

Extension headers need to be processed in the order they appear in the packet. However, the node that receives the information may not scan within a packet to look for a specific type of extension header and operate on that header before processing all previous headers.

There is one exception to this route, called the Hop-by-Hop Options header. It has information that must be looked at and operated on by each node throughout a packet's delivery path. This includes both the source and destination nodes. The Hop-by-Hop Options header must follow the IPv6 header immediately. You know it is present by the indication of the value zero in the Next Header field of the IPv6 header.

When a header is processed, a node must go to the next header, however if the Next Header value within the current header is not understood by the node, it may throw the packet away and send an ICMP Parameter Problem message to the source of the packet. Internet Control Message Protocol (ICMPv6) for the Internet Protocol Version 6 (IPv6) identifies a code value of 2 as being an unrecognized IPv6 option. The value should be 1 as the unrecognized next header type encountered. In both cases the ICMP type value would be 4—Parameter Problem. Furthermore, this same process will occur if a node comes across a Next Header value of zero within any header besides that of an IPv6 header.

It should be pointed out that each extension header is an integer multiple of 8 octets in length. To maintain an eight-octet alignment for all of the next headers, multiple octet fields contained in each extension header are aligned via their natural boundaries such as fields that have width n (where n = 1, 2, 4, or 8) octets. These octets are designated with an integer that is a multiple of n octets (starting from the beginning of the header.)

1.4. ROUTING HEADER

The IPv6 source uses the Routing header to list at least one intermediate node to be seen along the way to the packet's destination. In essence, this functionality is somewhat similar to IPv4's Source Route options. The Routing header is designated by a Next Header value of 43 in the header just prior to it.

If, when a received packet is being processed the node comes across a Routing header with an unknown Routing Type value, the specified behavior of the node is dependent upon the value of the Segments Left field.

Should the Segments Left be zero, then the node should ignore the Routing header and go directly to processing the next header in the packet. The Next Header field in the Routing header designates that packet's type.

Should the Segments Left not be zero, then the node needs to throw the packet away and transmit an ICMP Parameter Problem, Code 0. This refers to sending a message to the packet's Source Address in an effort to aim towards the unrecognized Routing Type.

Multicast addresses (each of the set of nodes) can not appear in a Routing header of Type 0, or in the IPv6 Destination Address field of a packet holding a Routing header of Type 0 as shown in Figure 1.2.

Should the bit number 0 of the Strict/Loose Bit Map have a value 1, the Destination Address field of the IPv6 header in the original packet needs to designate a neighbor of the originating node. Should the bit number 0 have a value 0, the creator may use any legal, non-multicast address as the starting Destination Address.

Fragment Header

The Fragment header is used by IPv6 to transmit packets greater than those that would fit in the path MTU to their destinations. In IPv4 fragmentation is different, due to the fact that only source nodes as opposed to routers along a packet's delivery path execute fragmentation in IPv6. The Fragment header is designated by a Next Header value of 44 in the prior header.

To send a packet that is too large to fit in the Path MTU to its destination, use a source node, which can segment the packet into fragments and transmit each fragment as an individual packet that may be reassembled at the receiving end.

With respect to each packet that will be fragmented, the source node creates an Identification value. The Identification must be unique from any other fragmented packet transmitted that has the same Source Address and Destination Address. When a Routing header is available, the Destination Address we are dealing with is the one for the final destination.

The first, large unfragmented packet is designated as the first packet and is composed of two parts: Unfragmentable and Fragmentable.

The Unfragmentable section is composed of the IPv6 header in addition to any extension headers which must be operated on by nodes on their way to the destination. This refers to all headers (e.g., Hop-by-Hop Options

Next Header	Hdr Ext len	Routing Type: 0	Segments Left
Reserved	Strict/Loose Bit Map		
Address: 1			
Address: 2			
Address: (n)			

Figure 1.2. Type 0 Routing
Header

header or Routing header.) Otherwise, if none of these are present there aren't any extension headers which can be used.

The Fragmentable section is composed of the remainder of the packet which includes any extension headers which must be processed only by the final destination nodes and the Upper-Layer header and data. The fragmentable section of the first packet is segmented into fragments. However, the last section may not if it is an integer multiple of 8 octets in length. The fragments are then transmitted in individual fragment packets (illustrated in Figure 1.3).

Fragment Composition

Fragment packets are composed of an unfragmentable section of the first packet. It has a Payload Length of the first IPv6 header altered to hold the length of this specific fragment packet. However, this does not include the length of the IPv6 header itself. The fragment header has a Next Header value that designates the first header of the Fragmentable section of the first packet.

The Fragment Offset holds the offset of the fragment that has 8-octet units that are germane to the beginning of the fragmentable section of the first packet.

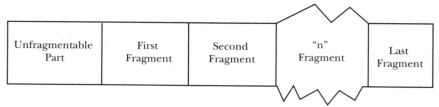

Figure 1.3. Fragment Packet

The actual fragment lengths (see Figure 1.4) need to be determined in such a way that the subsequent fragment packets meet the Path MTU to the packet destination.

When the packets reach their destination, the fragment packets are reassembled into their first unfragmented method. However, when packets are assembled there are several rules that must be observed.

The first packet is reassembled only from fragment packets that have the same Source Address, Destination Address, and Fragment Identification. The Unfragmentable section of the reassembled packet (seen in Figure 1.5) is composed of all headers except for the Fragment header of the first fragment packet. The first packet is that which has a Fragment Offset is zero. However it has alterations including the Next Header field of the last header of the unfragmentable section. It is achieved from the Next Header field of the original Fragment header.

The Payload Length of the reassembled packet is determined from the length of the Unfragmentable sections and the length and offset of the previous fragment. It is possible to compute the Payload Length of the reassembled original packet through the formula:

$$\text{PL\~Start} = \text{PL\~Begin} - \text{FL\~Begin} - 8 + (8 * \text{FO\~End}) + \text{FL\~End}$$

PL~Start = Payload Length field of reassembled packet.
PL~Begin = Payload Length field of beginning fragment packet.
FL~Begin = Length of fragment succeeding the Fragment header
           of beginning fragment packet.
FO~End   = Fragment Offset field of Fragment header of end
           fragment packet.
FL~End   = Length of fragment succeeding the Fragment header
           of end fragment packet.

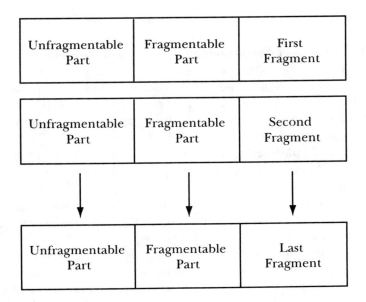

*Figure 1.4. Fragment Packet
Lengths*

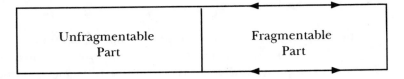

*Figure 1.5. Reassembled Initial
Packet*

The Fragmentable section of the reassembled packet is created from the fragments succeeding the Fragment headers within each of the fragment packets. The length of each fragment is determined by subtracting from each packet's Payload Length the length of the headers within the IPv6 header and fragments itself. However, its proportionate position in Fragmentable Part is determined from its Fragment Offset value. Yet, in the final reassembled packet the fragment header is not included.

Error Conditions

There are several error conditions that may occur when reassembling fragmented packets. One example is when there are not enough fragments received to complete the process of reassembling of a packet within one minute of the reception of the packet fragment which arrives first. Reassembling that packet needs to be canceled and all the fragments which have been received for that packet are thrown away.

When the length of a fragment, as determined from the fragment packet's Payload Length field, is not a multiple of 8 octets and the M flag (where the M flag means more fragments) of that fragment is 1, then that fragment needs to be thrown away. In addition, an ICMP Parameter Problem, Code 0, message needs to be sent to the source of the fragment, referring to the Payload Length field of the fragment packet.

When the length and offset of a fragment correspond to a Payload Length of the packet reassembled from that fragment would exceed 65,535 octets, then that fragment needs to be thrown away. In addition, an ICMP Parameter Problem, Code 0, message is transmitted to the source of the fragment, referring to the Fragment Offset field of the fragment packet.

Alternate Conditions

There are also certain conditions that are not expected to occur, but are not considered to be errors if they do arise. The number and content of the headers coming before the Fragment header of various fragments of the first packet may be different. Regardless of what type of headers are available before the Fragment header in each fragment packet, they are operated on when the packets arrive just before queuing the fragments for reassembly. It should be pointed out that only those headers in the Offset zero fragment packet are kept in the reassembled packet. The Next Header values in the Fragment headers of distinct fragments of the same original packet may be different. However, only the values from the Offset zero fragment packets are utilized during reassembly.

Destination Options Header

The Destination Options header is employed for purposes of carrying optional information which must be inspected only by a packet's destination nodes. The Destination Options header is designated by a Next Header value of 60 in the prior header.

Then the Next Header 8-bit selector determines the type of header just after the Destination Options header. In addition, it uses the same values as the IPv4 Protocol field.

There are two ways to encode optional destination information within an IPv6 packet. One is as an option in the Destination Options header, the other as an individual extension header. The Fragment headers as well as the Authentication header are samples of the individual extension header approach. The decision as to which method to use depends upon the type of action desired from a destination node which that not understand the optional information.

Should the requested action be that the destination node eliminate the packet and send an ICMP Unrecognized Type message to the packet's Source Address (only if the packet's Destination Address is not a multicast address)? Then the information may be encoded as a separate header or as an option in the Destination Options header whose Option Type has the value 11 in its highest order two bits. The choice is dependent upon which takes fewer octets, or which provides enhanced alignment or increased efficiency in parsing. Should another action be requested, the information needs to be encoded as an option in the Destination Options header whose Option Type has the value 00, 01, or 10 in its highest order two bits, designating the requested action.

1.5. SECURITY FACTORS

When dealing with any Internet protocol, it is important to specify the IP Authentication Header as well as the IP Encapsulating Security Payload, which will be used with IPv6. It is important that it conform with the Security Architecture for the Internet Protocol.

The Authentication Header (AH) yields both integrity and authentication for IP datagrams. It is important to note that the Security Architecture for the Internet Protocol designates the overall security plan for IP and yields important background for this specification.

The Encapsulating Security Payload (ESP) yields confidentiality for IP datagrams by encrypting the payload data to be protected. In fact, ESP utilizes the Cipher Block Chaining (CBC) mode of the US Data Encryption Standard (DES) algorithm.

All implementations that claim conformance or compliance with the Encapsulating Security Payload specification have to implement this in the DES-CBC transform. The Security Architecture for the Internet Protocol defines the overall security plan for IP and yields important background for this section.

1.6. TRANSITION MECHANISMS

One of the most important issues in this text involves IPv4 compatibility mechanisms that can be employed by IPv6 hosts and routers. This type of mechanism yields a complete implementation of both versions of IPv4 and IPv6. In addition, there is also the issue of tunneling IPv6 packets over IPv4 routing infrastructures. They are created to permit IPv6 nodes to hold on to total compatibility with IPv4. This should make the process of deployment of IPv6 in the Internet must easier. It will also assist in the transition of the whole Internet to IPv6.

The most important aspect of a successful IPv6 transition involves compatibility with a large installed base of IPv4 hosts and routers. In order to achieve compatibility with IPv4 as you deploy, IPv6 will smooth out the chore of transitioning the Internet to IPv6. This specification designates a fixed number of mechanisms which IPv6 hosts and routers may utilize in order to be compatible with IPv4 hosts and routers.

The specific mechanisms described here are intended to be used by IPv6 hosts and routers that must interoperate with IPv4 hosts and employ IPv4 routing infrastructures. You should expect that the majority of nodes in the Internet will require such compatibility for the foreseeable future.

Yet, IPv6 may be employed in some environments in which interoperability with IPv4 is not necessary. IPv6 nodes which must be used in specific environments do are not required to use or implement these specific mechanisms.

The mechanisms described above include a dual IP layer that yields total support for both IPv4 and IPv6 in both hosts and routers. In addition, there is also the implementation of IPv6 over IPv4 tunneling. There is also the method of encapsulating IPv6 packets within IPv4 headers in order to carry them over IPv4 routing infrastructures.

IPv6 tunneling is a method of creating a virtual link between two IPv6 nodes for transmitting data packets as payloads of IPv6 packets. The virtual link is called an IPv6 tunnel and shows up as a point to point link on which

IPv6 performs much like a link-layer protocol. The two IPv6 nodes play certain activities. One node encapsulates original packets received either from other nodes or from itself and forwards the resulting tunnel packets through the tunnel. The remaining node decapsulates the received tunnel packets and forwards the subsequent original packets to their destinations (maybe even itself.) The encapsulator node is called the tunnel entry-point node, and it is the source of the tunnel packets. The decapsulator node is referred to as the tunnel exit-point, as it is the destination of the tunnel packets. An IPv6 tunnel is a unidirectional mechanism in which tunnel packet flow occurs in one direction between the IPv6 tunnel entry-point and exit-point nodes The encapsulation of IPv6 packets in IPv4 packets basically employs the IPv4 network as a specialized media type.

Generic Packet Tunneling in IPv6 is indicative of the mechanism by which one protocol may be run over another. The standard IP mechanism indicates an address is associated with a specific interface [and needs to be held that a tunnel interface is not merely an abstraction. Yet, restricting the usage of IPv4 compatible addresses will ease the definition, implementation, and usage of this address form, and make the IPv4 to IPv6 transition easier.

There are two distinct methods of tunneling:

- Configured
- Automatic

Host to router default configured tunneling can be employed when the destination address is an IPv4-compatible IPv6 address. A policy decision may be established to prefer tunneling for part of the path and native IPv6 for part of the path, or alternatively to use tunneling for the entire path from source host to destination host. A source host may utilize the host to router configured default tunneling as long as the source address is an IPv4-compatible IPv6 address, the source host is aware of one or more neighboring IPv4 capable routers, and the source host has been configured with an IPv4 address of a dual router which can serve as the tunnel endpoint. Only then can the source host encapsulate the IPv6 packet in an IPv4 packet, using a source IPv4 address that is taken from the associated source IPv6 address. It can then use a destination IPv4 address that corresponds to the configured address of the dual router that serves as the tunnel endpoint.

An IPv4-compatible IPv6 address is when an IPv6 address is assigned to an IPv6/IPv4 node, which has the high order 96-bit prefix 0:0:0:0:0:0, and an IPv4 address in the low order 32-bits. The automatic tunneling mechanism uses IPv4-compatible addresses. An IPv6-only address is the other portion of the IPv6 address space. An IPv6 address has a prefix other than 0:0:0:0:0:0. A method employed in this transition involves IPv6-over-IPv4 tunneling. This technique of encapsulating IPv6 packets within IPv4 is done so that they can be carried across IPv4 routing infrastructures (the IPv4 header shown in Figure 1.6).

Configured tunneling involves IPv6-over-IPv4 tunneling is where the IPv4 tunnel endpoint address is determined by configuration information on the encapsulating node. Automatic tunneling involves IPv6-over-IPv4 tunneling where the IPv4 tunnel endpoint address is determined from the IPv4 address within the IPv4-compatible destination address of the IPv6 packet.

1.7. SETTING THE STANDARDS

There are certain types of nodes that will recur throughout this text. The first is the IPv4 only node that is either a host or router that implements only IPv4. In addition, an IPv4 only node will not recognize IPv6. The installed base of IPv4 hosts and routers that exist prior to the start of the transition involves only IPv4 nodes.

An IPv6/IPv4 node involves host or router which implements both IPv4 and IPv6. However, an IPv6 only node involves a host or router that implements IPv6, yet does not implement IPv4. An IPv6 node is basically any host or router that implements IPv6. IPv6/IPv4 and IPv6 only nodes are both IPv6 nodes. An IPv4 node, however, is any host or router that implements IPv4. IPv6/IPv4 and IPv4 only nodes are both IPv4 nodes.

IPv6 Addresses

IPv4 compatible IPv6 address is an IPv6 address (IPv6 header format shown in Figure 1.7) that is assigned to an IPv6/IPv4 node. It has the high order 96-bit prefix 0:0:0:0:0:0, as well as an IPv4 address in the low order 32-bits. The automatic tunneling mechanism employs IPv4 compatible addresses. An IPv6-only address has the remainder of the IPv6 address space. In addition, an IPv6 address has a prefix besides that of 0:0:0:0:0:0.

The notation 0:0:0:0:0:0 is that method by which IPv6 addresses are represented that is taken from the IPv4 dotted decimal notation. The address is represented as the hexadecimal equivalent of the 16 bit words that comprise the address or first 96 bits in this case.

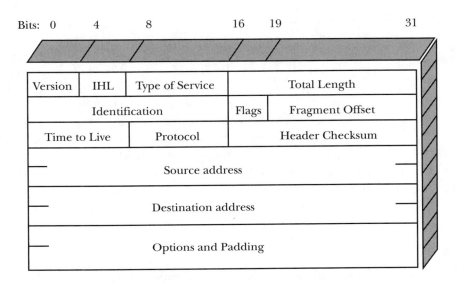

Figure 1.6. IPv4 Header

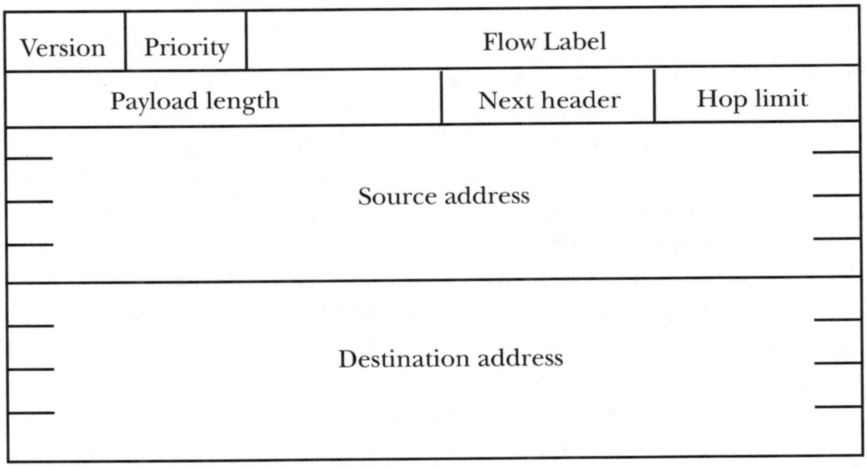

Figure 1.7. IPv6 Header Format

1.8. TRANSITION TECHNIQUES

One technique involves IPv6-over-IPv4 tunneling which involves encapsulating IPv6 packets within IPv4 in order for them to be conveyed across IPv4 routing infrastructures. One aspect involves configured tunneling which involves IPv6 over IPv4 tunneling where the IPv4 tunnel endpoint address is designated by configuration information on the encapsulating node.

However, automatic tunneling is a method where IPv6-over-IPv4 tunneling involves the IPv4 tunnel endpoint address to be designated from the IPv4 address within in the IPv4-compatible destination address of the IPv6 packet.

Addressing

The automatic tunneling mechanism employs a specific type of IPv6 address. It is designated as an IPv4-compatible address. An IPv4-compatible address is designated by an all zeros 96-bit prefix, and contains an IPv4 address in the low order 32-bits. Various IPv6 addressing formats are compared in Figure 1.8.

IPv4/IPv6 Address Format

IPv4 compatible addresses are reserved for IPv6/IPv4 nodes which handle automatic tunneling. Nodes that are configured with IPv4 compatible addresses may employ the total address as their IPv6 address can use the embedded IPv4 address as their IPv4 address.

The rest of the IPv6 address space which designates all addresses with 96-bit prefixes besides that of 0:0:0:0:0:0 are designated as IPv6-only Addresses.

The dual IP layer is the most direct method for IPv6 nodes to stay compatible with IPv4 only nodes. It provides a total IPv4 implementation. IPv6 nodes which yield a total method of IPv4 implementation besides that of their IPv6 implementation are designated as IPv6/IPv4 nodes. IPv6/IPv4 nodes have the capability to transmit and receive both IPv4 and IPv6 packets. They can directly interoperate with IPv4 nodes by utilizing IPv4 packets, as well as directly interoperating with IPv6 nodes by employing IPv6 packets.

1.8

Bits	3	n	m	o	p	125-*n-m-o-p*
	010	Registry ID	Provider ID	Subscriber ID	Subnet ID	Interface ID

Provider-based global unicast address

Bits	10	n	118-*n*
	1111111010	0	Interface ID

Link-local address

Bits	10	n	m	118-*n-m*
	1111111010	0	Subnet ID	Interface ID

Site-local address

Bits	96	32
	0000 0000	IPv4 address

IPv4-compatible IPv6 address

Bits	n	128-*n*
	Subnet Prefix	0000 0000

Subnet-router anycast address

Bits	8	4	4	112
	----------	Figs	Scop	Group ID

Multicast address

Figure 1.8. IPv6 Addressing Formats

The dual IP layer method may or may not be used together with the IPv6-over-IPv4 tunneling techniques. An IPv6/IPv4 node that supports tunneling may only work with configured tunneling or work with both configured and automatic tunneling. There are three types of configurations that can result from this technique:

- IPv6/IPv4 node that does not perform tunneling
- IPv6/IPv4 node that performs configured tunneling only
- IPv6/IPv4 node that performs configured tunneling and automatic tunneling.

Address Configuration

IPv6/IPv4 nodes may be configured with both IPv4 and IPv6 addresses since they can support both protocols. Although the two addresses can be related to each other, they don't have to be. IPv6/IPv4 nodes are configured with IPv6 and IPv4 addresses which are unrelated to each other.

When dealing with nodes that perform automatic tunneling, they are configured with IPv4 compatible IPv6 addresses. However, they may be viewed as individual addresses that can serve as both IPv6 and IPv4 addresses. The complete 128-bit IPv4 compatible IPv6 address is utilized as the node's IPv6 address, yet the IPv4 address embedded in low order 32-bits will perform as the node's IPv4 address.

The Dynamic Host Configuration Protocol (DHCPv6) yields a framework for passing configuration information through extensions, to IPv6 nodes. In addition, it yields the capability of automatic allocation of reusable network addresses as well as additional configuration flexibility. This protocol needs to be considered as a counterpart to the IPv6 Stateless Address Autoconfiguration protocol specification.

The IPv6/IPv4 nodes may employ the stateless IPv6 address configuration mechanism or DHCP for IPv6 in order to obtain their IPv6 address. This type of mechanism may yield either IPv4-compatible or IPv6-only IPv6 addresses.

IPv6/IPv4 nodes may employ IPv4 mechanisms to obtain their IPv4 addresses. However, IPv6/IPv4 nodes which execute automatic tunneling may also obtain their IPv4-compatible IPv6 addresses from an alternate resource of IPv4 address configuration protocols. A node can employ any IPv4 address configuration mechanism in order to obtain its IPv4 address, then it can map that address into an IPv4-compatible IPv6 address.

This method of configuration permits IPv6/IPv4 nodes to support the installed base of IPv4 address configuration servers. Its usefulness in arenas where IPv6 routers and address configuration servers have not yet been deployed is heightened.

The distinct algorithm used for acquiring an IPv4-compatible address by employing IPv4-based address configuration protocols involves the IPv6/IPv4 node which employs the standard IPv4 mechanisms or protocols to obtain its own IPv4 address.

These protocols include the Dynamic Host Configuration Protocol (DHCP), Bootstrap Protocol (BOOTP), Reverse Address Resolution Protocol (RARP), manual configuration, and basically any other mechanism which can correctly provide the node's own IPv4 address. The node utilizes this address as its IPv4 address. The end result is an IPv4 compatible IPv6 address with the nodes own IPv4-address embedded in the low order 32-bits. The node utilizes this address as its own IPv6 address.

IPv6 Implementations

The IPv4 Loopback Address is seen in many IPv4 implementations that recognize any given address 127.0.0.1 as a loopback address, or an address to grasp services which exist on the local machine. IPv4 packets addressed from or to the loopback address, however, are not to be sent onto the network. Instead, they must stay totally within the node. IPv6/IPv4 implementations actually see the IPv4-compatible IPv6 address ::127.0.0.1 (address representation as shorthand form) as an IPv6 loopback address. Packets which have this address must also keep completely within the node and may not have it transmitted onto the network.

The Domain Naming System (DNS) is also employed with both IPv4 and IPv6 in order to map hostnames into addresses. A new resource record type designated *AAAA* has been created for IPv6 addresses. Due to the fact that IPv6/IPv4 nodes need to be able to interoperate directly with both IPv4 and IPv6 nodes, it is required that they provide resolver libraries that are able to deal with IPv4 A records in addition to IPv6 AAAA records.

It is important to correctly work with records for IPv4-compatible addresses. When an IPv4-compatible IPv6 addresses is reserved for an IPv6/IPv4 host which handles automatic tunneling, both A and AAAA records are listed in the DNS. The AAAA record contains the full IPv4-compatible

IPv6 address, however the A record contains the low order 32-bits of that address. The AAAA record is required so that queries by IPv6 hosts can be satisfied. The A record is required so that queries by IPv4 only hosts, whose resolver libraries only handle the A record type, will locate the host.

The DNS resolver libraries on IPv6/IPv4 nodes need to be able to support both AAAA and A records. Whenever a query finds an AAAA record containing an IPv4-compatible IPv6 address as well as an A record containing the matching IPv4 address, the resolver library doesn't just send back both addresses. Instead, it has the following choices:

- Send back only the IPv6 address to the application
- Send back only the IPv4 address to the application
- Send back both addresses to the application.

The choice as to which address type to send in this case, or should both addresses be sent back in any specific order they are listed, can alter what type of IP traffic is created. Should the IPv6 address be returned, the node will talk with that specific destination through IPv6 packets or in many cases opt for encapsulated in IPv4. Should the IPv4 address be sent back, the dialog will utilize IPv4 packets.

The method by which the DNS resolver implementations support redundant records for IPv4-compatible addresses may be dependent upon whether that implementation handles automatic tunneling, or whether it is enabled.

When an implementation does not support automatic tunneling, it would not return IPv4-compatible IPv6 addresses to applications due to the fact that its destinations are usually only able to be reached through tunneling. However, those implementations which involve automatic tunneling that is supported and enabled may choose to return just the IPv4-compatible IPv6 address instead of the IPv4 address.

IPv6/IPv4 Tunneling

In many deployment settings, the IPv6 routing foundation is created over a period of time. However, while the IPv6 groundwork is being created, the existing IPv4 routing foundation can remain functional, and be used to convey IPv6 traffic. Tunneling, however, yields a method by which to utilize an existing IPv4 routing foundation to convey IPv6 traffic.

IPv6/IPv4 hosts and routers can tunnel IPv6 datagrams throughout regions of IPv4 routing topology by encapsulating them within IPv4 packets. Tunneling can be employed through Router to Router means where IPv6/IPv4 routers are interconnected via an IPv4 foundation. This foundation can tunnel IPv6 packets between the its two entities. The tunnel can reach across one segment of the end to end path that the IPv6 packet uses.

In addition, the Host to Router method involves the IPv6/IPv4 host to tunnel IPv6 packets to a go-between IPv6/IPv4 router which can be reached through an IPv4 foundation. This degree of tunnel reaches through the first segment of the packet's end to end path.

In addition, Host to Host is a method in which IPv6/IPv4 hosts are interconnected by an IPv4 foundation and can tunnel IPv6 packets between itself. The tunnel measures across the entire end to end path that the packet travels. Then the Router to Host is the method by which IPv6/IPv4 routers can tunnel IPv6 packets to their ultimate destination.

Tunneling

Tunneling techniques are often designated by a mechanism in which the encapsulating node determines the address of the node at the end of the tunnel. In both Router to Router and Host to Router, the IPv6 packet is tunneled to a router. The endpoint of this method of tunnel is a go-between router which must decapsulate the IPv6 packet and forward it on to its final destination. When tunneling to a router, the endpoint of the tunnel is distinct from the destination of the packet being tunneled. Therefore, the addresses in the IPv6 packet are being tunneled do not yield the IPv4 address of the tunnel endpoint.

The tunnel endpoint address needs to be designated from configuration information on the node performing the tunneling. Configured tunneling refers to the type of tunneling where the endpoint is explicitly configured. In both Host to Host and Router to Host the IPv6 packet is tunneled through its route to its final destination.

The tunnel endpoint is the node at which the IPv6 packet is addressed. Due to the fact that the endpoint of the tunnel is the destination of the IPv6 packet, the tunnel endpoint can be designated from the destination IPv6 address of that packet. Should the address be an IPv4 compatible address, then the low order 32-bits contains the IPv4 address of the destination node, which can be used as the tunnel endpoint address. This technique precludes the need to explicitly configure the tunnel endpoint address. Determining the tunnel endpoint address from the embedded IPv4 address of the packet's IPv6 address is called automatic tunneling.

The two tunneling techniques are automatic and configured. They differ in the way in which they determine the tunnel endpoint address. The majority of the underlying mechanisms are the same. The entry node of the tunnel or the encapsulating node establishes an encapsulating IPv4 header and transmits the encapsulated packet. However, the exit node of the tunnel or the decapsulating node gains the encapsulated packet, removes the IPv4 header, updates the IPv6 header (format shown in Figure 1.9), and operates on the received IPv6 packet.

1.9. CONCLUSION

In discussing IPv6, we must first look at the idea that the IPv4 addressing scheme is inadequate to meet the addressing needs of a globally growing Internet. One of the main benefits that this protocol offers far expanded addressing capabilities. In this chapter we have also discussed multicast routing and have dealt with all of the enhancements that this protocol offers.

IPv6 has been carefully overviewed with respect to extension headers, the exact header order, routing header, and fragment header and composition. Further, there are certain aspects we must carefully examine including error and alternate conditions.

One of the main aspects include security and how this protocol will provide a mechanism for transition from the old addressing scheme to the new version 6 method. The address format and configuration for IPv4 and IPv6 are specifically outline to foster the illustration which compares these two protocols and offers a new method to achieve an up to date method of mapping the Internet. We then proceed with IPv6 implementation and tunneling to make certain that your understanding of IPv6 is complete in this introductory section.

The next sections of this text will look at various aspects in which IPv6 can work in several operating systems. In determining the best method in which IPv6 works as the next generation of Internet protocol you can use the specifics to benefit your Internet installation.

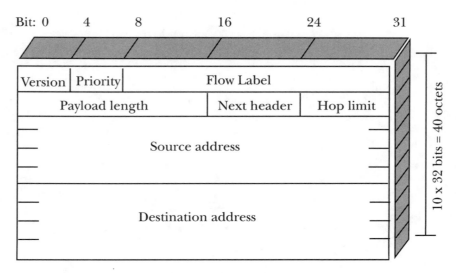

Figure 1.9. IPv4 Header Format
Measurement

Host Implementations

2

2.1. INTRODUCTION

IPv4, was created for small networks of engineers and scientists who perform mostly file transfer operations. IPv6 is the next generation of that basic
concept meant to permit the Internet to evolve to be a global, multimedia
network.

Using the existing 4 byte addresses employed in IPv4, the Internet is
estimated to run out of new addresses within the next decade or perhaps as
soon as 1998. Yet, when you take into account the sizable installed base of
IPv4 hosts and routers, it is important to create IPv6 in order to allow a
steady migration from IPv4. IPv6 augments addresses to 16 bytes in order to
permit for the enhancement of the Internet as it performs changes to
increase efficiency for both hosts and routers connected to a large scale network. IPv6 also integrates increased functionality to yield security, multimedia support, as well as plug and play capability. This level of functionality is
necessary to allow the Internet to grow even further.

2.2. ADDRESSING

IPv6 enhances IP addresses to 16 bytes from the current 4 bytes in IPv4. There are several benefits of larger addresses such as the ability to permit for increased growth of the Internet so as to enhance IP addresses to 16 bytes to make certain that the Internet won't be depleted of addresses in the long term.

There is an increased routing efficiency when dealing with longer IP addresses. It allows for assembling addresses via network hierarchies, access provider, geography, corporation, as well as other groupings. This type of collection would increase router look-up speed and decrease router memory requirements.

Furthermore, it works with non-IP addressing formats. The long address space yields sufficient area for translations of IPX, NSAP, Ethernet (components of an Ethernet network are shown in Figure 2.1), as well as other non-IP addresses into IPv6 addresses. This permits existing networks to connect to the Internet without a great deal of address reconfiguration and makes it easier for network managers to set-up, debugging, and monitor loads.

Multicast addressing in IPv6 is finding greater uses for its implementation. IPv6's new multicast address format permits for an enormous amount of multicast group code combinations. Each combination can designate two or more packet recipients. Besides that, the specific multicast address can be restricted to a single system, confined within a designated site, linked with a specific network link, or distributed globally.

IPv6 has a new type of address called an. *Anycast Address*. The IPv6 Anycast Address is a single value reserved for more than one interface, usually the property of different computers. A packet transmitted to an anycast address is routed to the closest interface that has that address, in accordance with the routing protocols' distance measurement.

Packet size optimization is essential prior to sending messages in IPv6. The source decides the highest packet size handled by all routers throughout the route to the destination. The source computer then segments the message into packets that do not need any fragmentation by routers, effectively decreasing the total load on the routers.

Multicasting decreases the load on hosts. The multicast function in IPv6 permits both hosts and routers to transmit neighbor discovery messages only to those machines which are registered to accept them. This effectively eliminates the need for all other machines to inspect and reject extraneous packets.

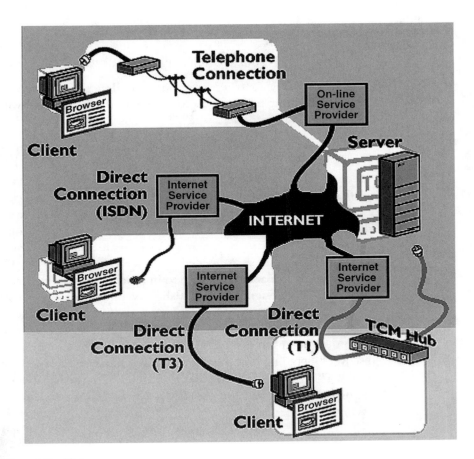

Figure 2.1. Ethernet Checklist

Multiple addresses permit route aggregation in IPv6 to have multiple addresses for each device interface. This makes route aggregation easy and quick. Should you host employ several access providers, it can have separate addresses aggregated within each provider's address space.

However, IPv4 addresses have hardly, if any, link to routing pathways. As a result, routers need to keep a large amount of tables of routing paths. Address aggregation in IPv6, however, permits routers to contain small tables of prefixes that send the packets to the correct access provider.

2.3. FLEXIBILITY

Flexibility in IPv6 is represented as two key aspects:

- Exercising control over options handling
- Permitting applications to designate the manner in which it treats unknown options

This yields IPv6 with the versatility to be augmented with new options in the future without forcing existing implementations to be forcibly updated to with regards to the new functionality. The ability to choose that routing is automatically determined (loose) or user specified (strict) throughout the entire travel route within IPv4 are two distinct methods. However, in IPv6 users can choose either loose or strict routing for each hop throughout the path. IPv6 integrates the flexibility to incorporate additional routing methods as needed.

Anycast addressing is a method in which IPv6 adds features which permit a source to designate that it wishes to contact any one machine from a group through a single address. Functional configuration is key to the IPv6 protocol for both hosts and routers who need to discover neighboring machines (neighbor discovery). IPv6 permits all the functions of neighbor discovery including both retries and time out parameters to be configured locally. This yields greater flexibility in addition to the capability of optimizing neighbor discovery for both the needs and constraints of each individual network.

2.4. UNICAST ADDRESS CONFIGURATION AND DISCOVERY

In order for IPv6 enabled computer systems (typical system configuration shown in Figure 2.2) to be able to configure itself, there are two methods in which this can occur. Number one, IPv6 can provide a stateful autoconfiguration method that is analogous to Dynamic Host Configuration Protocol (DHCP). Stateful autoconfiguration servers dynamically designate unique addresses to computers as they request them. It takes the information from a database of pre-allocated values.

IPv6 can also provide stateless autoconfiguration. This can be very important for mobile computing applications, IPv6 nodes have the power to create unique addresses by concatenating the link-local-address of the network connection it is using with an internal interface number (i.e., Ethernet or Token Ring MAC address network shown in Figure 2.3).

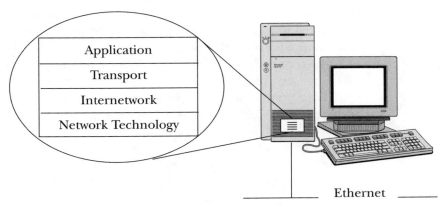

Figure 2.2. Typical System Configuration

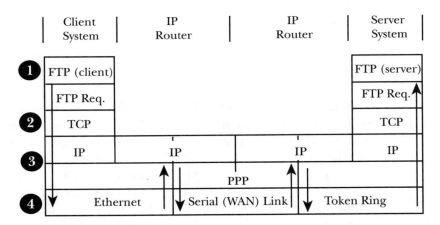

Figure 2.3. Ethernet on the Network

2.5. SECURITY ROUTINES

Due to the fact that IPv6 requires certain routines for packet-level encryption and authentication, applications can rely on having these functions at their disposal. Encryption encodes the data packet to stop any unauthorized users from viewing the message. Authentication checks to make certain that the source address was not forged in addition to checking that the packet has not been altered en route to its destination. IPv6 can also be configured to encrypt or authenticate specific data streams and automatically administer security to all communications across specific hosts. Users may also choose the default security algorithms or inquire about the use of additional algorithms.

Encryption is a central theme within IPv6 implementations, which includes 64-bit DES encryption. This algorithm uses a 64-bit symmetric secret key for packet level encryption. Users may also choose to just encrypt only the data portion of each packet or encrypt the whole packet as well as the header to ensure full confidentiality.

Authentication is a key issue in IPv6 as this protocol includes the MD5 algorithm for message authentication. This algorithm links the packet as well as the source's secret key to create a 128-bit number. Should the destination computer create the same number, it checks to see if that the message has gotten there in the same format that the user who sent the packet had specified.

2.6. MULTIMEDIA

IPv6 integrates several functions which make it possible to use the Internet to transmit video as well as other real-time data which need guaranteed bandwidth and latency to make certain that packets get to their destination regularly.

Multicast support is present within IPv6 to allow for a function that transmits messages to all hosts who sign-up to receive it. This function allows you to deliver video or other data at the same time to several users without throwing away bandwidth while transmitting to the entire network. IPv6 also incorporates the ability to restrict the extent of a multicast message distribution to a certain location, region, company, or other criteria. This effectively decreases bandwidth usage and yields greater security.

Bandwidth reservations hosts can set aside bandwidth throughout this route from source to destination. This function yields video or some alternate real-time data with an assured service quality level.

Packet prioritizing is where packets will be reserved a specified priority level. This makes certain that either voice or video transmission are not interrupted by lower priority packets.

2.7. PNP

Windows 95 and Macintosh have made Plug and Play (PnP) synonymous with ease of use. Until now, users or network managers had to manually configure each machine with its address and other network information. This method is difficult and can cause a great deal of errors for users. In addition, the process is a time consuming for network managers, and also requires that every machine be manually reconfigured in order to change network addresses.

IPv6 resolves these difficulties by integrating mechanisms which permit hosts to determine their own addresses and to automate address changes. Address discovery IPv6 permits hosts to determine their own address from a local router during boot-up. This prevents the need to manually configure addresses on each host. IPv6 also determines procedures for a host to allot an address for local site communications and for small sites without routers.

Network information discovery is something that IPv6 supports for DHCP (Dynamic Host Configuration Protocol). It allows the host to achieve all pertinent network information from a local router during startup.

Automated address changes are important due to the fact that network addresses are distributed by the router in IPv6. Therefore, if you need to change the address of the network, when switching access providers, you need to only update the router. Besides, all addresses include lifetimes, permitting the router to determine a time to switch addresses, making certain there will be a smooth transition to the new address without errors.

Support for mobile hosts is also an added advantage with more Windows laptop computer becoming powerful enough for on the road operation. IPv6 will integrate algorithms to automatically forward packets from a given base address to any other address. This permits users who are connected to the Internet from any location to automatically receive their messages from any location.

2.8. PRODUCTIVITY

Simplified headers exist so that IPv6 can make the packet header simpler by reducing it from 12 data elements in IPv4 to only 8 elements. This decreases the computation necessary to process headers and speeds up routing.

Fragmentation as well as other optional control functions are moved into Hop-by-Hop and End Destination extension headers which come after standard header. The options within the End Destination extension header are not operated on until it reaches final destination. This effectively decreases the computation needed to process IPv6 packets as they travel through each router.

2.9. HOST IMPLEMENTATIONS

AIX is IBM's operating system which now has an implementation of IPv6 running on AIX version 4.2. The IPv6 working group of WIDE project is creating three independent implementations based on BSD/OS version 2 is implementing BSDI/OS. Their goal is to yield full and free running codes and to obtain complete connectivity between IPv4 and IPv6.

Digital UNIX is Digital Equipment Corporation's operating system which has implemented a version of IPv6 on Alpha Digital UNIX. This implementation supports the Host specifications for IPv6. It can also perform as a router supporting packet forwarding and RIPv6. The IPv6 applications supported include:

- DNS Server and Resolver
- X Windows
- Altavista
- FTP
- Telnet
- Web Server and Browser
- Network debug
- Testing utilities

Implementation Background

The Internet Protocol (IP) provides the means of interconnecting millions of computers, however IP is showing the strain as today's networks trying to interconnect all of people who wish to be connected to the Internet. The Internet is growing phenomenally with regards to computer network applications. However, IPv6 will offer a greatly expanded addressing scheme, security enhancements, as well as other features that will simplify truly global interconnection.

The point of your overall implementation is to position the Internet Protocol within the TCP/IP protocol family, and define the most prominent limitations of IPv4. When dealing with the key features and technical characteristics of IPv6, it is important to determine how IPv6 will interoperate with IPv4 and then allow you to work towards migrating to IPv6 as well as how it will affect network managers and users.

IPv4 Compatibility

Due to the large installed base of IPv4 hosts and routers, the specifications for IPv6 incorporate mechanisms created specifically to foster a gradual transition from IPv4 to IPv6. IPv4 address translation is pertinent when IPv4 addresses are simply translated into IPv6 address by just adding an IPv6 address prefix of leading zeroes. IPv6 tunneled over IPv4 is also a key component for IPv6 hosts that will be able to communicate with each other through IPv4 routers by just encapsulating IPv6 packets within IPv4 packets.

IPv4 Limitations

Each TCP/IP network interface needs an individual IP address which IP routers employ to transmit packets across the various network cables that connect communicating systems. An IPv4 address is 32 bits in length and is capable of working with several million such interconnections, a number which is sufficient to handle the needs of the TCP/IP for now, but it is probable that we may start to run out of addresses as early as 1998.

IPv4 Addressing

IPv4 has a 32-bit address field that structures the networked into a two-level hierarchy:

- Network numbers
- Host numbers within network numbers

So as to ensure an addresses that is unique throughout the world, one central authority called the Internet Assigned Number Authority (IANA) assigns a unique network number to requesting organizations, where local authorities assign unique host numbers to its linked devices. In order to meet the needs of both large and small organizations to use the 32 available bit scheme most efficiently.

Unicast Addresses

IPv4 recognizes four types of unicast addresses that identify a specific network interface.

Class A addresses are composed of a 7-bit network number, succeeded by a 24-bit host number. Class A addresses are meant to be used by the world's largest organizations, each which can assign an extensive amount of unique addresses to its networked devices. With the exception of a few reserved and reassignable values, Class A addresses have been reserved.

Class B addresses are composed of a 14-bit network number, succeeded by a 16-bit host number. There can be as many as 16,384 organizations who can reserve Class B addresses, for supporting groups with up to 65,534 members (since address X.X.0.0 and X.X.255.255 are reserved — otherwise the amount would be 65,536 members.) Class B addresses are almost all reserved as well.

Class C addresses have 21-bit network numbers, and are meant for very small network communities which have a maximum of 254 connections or less. This is taken from a group of about two million possible values. Internet growth is controlled by assigning blocks of unused Class C addresses to new subscribers, in addition to re-using specific previously assigned addresses.

Class D IPv4 addresses are reserved for multicasting that is not strictly a multicast method and is not widely implemented. The Open Shortest Path First Protocol is based solely on multicast traffic and this accounts for a very large proportion of small to large IPv4 networks. Indeed those networks with large number of routers require OSPF in order to take advantage of the AREA features of this protocol. Finally, work continues with the recent introduction of the RIP version 2. It is in limited implementation success except where low demand routing in required over dial up links.

Class D addresses can be in some manner recognized by IPv4. As opposed to the other address classes, Class D address is not assigned to any specific interface, instead it designates the members of a logical group of interfaces. A packet that is meant for a Class D address will be delivered to all of its logical holders. Class D is basically a multicast addressing method, but IPv4 has certain restrictions in its implementation, and was never largely implemented in this way.

2.10. IPV4 FUTURE

Due to the fact that IPv4 can statistically handle over 4 billion possible values, the group is most definitely running out of addresses. This isn't due to insufficient bits, but results from the way the bits are handled under IPv4's simple network/host numbering methodology. IPv4 addresses lack from both squandering address assignment as well as exorbitant routing overhead.

The basic IPv4 address assignment system is not a very effective scheme. If the IPv4 methods were followed in the way in which they were originally laid out, any moderately sized organization with greater than 256 computers could apply for a Class B address, and consume as many as 64 thousand values. Any large organization could summarily consume Class A addresses and not use them to their fullest potential. In fact, that could result in the allocation of about 16 million of IPv4's available addresses.

This would have already happened if not for the TCP/IP community taking special measures, otherwise we would have run out of host numbers. Even worse, a great deal of those claimed addresses would not even be used. At this time, the stopgap introduction of the Classless Interdomain Routing Protocol (CIDR) allows for the assignment of Class C addresses in sequential aggregates to establish miniature Class B networks. This action has saved the IPv4 address pool, but this has proven to only be a short term solution until the next generation of Internet protocol can be instituted more fully.

If the original IPv4 architecture were still being used today, the Internet's routers would be jammed with the responsibility of maintaining millions of paths to Class C networks in individual locations. However, the CIDR employed an address aggregation methodology to restrict the growth of the Internet's routing tables, and extended the life of the IPv4 protocol.

IPv4 will ultimately fail in the next decade or two, making it more and more clear that the future of the Internet is in the hands of the newly revised IPv6 protocol.

Where did IPv4 Go Wrong?

The point at which the two-level addressing scheme went awry was in its inability to conceptualize what the modern network would be. It is at this point where IPv6 takes over.

2.11. NETWORK USERS

In order to see the modern network, it is important to look at the modern network user. The user falls into three types of classifications: Internet connects, non-Internet connects, and telecommuters.

Internet connects are users who work within an organization which is connected to the Internet, and are considered members of their organization's intranet. There can be millions of this type of organization all over the world, each with millions of users. Each intranet (members of the Internet) needs to have its own unique address. In addition, within the intranet, each host number also needs to be unique.

Non-Internet connects are users who work within an company that is not connected to the Internet, however, they are connected to their company's internal intranet. Millions of users exist in this situation who are strewn among millions of organizations. It is, however, a simple matter to install some network hardware and become a part of the Internet community without a problem. The difficulty lies in the number of intranet addresses that will need to change to make them unique within the Internet community as a whole.

Telecommuters are often seen as individual network users who are working from home or on the road. The Windows 95 and NT operating systems have simplified this type of connection through telephone lines or packet radio links. The questions remain as to what type of network and host numbers can be used and at what specific location. Since the user is mobile the concern is to how he can reasonably administer his address as he moves from location to location.

The problem was evident with IPv4's three Unicast address classes that were not able to map effectively to any of the above three groups of users.

Migrating to an IPv6 Implementation

The IPv6 addressing scheme is completely new, and is founded on the demographic aspects of the community it serves. In addition, it has the capability for upward compatibility from and interoperability with the existing IPv4 network architecture.

An intranet is one where an organization has its own private Internet type services but is not necessarily part of the public Internet itself. An intranet might have Web servers that internal personnel access for information regardless of what is available on the Internet.

IPv6 addresses are 128 bits in length. This structure is equivalent to the IPv4 addressing scheme squared two times—enough capacity to meet the exponentially growing demands of the Internet. However, more important is the size of the address is less important than its structure. IPv6 can understand and work with three types of unicast address including the provider based, site local use, and link local use which provide a new multicast address format and interject a new anycast address.

The *provider based* unicast addresses are designated by the Internet Service Provider (ISP) to any given organization, which offers a unique Internet addresses to all of its members that has an easy integration within the global Internet community. This was created as a portion of the CIDR, but the basic mechanism for designating these addresses through ISPs already exists.

The *site local* use addresses can be reserved for network devices that are inside an isolated intranet. However, if that company wishes to become a part of the Internet community, all of its site-wide local addresses automatically become unique provider addresses with only one administrative operation. This action is far easier than the associated IPv4 procedure, which often involves laboriously altering every address on each computer within the given intranet.

The *link local* use addresses are created to be used by individuals on one given communications link (i.e. laptop computer) users who are connected through phone lines, voice, ISDN, or packet radio links.

2.12. IPV4 COMPATIBILITY

In order to maintain TCP/IP, IPv6 needs to always work with IPv4 in both host computers and routers. However, with IPv6 implementations network administrators only need to upgrade the number of devices they can handle over given period of time. The IPv4-to-IPv6 specifications for any specific device will rely upon the vendor's implementation, migration, and the IPv6 foundation.

IPv6 is meant to work with IPv4, and this trend will continue to support existing TCP/IP applications. If a programmer wishes to take advantage of new IPv6 features he or she can port applications gradually to the new IPv6 APIs. IPv6 can also operate on the same machine at the same time with IPv4. However, unless specifically configured as an IPv6 only node, the IPv6 computer system will have the ability to communicate with its IPv4 enabled associates.

Finally, IPv6 yields a function that enables IPv6 packets to be tunneled through existing IPv4 routed networks. This ability allows system administrators to gradually migrate to IPv6 routing equipment while using their existing networks. It also allows you to use IPv4 Internet as a routing path to interconnect your IPv6 sites.

2.13. IPV6 OUTLINED

The most important factors which outline the designation of IPv6 packet headers is to have a simple methodology which avoids consuming a great deal of statically allocated but hardly used option fields. In addition, the architecture needs to permit for an easy addition of optional features.

IPv6 packet header format demonstrates enhanced address fields and small footprint. Once a packet option is needed, the next header field move towards the header extensions which support them. The simple foundation promotes a notable decrease in router overhead as opposed to the options format in IPv4.

The header of IPv6 contains the following fields:

- Version
- Priority
- Flow Label
- Payload Length
- Next Header

Version	Priority	Flow Label		
Payload length			Next header	Hop limit
Source address				
Destination address				

Figure 2.4. IPv6 Header
Format Fields

- Hop Limit
- Source Address
- Destination Address

IPv6 packet divisions will operate differently as opposed to that in IPv4. In the event where IPv4 routers can divide a sizable IP packet dynamically into smaller portions as it travels through a network, IPv6 routers will not be able to. Once the transition to IPv6 is final, the Internet will be composed only of networks with MTUs equal to or bigger than 576 bytes. While both IP packet segmentation and re-assembly are taken care of completely in the communicating hosts.

In terms of routing, the IPv6 header presents two important Quality of Service functions to the Internet Protocol:

2.14. FLOW LABELS

The flow is defined as a succession of packets transmitted from a unicast source to a unicast or multicast destination. The IPv6 flow label allows the flow's source to designate a logical succession of packets, while routers that handle this feature will be able to sustain a context for the flows that are traveling through the network. This allows for more optimized performance and traffic management, producing a faster and increasingly reliable network for users that was simply not available in IPv4.

2.15. PRIORITY

Packet Priority

Communicating hosts have the ability to designate packet priority. This functionality permits IPv6 routers to distinguish and work with TCP/IP applications that need increased response time. Applications that can benefit from this increased response time include the following applications:

- Telnet IP routing protocols
- SNMP network management traffic

SNMP does not prioritize traffic at the expense of real user's data. Instead, SNMP is a non-intrusive protocol.

These capabilities permit for several real-time network applications that could not have existed under IPv4.

IPv6 Security

The ability to offer security option is an integral part in any Internet protocol. Security features of concerns are at the router level of the TCP/IP architecture, at the point where they can take advantage of all TCP/IP applications that have been defined as extensions in the IPv6 header.

The IPv6 Authentication Header stops unauthorized hosts from sending traffic to specific locations at a point where the sender must log into the receiver in a secure manner. This extension places the burden of the authentication algorithm on those who implement the system. However, the advantage is that it greatly reduces someone trying to break into the network.

To stop sensitive traffic from being intercepted, IPv6 Encapsulating Security Header permits encryption of IPv6 traffic that is to be exchanged between two hosts. It is also independent of any algorithm, and its standard use of DES CBC encryption points towards more secure Internet traffic. Traffic can either be flow oriented or non-flow oriented as shown in Figure 2.5.

FLOW-ORIENTED TRAFFIC	SHORT-LIVED TRAFFIC
File transfer protocol (FTP) data	Domain Name System (DNS) query
TELNET session	Simple Mail Transfer Protocol (SMTP) data
Hypertext Transfer Protocol (HTTP) data	Network timing protocol (NTP)
Web image download	Point-of-presence (POP)
Multimedia audio/video	SNMP network management queries
Distribute Interactive Simulation (DIS) streams	

Flow-oriented data versus non-flow-oriented data

Figure 2.5. Flow-Oriented Traffic

The IPv6 security specification allows for the power of encapsulating the IP security payload within IPv4. This basically imitates the Next Header Payload field of IPv6. While these features are only optional IPv4, they are a required part of IPv6.

2.16. MANUFACTURERS

Digital employees are key within IETF with regards to developing IPv6 standards. Digital offers commercial IPv6 protocol stacks, for its Digital UNIX and OpenVMS computing platforms as well as for its family of high performance network routers.

Novell is creating a total IPv6 implementation that incorporates auto-configuration, mobility, security, multicast routing, OSPF, DHCP, PPP, and IPX integration. It will also handle socket and TLI programming interfaces.

Solaris 2 for Sun Microsystems Inc. is creating an IPv6 implementation for Solaris 2. This implementation will run on SPARC, x86, and Power PC machines. It involves a complete implementation of IPv6.

2.17. MENTAT IP NEXT GENERATION

Mentat, a member of the IETF IP Next Generation Working Group, is dealing heavily with the implementation of IPv6. Their implementation, MING, is for Mentat IP Next Generation, and delivers the analogous levels of performance and reliability. MING's goal is to be fully compliant with all official IPv6 standards.

MING is founded upon the Mentat TCP/IP for STREAMS and incorporates components that permit applications to utilize IPv6, IPv4, or IPv6 over IPv4 tunneling, effectively fostering an easy transition to IPv6. MING will work in any System V Release 4 (SVR4) compatible STREAMS environment. In combination with the Mentat Portable Streams, there is the added benefits of IPv6 on systems which do not have native STREAMS.

4.4BSD-Lite Derived Systems is working towards a complete IPv6 and IP Security implementation. Once more, all of the usual network applications such as telnet/telnetd, ftp/ftpd, tftp/tftpd,tcpdump, netstat, bind, route, ifconfig, discover, ping, ttcp, DHCPv6, and multicast are integrated in the implementation. Applications that have been modified allow users to take advantage of the IP Security features that are a mandatory part of IPv6. The implementation also incorporates the PF_KEY Key Management API.

2.18. CONCLUSION

In this chapter we glimpse into the IPv4 protocol, its inadequacies, and the migration and implementation of IPv6. This movement will allow for phenomenal growth in the Internet and will accommodate organizations and users for years to come. In terms of overall power, versatility, and security, IPv6 demonstrates an IP that will endure will future uses and keep backward compatibility with its predecessor as well.

We have looked into the background of IPv6 with respect to its addressing schemes, flexibility, and security. In terms of productivity, IPv6 is far more versatile and the comparisons drawn in this chapter with respect to version 4. In terms of IPv4's limitations and addressing structure, we see the need for version 6 and the reasons why IPv4 is destined to ultimately fail.

Router Implementations

3

3.1. INTRODUCTION

In this chapter we discuss router implementations for both networks and systems. We look at the dual IP layer procedure and proceed into testing of both IPv6 and IPv4 compatible addresses. The next sections deal with static tunnels, automatic tunnels, default tunneling, and automatic tunnel combinations. We finally look at security with respect to these router implementations and demonstrate how to refine your operational issues to protect your organization against information thieves.

3.2. ROUTER IMPLEMENTATIONS

Bay Networks is responsible for their version of an IPv6 implementation. Their IPv6 software functionality includes: IPv6 forwarding as well as forwarding of source routed packets, IPv6 Neighbor Discovery, IPv6 ICMP, IPv6 Stateless Autoconfiguration, total Support of IPv4 to IPv6 transition Mechanisms, configured static IPv6 in IPv4 Tunnels, automatic IPv6 in IPv4 Tunnels, IPv6 in IPv6 Tunnels, path MTU Discovery, RIPng (Dynamic IPv6 routing using RIP), IPv6 Static Routes, IPv6 over PPP, and IPv6 traffic filtering.

Digital Equipment Corporation, in its version of IPv6 routing for Distributed Routing Software, is used on the RouteAbout family of access and central site routers in addition to the DECswitch 900 family of Ethernet and FDDI switches. The RouteAbout and DECswitch products can be employed by themselves, as part of the MultiStack hub system, or in the DEChub 900 Multiswitch chassis. Digital's IPv6 routing implementation handles ICMPv6, Neighbor Discovery, RIPv6, forwarding of IPv6 packets, PPP for IPv6, as well as Static and Automatic tunnels.

Ipsilon Networks, Inc. has an IPv6 router based on FreeBSD. This solution will incorporate OSPFv6, flow id support, as well as multicast routing. The source code for this implementation will be widely available for non-commercial/operational usage.

Penril Datability Networks has complete IPv6 capability worked into its bridge/router software. The complete set of transition mechanisms will be supported.

3.3. ROUTING

One of the key aspects to IPv6 focuses on the routing aspects of the IPv6 transition. In this chapter we will look at the routing aspects of IPv4 to IPv6 transition. The methodology is designed to be compatible with the existing mechanisms for IPv6 transition.

When dealing with an extended IPv4 to IPv6 transition period, an IPv6 system has to work with the installed base of IPv4 systems. In this type of dual internetworking protocol environment, both IPv4 and IPv6 routing infrastructures will be available. At first, when IPv6 domains are deployed, they may not be globally interconnected through an IPv6 enabled Internet groundwork. Instead, they may be required to communicate via IPv4 only routing areas. However, in order to obtain dynamic routing in this type of mixed environment, there must be a means by which to globally transmit IPv6 network layer reachability information across various IPv6 routing regions. This same methodology can be employed in the final deployment of IPv4 to IPv6 transition to send IPv4 packets between isolated IPv4 only routing areas over an IPv6 groundwork.

The IPng transition yields a dual IP layer transition, expanded by using encapsulation as needed. There are several issues pertinent to routing related to this transition such as: routing for IPv4 packets, routing for IPv6 packets, IPv6 packets with IPv6 native addresses, IPv6 packets with IPv4 compatible addresses, operation of manually configured static tunnels, operation of automatic encapsulation, locating encapsulators, and making certain that routing is consistent with encapsulation.

The basic means that are needed to meet these goals include a dual IP layer Route Computation, a manual configuration of point to point tunnels, and route leaking to handle automatic encapsulation. The means by which routing of IPv4 and IPv6 occur involves dual IP layer routing. This indicates that routes are individually determined for IPv4 addresses as well as for IPv6 addressing.

When dealing with either IPv4 over IPv6 or IPv6 over IPv4 tunnels, it must be noted that they may be manually configured. If your organization is just commencing its transition this may be used to permit two IPv6 domains to work together over an IPv4 foundation. Manually configured static tunnels are seen as though they were a normal data link.

The incorporation of automatic encapsulation is useful when the IPv4 tunnel endpoint address is discovered from the IPv4 address within the IPv4 compatible destination address of an IPv6 packet. It needs a route between IPv4 routes and IPv6 routes for destinations that employ IPv4 compatible addresses. If you are dealing with a packet that begins as an IPv6 packet, but then is encapsulated in an IPv4 packet in the middle of its route from source to destination, then this packet needs to locate an encapsulator at the proper section of its path. In addition, this packet must follow a steady route throughout the entire path from source to destination.

The Dual IP Layer Procedure

Within the fundamental dual IP layer transition method, routers may support IPv4 and IPv6 routing individually. The other elements of this transition include DNS support and source host selection as to which has a packet format to transmit IPv4 or IPv6. Forwarding of IPv4 packets is founded on routes obtained through operating on specific IPv4 distinct routing protocols.

In the same way, forwarding of IPv6 packets as well as IPv6 packets with Ipv4 compatible addresses is founded on routes obtained through operating on IPv6 distinct routing protocols. This indicates that individual cases of routing protocols are employed for IPv4 and for IPv6. The packet forwarding process may be based upon static routing information or it may be gathered in an automated fashion analogous to the ES-IS mechanism that uses extensions to the Neighbor Discovery protocol.

Testing

Preliminary testing of IPv6 with IPv4 compatible addresses can be achieved but it would be prudent to permit forwarding of IPv6 packets without operating any IPv6 compatible routing protocol. In this event, a dual IPv4 and IPv6 router would be able to run routing protocols just for IPv4. At that time it could forward IPv4 packets with respect to routes it obtained from IPv4 routing protocols. In addition, it forwards IPv6 packets together with an IPv4 compatible destination address founded on the route for the equivalent IPv4 address.

The problem with this approach is that it does not precisely permit routing of IPv6 packets through IPv6 proficient routers as it routes around IPv4 only routers. Also, it does not yield routes for non-compatible IPv6 addresses. When using this method, the routing protocol will not inform the router as to whether the neighboring routers are IPv6 compatible. Yet, Neighbor Discovery can be used to obtain the solution needed. Should an IPv6 packet find it needs to be forwarded to an IPv4 only router, it can be encapsulated to the destination host.

3.4. STATIC TUNNELS

Tunneling methods are largely deployed for crossing a non-IP network layer protocols such as Appletalk, CLNP, and IPX over IPv4 routed groundwork. IPv4 tunneling is an encapsulation of arbitrary packets within IPv4 datagrams that are forwarded across IPv4 groundwork between tunnel endpoints.

When dealing with a tunneled protocol, a tunnel shows itself as a single hop link such as a router which can set up a tunnel across a network layer infrastructure. It can work over the tunnel as through it were a one hop, point to point link. When a tunnel is created, routers at the tunnel endpoints can set up routing neighborhoods and substitute routing information. In the end, manually configured points to point tunnels are operated on as though they were a simple point to point link.

3.5. AUTOMATIC TUNNELS

Automatic tunneling is utilized when IPv4 routing links both the transmitting and receiving nodes. The way automatic tunneling can function, is when both nodes are assigned IPv4 compatible IPv6 addresses. Automatic tunneling is advantageous when either the source or destination hosts don't possess any nearby IPv6 capable router. Any nearby router can include routers that are logically nearby due to a manually configured point to point tunnel or appears as a simple point to point link.

Automatic tunneling allows for its subsequent IPv4 packet to be forwarded by IPv4 routers as a standard IPv4 packet, via IPv4 routes obtained from routing protocols. There aren't any unique issues connected to IPv4 routing in this event. The issues involved with routing are those that relate to how the IPv6 routing performs in a way that is compatible with automatic tunneling. In addition, it also pertains to how the tunnel endpoint addresses are chosen during the encapsulation operation. Automatic tunneling is advantageous from a source host to the destination host, from the perspective of a source host to a router, as well as from a router to the destination host.

3.6. HOST TO HOST

When both the source and destination hosts utilize the Ipv4 compatible IPv6 addresses, it then becomes possible for automatic tunneling to be employed for the complete route from the source host to the destination host. In this event, the IPv6 packet is encapsulated within an IPv4 packet by the source host, and is then forwarded by routers as an IPv4 packet to the destination host. This action permits an initial deployment of IPv6 capable hosts to be completed prior to the update of any routers.

The source host can utilize host to host automatic tunneling so long as the following conditions exist:

- The source address is an IPv4 compatible IPv6 address.
- The destination address is an IPv4 compatible IPv6 address.
- The source host is not aware of at least one neighboring IPv4 capable router.
- The source and destination do not coexist on the same subnet.

After all of these conditions are met, then the source host may encapsulate the IPv6 packet within an IPv4 packet. It uses a source IPv4 address that is taken from the equivalent source IPv6 address. In addition, it utilizes a destination IPv4 address that is taken from the equivalent destination IPv6 address.

When the host to host automatic tunneling is employed, the packet is forwarded as a standard IPv4 packet along its complete route, and is then decapsulated. This could indicate that the IPv4 header is taken away, but only by the destination host.

When the source host has a neighboring IPv6 router or when the source and destination coexist on same subnet, automatic tunneling does not have to be employed. The packet can be transmitted in raw IPv6 form and forwarded through the standard IPv6 route.

3.7. DEFAULT TUNNELING

There are instances where the configured default tunneling can be employed to encapsulate the IPv6 packet when sending it from the source host to an IPv6 backbone. This action must have the source host configured with an IPv4 address to be used for tunneling to the backbone.

Configured default tunneling is especially helpful when the source host is not aware of any local IPv6 capable router. This indicates that the packet will not be able to be forwarded as a standard IPv6 packet instantly over the link-layer. When the destination host doesn't possess an IPv4 compatible IPv6 address, this indicates that host to host tunneling may not be employed.

Host to router configured default tunneling can be used even when the host is not aware of a local IPv6 router. In this event it is possible to decide whether the host wishes to transmit a native IPv6 packet to the IPv6 capable router or decide to transmit an encapsulated packet to the configured tunnel endpoint.

In the same way, a host to router default configured tunnel can be employed even when the destination address is an IPv4 compatible IPv6 address. This circumstance may indicate a case where tunneling is preferred for part of the route, while native IPv6 is a section of the path or perhaps employ tunneling for the total path from source host to destination host.

The source host may utilize host to router configured default tunneling so long as the following conditions have been met:

- The source address is an IPv4 compatible IPv6 address.
- The source host is not aware of at least one neighboring IPv4 capable router.
- The source host has been configured with a IPv4 address of an dual router which can act as the tunnel endpoint.

Once all of these conditions have been met, then the source host can encapsulate the IPv6 packet into an IPv4 packet, employing a source IPv4 address which is taken from the equivalent source IPv6 address, and utilizing a destination IPv4 address which is associated with the configured address of the dual router which is operating as the tunnel endpoint.

When host to router configured default tunneling is employed, the packet is forwarded as a standard IPv4 packet from the source host to the dual router which serves as the tunnel endpoint. The packet is then decapsulated by the dual router, and forwarded as a standard IPv6 packet by the tunnel endpoint.

3.8. CONFIGURED DEFAULT TUNNEL

The dual router which serves as the end point of the host to the router configured default tunnel needs to express its reachability into IPv4 routing enough to make the encapsulated packet be forwarded to it. The best method is for an individual IPv4 address to be designated as a tunnel endpoint. At least one dual router that has connectivity to the IPv6 backbone and is able to serve as tunnel endpoint can express a host route to this address into IPv4 routing in its associated area.

Each dual host within the IPv4 area is configured with the address of this tunnel endpoint and chooses a route to this address for the purpose of forwarding encapsulated packets to a tunnel end point. There are times where it is advantageous for certain hosts to choose one of many tunnel endpoints, while permitting all possible tunnel endpoints to act as backups in the event the selected endpoint is not reachable. In this event, each dual router (with IPv6 backbone connectivity) serves as possible tunnel endpoints with an individual IPv4 address reserved from a single IPv4 address block. It is this block where the IPv4 address block is designated. This may useful for either an organization administering the IPv4 in a large area, or for an organization administering IPv6 in a local area.

It is possible that there will be far less than 250 dual routers that serve as tunnel endpoints. Therefore, it is prudent to use several IPv4 addresses chosen from a single 24 bit IPv4 address prefix for this situation. Each dual router then publicizes two routes that go in the IPv4 area:

- A host route associated with the tunnel endpoint with an address exactly assigned to it.
- A standard prefix route to the equivalent IPv4 address block

Individual dual hosts within the IPv4 specific area are configured with a tunnel endpoint address that is associated with using a selected tunnel endpoint. Should the equivalent dual router be in use, then the packet will be sent to it with respect to the host route that it is publicizing into the IPv4 specific area. Should the equivalent dual router be non-functional, then the alternate dual router acts as a possible tunnel endpoint. In this case, the packet will be sent to the closest working tunnel endpoint.

3.9. ROUTER TO HOST

There are times when the source host may have straight connectivity with at least one IPv6 capable router, although it is possible that such connectivity may be unavailable. In this event, so long as the destination host has an IPv4 compatible IPv6 address, standard IPv6 forwarding can be employed for a portion of the packet's route. The router to host tunneling can be employed to get the packet from an encapsulating dual router to the destination host.

The most difficult aspect is that IPv6 routing that is needed to transfer the IPv6 packet from the source host to the encapsulating router. In order for this to occur, the encapsulating router needs to publicize its reachability for the proper IPv4 compatible IPv6 addresses into the IPv6 routing area. This method allows IPv6 packets as well as IPv4 compatible addresses to be routed via routes determined from native IPv6 routing. This method implies that encapsulating routers must work their way into IPv6 routing distinct route entries which are associated with IPv4 compatible IPv6 addresses which are property of dual hosts, which can be found in neighboring IPv4 specific areas. This necessitates manual configuration of the encapsulating routers to handle which routes will be sent into IPv6 routing protocols.

The nodes within the IPv6 routing area would employ this type of route to forward IPv6 packets along the routed path towards the router that leaked the route in the first place. Then, packets are encapsulated and forwarded to the destination host via standard IPv4 routing. With respect to the extent of IPv4 only and dual routing regions, the leaking of routes can be somewhat simple or perhaps more complex depending on the following situations.

If you look at a dual Internet backbone that is linked through an individual or couple of dual routers to an IPv4 specific stub routing domain, then you may find that there exists one summary address prefix that is being publicized on the Internet backbone. This is meant as an abstract with regards to IPv4 reachability in the stub domain. In this event, the border routers would be configured to declare the IPv4 address prefix into the IPv4 routing within the backbone. In addition, it also declares the associated IPv4 compatible IPv6 address prefix into IPv6 routing inside the backbone.

It is even harder to deal with the border betwixt a dominant Internet backbone that is IPv4 specific, and a dominant Internet backbone which handles both IPv4 and IPv6. This is one case that must have the complete IPv4 routing table sent into the IPv6 routing inside the dual routing domain. This indicates something that is twice the size of the routing tables in the dual domain. Manual configuration is needed to find out which of the addresses within the Internet routing table incorporates one or more IPv6 capable systems, and only these specific addresses can be publicized in IPv6 routing within the dual domain.

3.10. AUTOMATIC TUNNEL COMBINATION

Clearly tunneling is useful only if communication can be achieved in both directions. However, different forms of tunneling may be used in each direction, depending upon the local environment, the form of address of the two hosts which are exchanging IPv6 packets, and the policies in use.

When IPv6 capable hosts do not have any local IPv6 router, they require an IPv4 compatible IPv6 address so as to utilize its IPv6 capabilities. Therefore, there are no entries for IPv6 capable hosts that possess an incompatible IPv6 address and don't have connectivity to any local IPv6 router. These type of hosts would be able to communicate with different IPv6 hosts within the same local network without employing a router.

IPv4 and IPv6 Routing within the Domain

When route leaking is used, then IPv4 routes acquired by an inter-region dual router may have to be injected into an IPv6 routing area. This type of operation within the same area of a dual router may utilize BGP-4 for IPv4 routing within the same domain (inter-domain). The Inter-Domain Routing Protocol (IDRP) has embraced IPv6 inter-domain routing, IDRP may need to propagate the IPv4 route into IPv6 routing.

When routes are obtained with BGP and are injected into IDRP, it is prudent to preserve routing attributes that are equivalent with the routes so as to lessen the effect of the inter-region route leaking onto the routing integrity. Due to the fact that nearly all routing attributes are conveyed in BGP-4, it is important to note that they are also present in IDRP. The process of mapping BGP-4 attributes to the IDRP attributes is direct, but since addresses and routing domain identifiers are conveyed by IDRP and BGP-4. They are designated from different number spaces which need to make certain that 32-bit IPv4 addresses and 16-bit routing domain identifiers are distinct in the larger IPv6 number space. In terms of IPv4, this concept refers to Autonomous System numbers.

IPv6 domain identifiers are designated from the 128-bit IPv6 address space. In addition, IPv6 addresses with 96 leading zero bits are restricted to representing addresses assigned from the IPv4 address space. In fact, it is common to reserve IPv6 addresses to be used as routing domain identifiers with 112 leading zero bits to individually represent IPv4 Autonomous System numbers.

3.11. SECURITY

When you employ tunneling be aware that the process may breach firewalls of the fundamental routing foundation. IPv6 along with the IETF will serve to replace IPv4 for the foreseeable future. As IPv6 was developed, sets of IPv4 compatible IPv6 addresses were defined. These addresses are 128 bits in length and are composed of a fixed 96-bit prefix that holds an embedded 32-bit IPv4 address in the low order portion of the address.

3.12. OPERATIONAL ISSUES

A backbone router is a router that contains all IPv4 routes excluding the default route. A backbone router can convey nearly 50,000 IPv4 routes, as well as around 30,000 routes, that are external to the router's own network. On the internal side it can convey nearly 20,000 routes which are on the routers own network but cannot be aggregated. There are several activities accomplished by a router which have costs that are equivalent to the complete structure of the routing table. The combination of both size and growth rate of the complete set of IPv4 routes are an important operational issue for backbone networks.

In the existing IPv4 backbone, the amount of the IPv4 routing table is a critical operational decision. Even though the deployment of CIDR has extensively lowered the rate of increase of the total set of IPv4 routes, the total amount of this type of route continues to increase.

IPv6 deployment within a backbone will expand the amount of complete routes, which backbone routers need to convey. IPv6 addresses have the ability to be aggregated more effectively than IPv4 routes. The operational issues involved in the deployment of a second network-layer protocol can be mitigated. Yet, with each IPv6 routing prefix being 128 bits long as opposed to 32 bits for an IPv4 routing prefix, the total size of a routing table entry can fluctuate extensively in various implementations of IPv6 routing.

However, the process of carrying an IPv4 prefix natively, as though it were an IPv6 prefix, can be enough reason to expand the routing table size. When an IPv6 route entry is the same size as an IPv4 route entry, the router would require double the memory for the routing table. In fact this can present itself to be a crucial operational issue in routers without a default route.

The Alternative

There are three alternatives to your operational issues described in the preceding section.

- Inaction: The easiest and least invasive approach is to simply not do anything. This involves specific actions to prevent backbone routing tables from expanding in size. This solution may function if backbone operational networks acquire and deploy routers that are able to support the critically larger amount of backbone routes.
- Route Filtering: This alternative is best served under the system administrator who wishes to handle this operational issue for the purpose of filtering the routes which they receive through their routing protocols. This makes certain that IPv4 compatible IPv6 prefixes that are not allowed into the routing table and are not reproduced within that administrator's routing domain. This solution may function but may take up a great deal of a the router's resources. The only drawback to this operation is that of the forwarding rate of the routers involved in such filtering.
- Don't convey IPv4 compatible Routing Prefixes: This final option simply avoids conveying IPv4 compatible IPv6 routing prefixes as though they were native IPv6 routing prefixes. This option permits the routing protocol specifications to forbid IPv4 compatible IPv6 routing prefixes as native IPv6 prefixes. However, native IPv4 prefixes that were designated as IPv4 prefixes could be carried by a routing protocol which handles integrated routing. This alternative involves a dual stack of both IPv4 and IPv6 router which receives a native unencapsulated IPv6 packet that is meant for an IPv4 compatible IPv6 address which doesn't have an IPv6 route for that specific IPv4 compatible IPv6 address. It would then instantly encapsulate

that IPv6 packet within IPv4 and forward it in a tunneled configuration to the IPv4 destination address. This operation involves
expanded cost because of encapsulation in the outer edge routers.
In addition, it would kill any IPv4 compatible IPv6 addresses as a possible origin of significantly expanded routing tables for the backbone routers.

Due to the actuality of the IPv4 route within an IPv4 routing table, you
will find it will not yield any data regarding the next hop. In addition, it is also
capable of handling IPv6 packets, encapsulation of the IPv6 packet within the
IPv4 packet before forwarding is required. This is true except if the forwarding node has specific information regarding the next hop address pertaining
to the IPv4 route. Furthermore, it is also able to support IPv6 packets.

3.13. PROPOSAL

The IPv6 capable routing protocols specify that router implementations
cannot have the default of inserting any portion of its logical IPv4 routing
table within its logical IPv6 routing table. These outlined parameters take
into account the operational issue as well as the specifications which repel
implementers from allowing cross protocol route leakage to happen.
Should the operator of the router decide to intentionally select to leak IPv4
compatible IPv6 routes within the IPv6 routing table, he or she would find
that that action is possible provided the results are understood.

Dual stack routers which do not possess an explicit route for an IPv4
compatible IPv6 address will need to encapsulate all IPv6 packets forwarded
to an IPv4 compatible IPv6 destination address within IPv4. It may then
employ the IPv4 routing table to lookup routes to IPv4 compatible destination addresses.

3.14. SECURITY APPROACHES

One aspect that is available is to take out an operational network via improper
leakage of invalid routes. Furthermore, you can take out an operational network simply by leaking more routes than that network's routing systems are

able to support. Either of these options can occur through operator error or through tampering or hacker sabotage. Deliberate leakage of numerous routes into a network's routing system including that which the receiving network stops proper operation is indicative of a denial of service attack.

3.15. IPV6 ROUTER ALERT

Another aspect that is crucial involves the IPv6 Hop-by-Hop Option type, which alerts transit routers to carefully inspect the contents of an IP packet. This is appropriate for protocols addressed to a destination, but also need specialized processing in routers across the path.

IPv6 utilizes optional headers that enhance its ability and eliminate the IPv4 restriction on the number of options that can exist. Due to several optional headers which can be present in between the base IPv6 header as well as the final payload, increased parsing effort is required to designate the type of upper layer information that is to be present within a specified IPv6 packet. There is also some control packets that are of interest to routers. They are addressed to the same destination as those of data packets (the next TCP header is seen in Figure 3.1) that are property of a given session.

It is prudent to forward the data only packets as rapidly as possible. This makes certain that the router operates control packets correctly. The router cannot freely switch packets that hold optional headers quickly due to the fact that it needs to determine whether or not the upper layer information is control information required by the router. It is the parsing which is needed to determine this that makes the packet to move across its slow path. This path is illustrated by Figure 3.2 in a sample LAN network.

Impact on Protocols

For this alternative to produce the desired effect, it needs to be valid in protocols which anticipate routers to perform important processing os. n packets which are not directly addressed to them. All of the IPv6 packets that hold an ICMPv6 Group Membership message that needs to hold this alternative within the IPv6 Hop-by-Hop Options header of these packets. In addition, all IPv6 packets which hold an RSVP message need to have this option within the IPv6 Hop-by-Hop Options header of such packets.

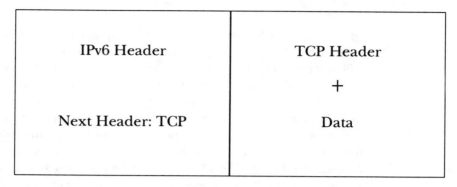

Figure 3.1. Next Header:TCP

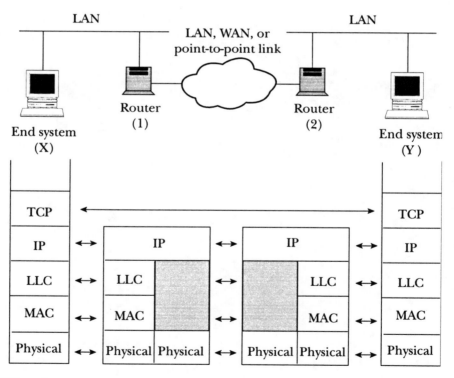

Figure 3.2. LAN Network

3.16. CONCLUSION

In this chapter we have discussed router implementations with some background on IPv6 specifically. Tunneling is then discussed in detail with specific reference to static, automatic, and default tunnels. The last sections of this chapter deal with statements on both operational and security issues.

It is important to produce the correct routing aspects for IPv6. Realizing that in the next few years we will be in a constant state of transition from the older IPv4 protocol, it is important to test the routing pathways, learn the alternatives, and plan for the issue of coexistence in the near future. IPv6 will handle a great deal more routing techniques than did its predecessor, however to fully take advantage of that functionality the conditions outlined in this chapter must be fully explored to take advantage of the enhancements in version 6 over version 4.

Piecing Together a Protocol

4

4.1. INTRODUCTION

The primary concern today is with the future direction for the replacement for the existing version of the Internet Protocol (IPv4). When choosing the next generation of the Internet protocol it is important that the specifications take into account all proposals, selection criteria, and the overall decision process. This includes specific technical information of IPv6 including the next generation transition and address auto-configuration.

4.2. ADDRESSING ARCHITECTURE

When discussing the true specification of the IPv6 protocol, it is important to take a detailed look into the addressing architecture of this next generation protocol. This chapter designates several Internet standards that track the IP protocol for the Internet community.

The IPv6 specification determines the addressing architecture of IPV6. This chapter incorporates the IPv6 addressing model, text representations of IPv6 addresses, definition of IPv6 unicast addresses, anycast addresses, multicast addresses (shown in Figure 4.1), and IPv6 nodes required addresses.

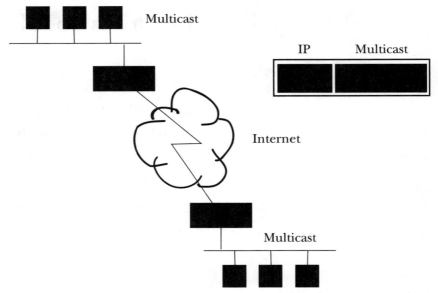

*Figure 4.1. Multicast and the
Internet*

Anycast Addresses

Anycast addresses identify a set of interfaces, usually belonging to various nodes. A packet transmitted to an anycast address is delivered to one of the interfaces specified by the address. This is usually the nearest interface, and is determined by how the router measures distance. This makes routing more efficient because the address itself can specify intermediate hops routed to a destination, rather than having the router determine the route.

Multicast Addresses

Multicast addresses determine a set of interfaces which belong to various nodes. Packets sent to a multicast address are delivered to *all* interfaces identified by that address. This is useful in several ways, such as sending discovery messages to only the machines that are registered to receive them. One specific multicast address can be restricted to a single system, confined to a specific site, associated with a particular network link, or distributed

Bits	8	4	4	112
	11111111	Flags	Scope	Group ID

Figure 4.2. Multicast Address
Format

world-wide. Note that IPv6 has no broadcast addresses and uses multicasting instead (address format shown in Figure 4.2).

4.3. IPV6 ADDRESSING

IPv6 addresses are 128-bit identifiers with regards to both interfaces and sets of interfaces. The three types of addresses include:

- Unicast: This is an identifier for an individual interface. A packet is transmitted to a unicast address and it is send to the interface identified by that address (format shown in Figure 4.3).
- Anycast: This is an identifier for a set of interfaces that are property of different nodes. A packet is transmitted to an anycast address, and is then delivered to an interfaces identified by that address. It is actually sent to the closest one as designated by the routing protocols' measure of distance.
- Multicast: This is an identifier for a set of interfaces that is property of different nodes. The packet is transmitted to a multicast address, and is delivered to all interfaces identified by that address.

Since there aren't any broadcast addresses in IPv6, their function is outdated by multicast addresses.

4.4. ADDRESSING MODEL

IPv6 Addresses of all kinds are reserved for interfaces, but not nodes. Due to the fact that each interface is the property of an individual node, any of that node's interfaces' unicast addresses can be employed as an identifier for the node.

Bits	n	128-n
	Subnet prefix	0000 0000

Figure 4.3. Unicast Address
Format

An IPv6 unicast address points to an individual interface. An individual interface can be reserved for several IPv6 addresses of any kind including:

- unicast
- anycast
- multicast

This methodology has two very important exceptions such as:

- An individual address may be designated for several physical interfaces should the implementation consider the several physical interfaces as though it were one interface when giving it to the Internet layer. This is beneficial for load sharing across several physical interfaces.
- Routers may have interfaces which haven't any IPv6 address designated to the interface on point to point links. This removed the need to manually configure and advertise the addresses. Addresses are not required for point-to-point interfaces on routers should those interfaces not be used as the origins or destinations of any IPv6 datagrams.

IPv6 expands on the IPv4 methodology in a way such that a subnet is equivalent with a link. Several subnets may be reserved for the same link.

Text Depiction

There are three standard methods to portray IPv6 addresses as text strings. The first form is designated as #:#:#:#:#:#:#:#, where the "#s" are the hexadecimal values of the eight 16-bit words of the address.

The second method relies upon the fact that it is not required to write the leading "0s" in a separate field. There needs to be at least one numeral for each field except with regards to the method of reserving specific types of IPv6 addresses. In fact, it is usual for addresses that have lengthy strings of zero bits.

This method makes writing addresses that have zero bits simpler is through the use of a special syntax available to compress the zeros. Using

"::" demonstrates that there are several groups of 16-bits of zeros. The "::" may only show up one time in an address. The "::" may also be used to compress the leading and/or trailing zeros within an address.

There is also another option form which may actually turn out to be somewhat easier when working with a mixed environment of IPv4 and IPv6 nodes is #:#:#:#:#:#:$.$.$.$, where the "#s" are the hexadecimal values of the six high-order 16-bit pieces of the address, and the "$s" are the decimal values of the four low-order 8-bit pieces of the address represented in IPv4.

4.5. ADDRESS CLASSIFICATION

The leading bits in the address designate this of IPv6 address. The variable length field that composes these leading bits is designated as the Format Prefix (FP).

Unicast addresses are different from multicast addresses due to the value of the high-order octet of the addresses. For example, a value of FF (11111111) describes an address as a multicast address. However, any other value designates an address as a unicast address. Anycast addresses are reserved from the unicast address space, they are not syntactically identifiable from unicast addresses.

4.6. UNICAST ADDRESSES

The IPv6 unicast address is contiguous bit-wise maskable, very much like IPv4 addresses under Class-less Interdomain Routing (CIDR). Furthermore, there are numerous methods of unicast address assignment in IPv6 including:

- global provider based unicast address
- geographic founded unicast address
- NSAP address
- IPX hierarchical address
- Site-Local-use address
- Link-Local-use address
- IPv4-capable host address.

IPv6 nodes have varying amounts of information regarding the internal structure of the IPv6 address. In fact, this knowledge is dependent on the role the node plays — whether it be the host or the router. At the very least, a node may believe that unicast addresses have no internal structure whatsoever. An even more complex host may understand subnet prefixes for the links it is associated with and where various addresses may have different values for x bits.

These same hosts may understand other hierarchical boundaries within the unicast address. Although it may be a very straightforward router with no conception of the internal structure of IPv6 unicast addresses, routers will have greater knowledge of at least one of the hierarchical boundaries routing operation protocols. The boundaries it knows will be different from router to router, depending upon the position the router maintains in the routing hierarchy.

Addressing Concerns

The address 0:0:0:0:0:0:0:0 is designated as the unspecified address and should never be assigned to any node. This is indicative of the absence of an address. This is best demonstrated in the Source Address field of any IPv6 datagrams transmitted by an initializing host prior to obtaining its own address. The unspecified address must not be employed as a destination address of IPv6 datagrams or in IPv6 Routing Headers.

The unicast address 0:0:0:0:0:0:0:1 is designated as the loopback address. It can be employed by a node to transmit an IPv6 datagram to itself. However, it will never be assigned to any interface.

The loopback address cannot be employed as the source address in IPv6 datagrams that is transmitted beyond the single node. An IPv6 datagram that has a destination address of loopback can also never be transmitted outside of a single node.

An IPv6 Address (header to Extension header route shown in Figure 4.4) with Embedded IPv4 Address is best seen through the IPv6 transition mechanisms. They incorporate a method by which hosts and routers dynamically tunnel IPv6 packets across an IPv4 routing foundation. IPv6 nodes that use this method to designate specific IPv6 unicast addresses can convey an IPv4 address in the low-order 32-bits. This kind of address is called an IPv4 compatible IPv6 address.

Another kind of IPv6 address carries an embedded IPv4 address used to designate the addresses of IPv4 only nodes as IPv6 addresses. The high-order sections of this type of address are reserved for registries, who then

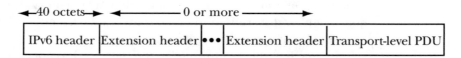

Figure 4.4. IPv6 Header to Extension Header Route

reserve portions of the address space to providers, who in turn assign portions of the address space to subscribers.

The registry ID designates the registry that determines the provider section of the address. The designation registry prefix is analogous to the high-order portion of the address up to and including the registry ID.

The provider ID determines a particular provider that designates the subscriber section of the address. The phrase provider prefix designates the high-order portion of the address up to and including the provider ID.

The subscriber ID identifies multiple subscribers who are linked to the provider designated by the provider ID. The term subscriber prefix points to the high-order portion of the address up to and including the subscriber ID.

The intra-subscriber section of the address is designated by an individual subscriber and is organized with respect to the subscriber's local Internet area. In fact, most subscribers will decide to segment their intra-subscriber section of the address into a subnet ID and an interface ID. In this event, the subnet ID designates a specific physical link as well as the interface ID that determines an individual interface on that subnet.

4.7. LOCAL-USE UNICAST ADDRESSES

There are two different kinds of local-use unicast addresses that are listed:

- Link-Local
- Site-Local

The Link-Local addresses are used on an individual link, while the Site-Local is used within a single site. The Link-Local address is used for addressing on a single link for design including an auto-address configuration, neighbor discovery, or when no routers are present.

Site-Local addresses can be employed for sites or organizations that are not now, but will be connected to the Internet. It is not necessary to allocate an address prefix from the Internet address space. IPv6 Site-Local addresses employed however. When the company connects to the Internet, they may form global addresses by substituting the Site-Local prefix with a subscriber prefix. Routers, however, will not be able to forward packets that have Site-Local source addresses beyond the site.

4.8. ANYCAST ADDRESSES

An IPv6 anycast address is a type of address that has been designated to more than one interface. This address is usually the property of different nodes. In addition, it has the property of a packet that has transmitted to an anycast address, and is routed to the closest interface which has that address. These rules are determined according to the routing protocols' ability to measure distance.

Anycast addresses are reserved from the unicast address allotment, via a designated unicast address formats. Anycast addresses are syntactically the same as unicast addresses. After a unicast address is reserved for greater than one interface, it becomes an anycast address. The nodes in which the address is designated needs to be specifically configured so that it is clearly an anycast address.

Anycast Address Uses

The anycast addresses is expected to designate the set of routers that are property of an Internet service provider. These types of addresses can be employed as intermediate addresses within an IPv6 Routing header. This causes a packet to be transmitted through a specific provider or sequence of providers. There are also alternative options that determine the set of routers that are linked to a specific subnet, or the set of routers that yield an entry into a specific routing domain.

There are few actual circumstances where complete, widespread, and discretionary use of Internet anycast addresses is possible. There are also some known complications and problems that can result when employing them in their full conceptual application. Due to this lack of real world experience with possible difficulties, the following limitations have been placed on IPv6 anycast addresses:

- An anycast address cannot be employed as the source address of an IPv6 packet.
- An anycast address cannot be designated to an IPv6 host. Specifically, it can be designated to an IPv6 router only.

The Subnet-Router anycast address has a designated format that includes the subnet prefix. The prefix that determines a particular association exists within the anycast address. This type of anycast address is syntactically indistinguishable from a unicast address for an interface on the association with the interface identifier (e.g., IEEE MAC address) configured to 0.

Packets transmitted to the Subnet-Router anycast address will be sent to one router on the subnet. The routers are necessary to maintain the Subnet-Router anycast addresses for the subnets that have interfaces.

The Subnet-Router anycast address is utilized for applications in which a node requires the ability to communicate with one of a set of routers on a remote subnet. This is especially useful if a mobile host requires the ability to communicate with one of the mobile agents on its home subnet.

4.9. MULTICAST ADDRESSES

An IPv6 multicast address is an identifier for an aggregate of nodes. The node may be the property of any amount of multicast aggregates. Simply put, a multicast address is the property of a group of nodes.

4.10. REQUIRED ADDRESSES

A host must be able to recognize these addresses as identifying itself:

- Link-Local Address for each individual interface
- Designated Unicast Addresses
- Loopback Address

- All Nodes Multicast Address
- Solicited Node Multicast Address for each of designated unicast and anycast addresses
- Multicast Addresses of all other groups to which the node belongs.

A router needs to recognize the following addresses as identifying itself:

- Link-Local Address for each interface
- Designated Unicast Addresses
- Loopback Address
- Subnet-Router anycast addresses for the links it has interfaces
- Other Anycast addresses with which the router has been configured
- All Nodes Multicast Address
- All Router Multicast Address
- Solicited Node Multicast Address for each of its designated unicast and anycast addresses
- Multicast Addresses of all other aggregates which are property of the router.

The only address prefixes that need to be determined within an implementation include:

- Unspecified Address
- Loopback Address
- Multicast Prefix (FF)
- Local-Use Prefixes (Link-Local and Site-Local)
- Pre-Defined Multicast Addresses
- IPv4Compatible Prefixes

Any implementation needs to take into account that all other addresses are unicast unless precisely configured as an anycast address.

Testing Address Allocation

The address format for the IPv6 test address (consistent with the provider-based unicast address allocation 'PRVD') is compatible with the provider unicast address allocation. The current autonomous system number is designated as the provider yielding Internet service to the IPv6 testers organization. The values for the autonomous system number of an organization's provider can be achieved from a specific provider, or can be looked up in the whois database maintained by internic.net.

4.11. IPV4 ADDRESS

The IPv4 address is a network address based upon the existing IPv4 routable address for the subscriber for whom the interface is connected. It is established by taking the high order 24 bits of the IPv4 address.

This method by which values are created for this field only works for subscribers which have IPv4 subscriber prefixes less than or equal to 24 bits length. When there are subscribers who employ IPv4 addresses with longer subscriber prefixes, this may prove to be a conflict but only under unusual circumstances. Subscribers with subscriber prefixes bigger than 24 bits should employ the leftover bits in the IPv4 prefix as the high order bits in the Subnet Address field.

4.12. SUBNET

The Subnet ID designates a particular physical link on which the interface is situated. There can be several subnets on the same physical link. A distinct subnet is not able to reach across multiple physical links. Designating values for this field is the responsibility of each subscriber. A choice can involve an algorithm to create values for this field to use the bits in the IPv4 address, which determines the IPv4 subnet. The subnet cannot span multiple physical links. The IPv4 specification does make particular reference for multi-homed hosts.

Interface ID

This is the singular identifier of the interface on the link. It often corresponds to the 48-bit IEEE 802 MAC address of the interface.

4.13. ADDRESS RESOLUTION

Address resolution is the means by which a node designates the link-layer address of a neighbor only by knowing its IP address. Address resolution is accomplished only on addresses that are designated to on the same link and for which the sender is not aware of a corresponding link-layer address. Address resolution is not, however, executed on multicast addresses. The IPvX address sends multicast packets at the link-layer. (Address resolution does not take place for multicast addresses.)

4.14. INTERFACE INITIALIZATION

Once a multicast capable interface is enabled, the node needs to connect to all multicast address nodes on that interface. In addition, the solicited node multicast address is the same as each of the IP addresses on that interface.

The set of addresses given to an interface may vary over a period of time. New addresses may be added and previous addresses may be eliminated. The node needs to connect and abandon the solicited node multicast address analogous to the new and old addresses. Remember that several unicast addresses may map into the same solicited node multicast address. However, a node cannot leave the solicited node multicast group until all designated addresses analogous to that multicast address have been eliminated.

4.15. TRANSMITTING NEIGHBOR SOLICITATIONS

When a node transmits a unicast packet to a neighbor, it is not aware of the neighbor's link-layer address, but does enable address resolution. In terms of multicast-capable interfaces (that involve establishing a Neighbor Cache entry in the incomplete state and sending a Neighbor Solicitation message marked for the neighbor) the solicitation is transmitted to the solicited-node multicast address in the same way as the marked address.

The source address of the packet initiating the solicitation is analogous to one of the addresses designated to the outgoing interface. This address needs to be placed in the IP Source Address of the outgoing solicitation.

However, any of these addresses dedicated to the interface needs to be employed. When you use an initiating packet's source address, this makes certain that the recipient of the Neighbor Solicitation installs the IP address in its Neighbor Cache which is most likely to be used in succeeding return traffic that is property of the prompting packet's connection.

When the solicitation is sent to a solicited node multicast one event happens but in other events the same event can happen as well. The Source Link-Layer Address option contains the link-layer address of the sender of the packet. It is used in the Neighbor Solicitation, Router Solicitation, and Router Advertisement packets. The Target Link-Layer Address option has the link-layer address of the target. It is employed in Neighbor Advertisement and Redirect packets. These options need to be quietly ignored for other Neighbor Discovery messages.

In any other event, it must have its link-layer address as a Source Link-Layer Address option. This incorporates the source link-layer address in a multicast solicitation, as it is needed to provide the target an address to where it can send the Neighbor Advertisement.

As you wait for address resolution to be processed, the sender needs retain a small queue of packets waiting for address resolution to finish for each neighbor. The queue is required to contain one or more packets and can hold more. The number of queued packets per neighbor, if possible, needs to be limited to a minimal value. When a queue overflows, the new item needs to replace the oldest entry. When address resolution finishes, the nodes send out any queued packets.

Neighbor Solicitations

A proper Neighbor Solicitation is where the Target Address isn't a unicast or anycast address designated to the receiving interface. As soon as the recipient receives a valid Neighbor Solicitation targeted at the node, it needs to update the Neighbor Cache entry for the IP Source Address of the solicitation so long as the Source Address isn't the unspecified address. Should an entry not exist, the node is required to create a new entry and set its reachability state to "stale."

When a cache entry does exist, it is updated with a different link-layer address and its reachability state then needs be set to "stale." If the solicitation has a Source Link-Layer Address option, the entry's cached link-layer address needs to be replaced with the one in the solicitation.

When the Source Address is the unspecified address, the node cannot create or update the Neighbor Cache entry. However, once updates to the Neighbor Cache are complete, the node transmits a Neighbor Advertisement response.

Solicited Neighbor Advertisements

When a node transmits a Neighbor Advertisement it is because a valid Neighbor Solicitation points to one of the node's designated addresses. The Target Address of the advertisement is duplicated from the Target Address of the solicitation. Should the solicitation's IP Destination Address be a unicast or anycast address, the Target Link-Layer Address option is not to be included. However, the neighboring node's cached value needs to be current to allow for a solicitation to have been received. Should the solicitation's IP Destination Address be a solicited-node multicast address, the Target Link-Layer option needs to be integrated in the advertisement.

Should the Target Address be either an anycast address or a unicast address (where the node is supplying proxy service or if Target Link-Layer Address option is not incorporated in the outgoing advertisement) the Override flag must be set to 0. If it is not, it must be set to 1. The correct setting of the Override flag makes certain that nodes yield preference to non-proxy advertisements, even when they are received after proxy advertisements.

Should the source of the solicitation be an unspecified address, the node needs to set the Solicited flag to 0 and multicast the advertisement to the all-nodes address. If this does not happen, the node needs to set the Solicited flag to 1 and unicast the advertisement to the Source Address of the solicitation.

Neighbor Advertisements

When either means of solicitation or unsolicitation receives a valid Neighbor Advertisement, the Neighbor Cache is inspected for the target's entry. Should no entry exist, the advertisement must be silently discarded. It is not necessary to create an entry in this event due to the fact that the recipient has not prompted any communication with the target.

When the correct Neighbor Cache entry has been found, the particular actions that are involved are dependent upon the state of the Neighbor Cache entry as well as the flags in the advertisement. Should a cached link-layer address already be available, a node may instead decide to ignore the received advertisement and proceed using the cached link-layer address.

Should the target's Neighbor Cache entry be in the "incomplete" state, the receiving node records the link-layer address in the Neighbor Cache entry and transmits any packets queued for the neighbor which is waiting for address resolution. Should the Solicited flag be set, the reachability state for the neighbor needs be set to "reachable," if it is not it will need to be set to "stale."

If the target's Neighbor Cache entry is a state other than "incomplete" at the time which the advertisement is received, the advertisement's Override flag's setting designates whether the Target Link-Layer Address option substitutes for the cached address. Should the Override flag be set, the receiving node is required to install the link-layer address into its cache. Should the flag be 0, the receiving node will not install the link-layer address into its cache. An advertisement's sender sets the Override flag at the time when it wants its Target Link-Layer Address option to substitute the cached value in Neighbor Cache entries, despite their current contents.

Should the target's Neighbor Cache entry be in any state other than "incomplete" at the time in which the advertisement is received, the advertisement's Solicited flag setting designates what the entry's new state needs to be. Should the Solicited flag be set, the entry's state is must be set to "reachable." Should the flag read 0, the entry's state needs to be set to "stale."

An advertisement's Solicited flag may only be set if the advertisement is a response to a Neighbor Solicitation. Due to the fact that Neighbor Unreachability Solicitations are sent to the cached link-layer address, a receipt of a solicited advertisement designates that the forward path is operational. Yet, receipt of an unsolicited advertisement indicates that a neighbor has urgent information to broadcast such as a changed link-layer address.

Regardless, if the new link-layer address is installed in the cache, a node needs to verify the reachability of the path it is currently working with when it transmits the next packet. In this way, it can easily locate a working path if the existing path has ceased due to an event such as an unsolicited Neighbor Advertisement being sent to announce a link-layer address change.

When the cached link-layer address is updated, the receiving node needs to inspect the Router flag in the received advertisement. It can then update the Router flag in the Neighbor Cache entry to illustrate whether the node is a host or router. The neighbor had been used as a router previously, yet the advertisement's Router flag is now set to 0. The node needs to remove that router from the Default Router List and update the Destination Cache entries for all destinations that employ that neighbor as a router.

Unsolicited Neighbor Advertisements

During the times at which a node is able to decide that its link-layer address has been altered as in the case of a hot swap of an interface card, it can decide to communicate to its neighbors the new link-layer address. In this event, a node can send up to the maximum of unsolicited Neighbor Advertisement messages to the all-nodes multicast address.

The Target Address field within an unsolicited advertisement is set to an IP address of the interface, while the Target Link-Layer Address option is furnished with the new link-layer address. The Solicited flag needs to be set to 0, so as to avoid disorienting the Neighbor Unreachability Detection algorithm. Should the node be a router, it needs to set the Router flag to 1, if it does not it needs to set it to 0. The Override flag can be set to either 0 or 1. Regardless of the case, the neighboring nodes will instantly change the state of their Neighbor Cache entries for the Target Address to "stale." This causes them to verify the path for reachability.

Should the Override flag be set to 1, neighboring nodes will install the new link-layer address in their caches. If not, they will disregard the new link-layer address, selecting to look for the cached address.

A node that has several IP addresses designated to an interface which can multicast a separate Neighbor Advertisement per each address. In this event, the node can interject a minimal delay between the sending of each advertisement to decrease the likelihood of the advertisements being lost due to congestion.

In addition, proxies can multicast Neighbor Advertisements when its link-layer address is altered or when it is configured to proxy for an address. If there are several nodes which yield proxy services for the same set of addresses the proxies need to support a means by which it stops several

IP Priorities for Congestion-Controlled Traffic
0 no specific priority
1 background traffic (news)
2 unattended data transfer (e-mail)
3 reserved
4 attended bulk transfer (FTP)
5 reserved
6 interactive traffic (telnet, windowing)
7 control traffic (routing, network management)

Figure 4.5. Congestion-Controlled Priorities

proxies from multicasting advertisements for any one given address. This is primarily to decrease the likelihood of exorbitant multicast traffic. Furthermore, if a node is the property of an anycast address, it can multicast unsolicited Neighbor Advertisements for the anycast address while the node's link-layer address is altered.

Due to the fact that unsolicited Neighbor Advertisements cannot reliably update caches in all nodes, they need only be looked upon as a performance optimization to briskly update the caches in the majority neighbors. The Neighbor Unreachability Detection algorithm makes certain that all nodes acquire a reachable link-layer address. The only drawback is that the delay may be somewhat lengthier.

Neighbor Advertisements for Anycast

Due to the fact that an anycast address is syntactically analogous to a unicast address, nodes operating on address resolution or Neighbor Unreachability Detection on an anycast address look at it as though it were a unicast address without any abnormal processing occurring.

Should the nodes have an anycast address designation to an interface, they are looked upon as though they were unicast addresses except for two points.

- Neighbor Advertisements transmitted in response to a Neighbor Solicitation need to be delayed by a random time between 0 and the maximum delay time in order to reduce the likelihood of network congestion.
- The override flag in Neighbor Advertisements needs to be set to 0. In this way, when several advertisements are received, the first received advertisement is used first as opposed to using the most recently received advertisement first. In essence first come first served.

Note that Neighbor Unreachability Detection (just as with unicast addresses) makes certain that a node rapidly detects when the current binding for an anycast address is invalid.

The Proxy Neighbor Advertisements

In some restricted cases, routers can proxy for other node(s). This happens through Neighbor Advertisements that are indicative of its willingness to accept packets which are not specifically addressed to itself. In fact, a router may accept packets for a mobile node which has moved off link. This method is used by proxy, and is analogous to the means used with anycast addresses.

A proxy needs to connect to the solicited-node multicast address that concurs with the IP address designated for that node that it is proxying for.

Any solicited proxy Neighbor Advertisement messages are required to have the Override flag set to 0. This makes certain that should the node itself be present on the link, its Neighbor Advertisement which has the Override flag set to 1 will have priority over any advertisement received from a proxy. A proxy can send unsolicited advertisements with the Override flag set to 1, however this may make the proxy advertisement override a valid entry established by the node itself.

4.16. CONCLUSION

Addressing allocation is a key concept in the IP version 6 protocol. The architecture, addressing, and the overall model are exceedingly crucial aspects to understanding IPv6 and how it functions. Unicast and multicast addresses explain specifics regarding how packets are handled and give a more detailed look into the various aspects and methods by which IPv6 operates.

The IPv6 addressing architecture is covered in this chapter along with unicast, anycast, and multicast types of addressing. Various address classifications are specified with NSAP, IPX, Site-Local, and Link-Local types of addresses. This section continues with a discussion about solicited neighbor advertisements, unsolicited neighbor advertisements, and proxy neighbor advertisements.

Finally, we look at some aspects of neighbor discovery and the way in which IPv6 handles communication aspects. We see the actual architecture described in the preceding section of this chapter put to use in its ability to use its addressing to talk with its neighbors and link the aspects of IPv6 together.

Internet Protocol Addressing

5

5.1. INTRODUCTION

This chapter deals with the architecture used in allocating IPv6 unicast addresses in the Internet. The Internet can be conceptualized as a collection of hosts interconnected through transmission and switching facilities. The control over the aggregate of hosts, transmission, and switching facilities is what constitutes the networking resources of the Internet. This is not a homogeneous mix, but it is distributed throughout several administrative powers.

Domains that share their resources with other domains are referred to as network service providers. Domains that use other domain's resources are designated as network service subscribers. A domain may perform as a provider and as a subscriber at the same time.

In IPv6 unicast address allocation within the Internet there are two distinct aspects:

- The set of administrative requirements for acquiring and allocating IPv6 addresses
- The technical aspect of such assignments, composed for the most part intra-domain routing (within a routing domain) and inter-domain routing (between routing domains).

In the Internet, there exists several routing domains (the subscribers) including corporate and campus networks that are attached to transit networks in only a small number of precisely controlled access points (the provider).

There are several benefits of encoding some topological data in IPv6 addresses to extensively decrease routing protocol overhead. The preferred mapping is between Internet service providers/service subscribers and IPv6 addressing and routing components. The best segmentation of IPv6 address assignment is through service providers such as backbones, regionals, and service subscriber sites. In addition, the allocation of the IPv6 addresses (illustrated in Figure 5.1) by the Internet Registry and the selection of the high-order section of the IPv6 addresses in leaf routing domains which are linked to more than one service provider, backbone, or regional network is significantly improved through this addressing structure.

5.2. ADDRESS DESIGNATION

There is a distinct plan for address designation which involves embedding address spaces from alternate network layer protocols (i.e., IPv4) within the IPv6 address space and the addressing architecture for embedded addresses including multicast. In addition, there is address allocation for mobile hosts and identification of distinct administrative domains in the Internet.

There is also an established policy for creating registered information which is available to third parties including the entity with specific IPv6 address or where a section of the IPv6 address space has been allocated.

A routing domain or site should be organized by: internal topology, allocated portions of its IPv6 address space, relationship between topology and addresses, as well as the methodology involves for assigning host IPv6 addresses.

Routing Problems

IPv6 segments routing problems into these areas:

- Routing exchanges between end systems and routers
- Routing exchanges between routers in the same routing domain
- Routing among routing domains.

Allocation Space	Prefix (binary)	Fraction of Address Space
Reserved	0000 0000	1/256
Unassigned	0000 0001	1/256
Reserved for NSAP Allocation	0000 001	1/128
Reserved for IPX Allocation	0000 010	1/128
Unassigned	0000 011	1/128
Unassigned	0000 1	1/32
Unassigned	0001	1/16
Unassigned	001	1/8
Provider-Based Unicast Address	010	1/8
Unassigned	011	1/8
Reserved for Geographic-Based Unicast Addresses	100	1/8
Unassigned	101	1/8
Unassigned	110	1/8
Unassigned	1110	1/16
Unassigned	1111 0	1/32
Unassigned	1111 10	1/64
Unassigned	1111 110	1/128
Unassigned	1111 1110 0	1/512
Link Local Use Addresses	1111 1110 10	1/1024
Site Local Use Addresses	1111 1110 11	1/1024
Multicast Addresses	1111 1111	1/256

Figure 5.1. Address Allocation

In order to best understand the administrative policy for IPv6 address assignment, the primary goal regarding the use of hierarchical routing is to acquire a level of routing data abstraction (summarization) in order to decrease the CPU, memory, and transmission bandwidth depleted in sustaining routing.

The concept behind routing data abstraction can be used for different types of routing information. One type is called *reachability information*, it points to the set of reachable destinations. Both abstraction of reachability information determines what IPv6 addresses will be reserved with respect to topological routing structures.

Reachability information abstraction occurs at the boundary in between hierarchically grouped topological routing structures. An element lower in the hierarchy indicates summary reachability information to its parents.

When dealing with routing domain boundaries, IPv6 address information is exchanged with other routing domains. When IPv6 addresses within a routing domain are all drawn from non-contiguous IPv6 address spaces without abstraction, then the address information is exchanged at the boundary which is composed of an explicit list of all the IPv6 addresses.

Optionally, if the routing domain takes its IPv6 addresses for all the hosts within the domain from an individual IPv6 address prefix, boundary routing information may be summarized into the single IPv6 address prefix. This allows for a significant data reduction and permits increased scaling.

As routing domains are interconnected via a non-hierarchical method, it is extremely probable that no more abstraction of routing data will happen. When routing domains are without designated hierarchical relationship, administrators do not have the power to designate IPv6 addresses within the domains out of a common prefix for the intention of data abstraction. This results in a plain form of inter-domain routing. Routing domains require specific information regarding alternate routing domains to which they wish to route to. This can function well in small and medium sized Internets. Unfortunately, this does not scale to very large Internets.

IPv6 will likely reach out to numerous routing domains in the United States and even more abroad. This requires an increased degree of the reachability information abstraction beyond what can be acquired at the routing domain level.

Within the Internet it may be possible to drastically restrict the volume and the complexity of routing information. This can be accomplished by utilizing existing hierarchical interconnectivity. This provides you with the means for a group of routing domains to be each designated with an address prefix from a shorter prefix designated to another routing domain whose responsibility is to interconnect the group of routing domains. Each member of the routing domains group can now utilize its longer prefix from which it designated its addresses.

This is best illustrated through a set of routing domains that are all linked to an individual service provider domain such as a regional network and can employ that provider for all external inter-domain traffic. A short prefix can be sent to the provider, as it will then provide a somewhat longer prefix. This prefix is sent to each of the routing domains to which it interconnects. This permits the provider, as it tells the other routing domains of the addresses that it can reach, to abstract the reachability information for a sizable amount of routing domains into a single prefix. This method can permit a large amount of reduction of routing information. This can effectively increase scalability of inter-domain routing.

This method is brought through several levels of change. Routing domains at any given level in this hierarchy may utilize their prefix as the foundation for subsequent sub-allocations. This is dependent upon the fact that the IPv6 addresses stay within the overall length and structure constraints.

What you see is that the amount of nodes at each lower level of the structure is inclined to greatly increase. Therefore, the most significant increase in the reachability information abstraction happens when the reachability information collection happens near the edges of the collection. In essence, there is a point where data abstraction stops yielding extensive benefits. Determining the point at which data abstraction ceases to be of benefit needs to be carefully considered with respect to the number of routing domains. This is compared to the amount of routing domains and address prefixes which can be easily and effectively supported through dynamic inter-domain routing protocols.

Control vs. Chaos

One aspect of Internet support focuses on decentralized address administration. There is a careful balance between IPv6 addresses requirements (for efficient routing) and the requirement for decentralized address administration. It is important to develop a consistent addressing plan at any given level within the Internet, as it needs to focus on the alternatives.

Administrative decentralization is best illustrated if the IPv6 address prefix X designates a section of the IPv6 address space allocated for North America. All of the addresses that are within this prefix can be reserved along topological boundaries to sustain the increased data abstraction. Then, inside this prefix, addresses may be allocated on a per-provider method that is based on a significant boundary such as location.

If you were to imagine that this prefix is allocated on a per-provider basis, subscribers who exist within North America utilize sections of the IPv6 address space that is beneath the IPv6 address space of their service providers. Inside a routing domain, addresses for subnetworks and hosts are allocated from individualized IPv6 prefix designated to the domain with respect to the addressing plan for that domain.

5.3. ADDRESS ADMINISTRATION

Internet routing components include service providers such as backbones and regional networks. While service subscribers such as sites or campuses are allocated in a specific structure. It is considered standard that mapping from these components to IPv6 routing components is best served when providers and subscribers act as routing domains.

A subscriber or site may optionally decide to work as a section of a domain created by a service provider. Most sites will decide to operate as a section of their provider's routing domain with the ability to exchange routing information directly with the provider. The site is still given a prefix from the provider's address space, and the provider will advertise its own prefix into inter-domain routing.

When dealing with this type of mapping, it is important to determine where address administration and allocation should be performed to meet both administrative decentralization and data abstraction. In fact, the answer lies in either some portion within a routing domain, at the leaf routing domain, at the transit routing domain (TRD), and/or at an alternative with more standard boundaries.

A section within a routing domain is analogous to any arbitrary connected set of subnetworks. Should a domain be composed of several subnetworks, they are interconnected through routers. Leaf routing domains are analogous to sites where the primary purpose is to yield intra-domain routing services. Transit routing domains are deployed to convey transit or inter-domain traffic such as backbones and providers are TRDs. There are even more general boundaries that are seen as extensive collections of TRDs.

The most significant difficulty in transmitting and operating on reachability information is at the highest point of the routing hierarchy, where reachability information starts to collect. Providers on the Internet must manage reachability information for all subscribers who are directly linked to the provider. Traffic sent to other providers is usually routed to the back-bones that happen to act as providers too. The backbones must be aware of the reachability information for all associated providers as well as their connected subscribers.

The biggest benefit in abstracting routing information at any level of the routing structure is bigger at the highest levels of the structure. There is hardly any immediate benefit to the administration that performs the abstraction, as it needs to sustain routing information separately on each linked topological routing hierarchy.

There is a notable distinction when the provider sends out routing information to other providers such as for a backbone or TRDs. First, the provider is not able to aggregate the site's address into its own prefix, instead the address needs to be specifically listed in routing exchanges. The end result is another burden to other providers that have to exchange and maintain this information.

In addition, each provider including a backbone or TRD has a single address prefix for the provider, which comprises the new site. This eliminates the exchange of additional routing information to determine the new site's address prefix. Therefore, any benefits go to other providers who maintain routing information regarding this site and provider.

IPv6 Address Administration

When individual hosts reserve their IPv6 addresses from several unrelated IPv6 address spaces, there won't be any data abstraction outside of what is part of existing intra-domain routing protocols. If you were to say that a routing domain employs three separate prefixes designated from three unique IPv6 address spaces linked with three separate associated providers. Then you might find the end result has a negative impact on inter-domain routing. This is specifically true for other domains which have the requirement of maintaining routes to this domain. In addition, there is no common prefix which can be employed to portray these IPv6 addresses. In essence, no summarization can occur at the routing domain boundary. Once this routing domain advertises addresses, a detailed list of the three separate prefixes must be employed.

The amount of IPv6 prefixes that leaf routing domains can advertise measures to be about the amount of prefixes designated to the domain. The amount of prefixes a provider's routing domain can advertise is nearly the amount of prefixes linked to the client leaf routing domains. In addition, a backbone would be summed throughout all linked providers. Increased structural information is an aspect the Internet sorely needs in order for continued growth and expansion to occur.

5.4. LEAF ROUTING DOMAIN

The largest amount data abstraction occurs at the lowest levels of the structured hierarchy. By giving each leaf routing domain a contiguous block of addresses from its provider's address block, the result is the largest expansion in abstraction. When dealing with the outside the leaf routing domain, the set of all addresses reachable in the domain can then be portrayed by an individual prefix. In addition, all destinations reachable within the provider's prefix can be portrayed by a single prefix.

If you look at an individual campus that has a leaf routing domain, you would find it currently needs four separate IPv6 prefixes. However, they can be provided with an individual prefix that yields the same amount of destination addresses. In addition, since the prefix is a subset of the provider's prefix, they don't force any additional burden onto the higher levels of the routing hierarchy.

There is a tight coupling between hosts and routing domains. The routing domain portrays the only path between a host and the remainder of the internetwork. Therefore, you have to look at this coupling in a way that extends to incorporate a common IPv6 addressing space. Therefore, the hosts within the leaf routing domain need to take their IPv6 addresses from the prefix designated to the leaf routing domain.

5.5. TRANSIT ROUTING DOMAIN

There are two types of transit routing domains:

- Direct providers
- Indirect providers

Many of the subscribers of a direct provider include domains which act only as service subscribers. In essence, they carry no transit traffic. Several of the subscribers of an indirect provider are domains that perform similarly to service providers. A backbone is an indirect provider, while an NSFnet regional is illustrative of a direct provider.

Direct Service Providers

In a provider-addressing scheme, direct service providers need to use their IPv6 address space for designating IPv6 addresses from an individual prefix to the leaf routing domains which they serve. The benefits received from data abstraction is much more than in the event of leaf routing domains, and the additional amount of data abstraction yielded by this method may be required in the near future.

In order to describe this concept, think about the direct provider who serves 200 clients (network clients shown in Figure 5.2). When each client reserves its addresses from four independent address spaces then the total number of entries which are required to take care of routing to these clients is 800 (200 clients multiplied by four providers). When each client receives his addresses from a single address space, then the total number of entries would be only 200.

There will be a growing amount of routing domains in the Internet which will increase so that it will not be possible to route on the grounds of a flat field of routing domains. It is then very important to yield an increased amount of information abstraction with IPv6.

Direct providers may provide a part of their address prefix to leaf domains. This is primarily founded on the basis that an address prefix is given to the provider. This causes direct providers to advertise to other providers a small amount of the number of address prefixes that are required if they specified the individual prefixes of the leaf routing domains. This points to a great deal of savings given the expected scale of global internetworking.

The efficiencies acquired in inter-domain routing foster the retrieval of IPv6 address prefixes taken from the IPv6 address space of the providers. When a direct service provider is linked to another provider through several attachment points, then it may sometimes be beneficial for the direct provider to exercise a specific amount of control over the link between the attachment points and flow of the traffic destined to a specific subscriber.

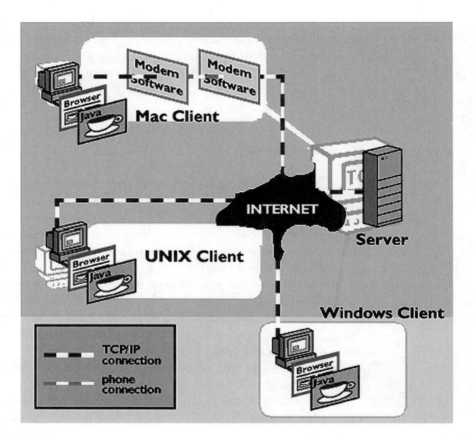

Figure 5.2. Network Clients

This type of control can be made easier by primarily partitioning all the subscribers into groups. This allows specific traffic meant for all the subscribers within a group to flow through a specific attachment point. When the partitioning is complete, the address prefix of the provider is segmented along the group boundaries. A leaf routing domain that can accept prefixes taken from its direct provider acquires a prefix from the provider's address space subdivision linked with the group the domain belongs to.

When looking at the attachment point that lies between the direct and indirect providers, the direct provider advertises both an address prefix which is associated with the address space of the provider. In addition, one or more address prefixes which are associated with the address prefix linked with each segment. The subsequent prefixes are the same as the former prefix, however they are longer than the earlier prefix.

Backbones

It is not usual practice for a direct provider to take his address prefixes from the IPv6 space of an indirect provider or backbone. The benefit in routing data abstraction is somewhat minuscule. The amount of direct providers numbers in the tens and an order of magnitude increase would not precipitate an overwhelming strain on backbones. In addition, you might think that over time an increased direct interconnection of the direct providers, leaf routing domains directly linked to the backbones, and international links are directly linked to the providers. In fact, the separation between direct and indirect providers is somewhat fuzzy.

There is another drawback to the allocation of IPv6 addresses from a backbone prefix, it is that the backbones and its associated providers are looked upon as being independent. Providers can take their long haul service from at least one backbones, or may switch backbones. This can happen to provide a more cost-effective service if available. When you have IPv6 addresses derived from a backbone it is not compatible with the overall association.

5.6. ROUTING DOMAINS

In the previous section we saw a method for allocating IPv6 addresses with respect to direct or indirect provider connectivity. This permits a large amount of information reduction to be gained for those routing domains which are linked to a single TRD. Specifically, this type of domain may choose its IPv6 addresses from the direct provider. This gives the provider (when announcing the addresses) with the ability to reach to other providers, to utilize an individual address prefix to designated a large amount of IPv6 addresses associated multiple routing domains.

In addition, you have to consider routing domains that are linked to several providers. This type of multi-homed routing domains can be composed of single site campuses as well as organizations who are linked to several backbones, large organizations that are linked to various providers at varying locations in the same country. This might also include multi-national organizations who are linked to backbones in a variety of countries worldwide.

Dealing with Multi-Homed Domains

One solution for each is composed of multi-homed organizations that acquire its IPv6 address prefix individually from the providers to whom it is linked. This permits each multi-homed organization to base its IPv6 assignments on an individual prefix. This also allows them to summarize the set of all IPv6 addresses reachable within that company through a single prefix.

The drawback to this method due to the fact that the IPv6 address for that company has no relationship to the addresses of any specific TRD, the TRDs to which this organization is linked will have to advertise the prefix for this organization to other providers. In addition, other providers will have to sustain a specific entry for that company in their routing tables.

An alternate method for multi-homed companies is that they are designated with a separate IPv6 address space for each connection to a TRD. In addition, they are designated with a single prefix to some subset of its domains founded on the closest interconnection point. One of the drawbacks to this alternative is that the backup routes to multi-homed companies are not automatically sustained.

These solutions have different effects on policies. If you were to look at any given country that has a law pertaining to traffic from a source within that country to a destination within the same country must always remain entirely within the country. In the first method, it is not possible to determine from the destination address if the destination is within the country. In the alternate method, then a separate address needs be designated to those hosts which are within country one. This permits for routing policies to be observed.

There is also another solution approach that assigns each multi-homed organization to a single address prefix, founded on one of its connections to a TRD. There are other TRDs in which the multi-homed company is linked to sustain a routing table entry for the organization. However, they are selective with regards to which other TRDs are informed of this route. These methods will yield a single default routing entry that all TRDs will understand how to reach. This presumes that all TRDs will sustain routes to each other while yielding a more direct routing in most events.

This solution may prove to be appropriate to a certain cross section companies who have deployed their own provider. In this method, each multi-homed organization in a given organizational group would employ address assignment based on its other attachments to TRDs. The organization would need to sustain routes to the routing domains linked with several member organizations. In the same way, all members of a given company would be required to sustain a table of routes to the other members through the organization's provider. Since the company's provider does not inform other general worldwide TRDs of what addresses it can reach the large set of routing prefixes must be maintained only in a few places. The addresses reserved for the various organizations are members of the group that would provide a default route through each members other attachments to TRDs, while permitting communications within the organization to use the preferred path.

One other method involves the designation of a specific address prefix for routing domains that are linked to two or more distinct routing domains. This type of solution is going to be important when use of public data networks becomes more common. Specifically, it is likely that at sometime a substantial percentage of all routing domains will be linked to public data networks. In this case, a great deal of all government-sponsored networks can have a set of customers which overlaps substantially with the public networks.

5.7. SOLUTION OPTIONS

There are several solutions to the difficulty of designating IPv6 addresses to multi-homed routing domains. Each of these solutions has various benefits and drawbacks. Each solution yields a different cost on the multi-homed organizations, and on the TRDs. This also incorporates those to which the multi-homed organizations are not attached.

These solutions also require each TRD to create a policy regarding the specific conditions to accept addresses that are not based on its own address prefix, as well as how such non-local addresses will be operated on. Another policy can include non-local IPv6 address prefixes will be accepted from any attached leaf routing domain. However, they are not advertised to other TRDs. In a less conventional policy, a TRD can accept such non-local prefixes and exchange them with a defined set of other

TRDs. Several policies involve costs to TRDs, which may be described in those policies.

Zero-Homed

There are several links which interconnect two routing domains in a way that private link usage may be restricted to carrying traffic only between the two routing domains.

There are several organizations that have internal communications networks that are not connected to any service providers. This type of organizations can have a number of private links that they use for communications with other organizations. These types of organizations do not participate in global routing, however they are pleased with reachability to those organizations in which they have created private links. This is designated as zero-homed routing domains.

Zero-homed routing domains are looked at as the degenerate case of routing domains with private links. However, they do not present a problem for inter-domain routing. The routing information exchanged via the private links notices very restricted distribution, this is only to the routing domain at the other end of the link. There are no address abstraction requirements beyond those intrinsic in the address prefixes exchanged throughout the private link.

The zero-homed routing domains utilize valid globally unique IPv6 addresses. The routing domain is connected in an Internet which subscribes to the IPv6 addressing plan. This domain need to have the ability to make a distinction between the zero-homed routing domain's IPv6 addresses as opposed to any other IPv6 addresses that it may need to route to. The only method in which this can assured is if the zero-homed routing domain employs unique IPv6 addresses.

These unique addresses represent extremely important aspects in order to distinguish between destinations in the Internet. Unique addresses are not always enough to guarantee world-wide connectivity. Should a zero-homed routing domain be connected to the Internet, the block of addresses employed within the domain may not be related to the block of addresses allocated to the domain's direct provider. The way in which to maintain the increased granted by structural routing and address assignment. The zero-homed domain must then change addresses designated to the systems within the domain.

5.8. AGGREGATION

An even higher level of the structural hierarchy may be employed in this addressing scheme to reduce the amount of routing information required for world-wide routing. Continental aggregation is beneficial due to the fact that continental boundaries yield natural barriers to topological connection and administrative boundaries. It therefore presents a natural boundary for another level of aggregation of inter-domain routing information. In order to utilize this, it is necessary that each continent be assigned an appropriate contiguous block of addresses. Providers inside a continent would allocate their addresses from this space.

The advantages of continental aggregation is that it assists in the absorption of the chaos injected within continental routing due to the cases where an organization must use an address prefix that can be advertised beyond its direct provider. If the address is removed from the continental prefix, the additional cost of the route is not propagated beyond the point where continental aggregation occurs.

As opposed to the providers case, the aggregation of continental routing information is not necessary completed in the continent to which the prefix is allocated. The cost of inter-continental links and trans-oceanic links is exceedingly large. If aggregation is executed on the near side of the link, then routing information regarding the unreachable destinations within that continent can only live on that continent. Optionally, if continental aggregation is done on the far side of an inter-continental link, the far end can operate on the aggregation and introduce it into continental routing. Therefore, destinations which are part of the continental aggregation and do not have a specific prefix can be cast aside prior leaving the continent where it was created.

Local Use Addresses

There are several domains which have hosts that will not require with world-wide unique IPv6 addresses. A domain that chooses to use IPv6 addresses out of the private address space is capable of doing so without address allocation from any authority. On the other hand, private address prefix to not require to be advertised throughout the public section of the Internet.

In order to employ private address space, a domain must decide which hosts don't need to have network layer connectivity beyond the domain in the near future. These type of hosts will be designated as private hosts, and may employ the private addresses when it is amenable to do so. Private hosts can talk with all other public and private hosts. Unfortunately, they can not have IPv6 connectivity with any external host. Without possessing external network layer connectivity, a private host still has the ability to access external services through application layer relays. Public hosts don't have connectivity to private hosts outside of their own domain.

Since private addresses have no world wide definition, reachability information linked with the private address space won't be reproduced on inter-domain links, and packets with private source or destination addresses need not be forwarded via these type of links. Routers within domains that don't use private address space, specifically those of Internet service providers, are thought to be configured to filter out routing information which conveys reachability information linked with private addresses. If this type of router obtains such information, the rejection will not be looked at as a routing protocol error. Besides that, indirect references to private addresses need to be restricted to within the enterprise that employs these addresses.

Policy Routing

It is thought that inter-domain routing protocol will have problems when trying to aggregate several destinations with disparate policies. Similarly, the ability to aggregate routing information without violating routing policies is crucial. It is then believed that address allocation authorities try to allocate addresses so that aggregates of destinations with the same policies can be created easily.

5.9. CONCLUSION

It is important to carefully look at the addressing structures to work on route optimality, routing algorithm efficiency, ease and administrative efficiency of address registration, and what addressing authority assigns considerations for what addresses.

In addition, address allocation is crucial so that a disparate set of TRDs such as backbone networks, several regional or national networks, as well as several commercial Public Data Networks will provide public inter-connectivity between private routing domains.

In this chapter we have discussed the IPv6 address designation along with the various routing problems which can result within this new protocol version. We continue with IPv6 address administration with a focus on leaf routing domains and transmit routing domains. In terms of transmit routing domains this chapter deals with both direct and indirect providers. The discussion then turns to routing domains and how to deal with multi-home routing domains. The direction of this text then turns to finding solutions options to illuminate IPv6 even further.

Address Types

6

6.1. INTRODUCTION

The Internet is a world-wide medium which can be conceptualized as a group of hosts interconnected through transmission and switching facilities. Managing the collection of hosts and the transmission and switching facilities which make up the networking resources of the world wide Internet is not homogeneous, it is instead a distributed environment among multiple administrative authorities. Resources under control of one administration within a contiguous segment of network topology form a domain.

Domains which both uses the same resources with other domains are referred to as network service providers. Domains that employ other domain's resources are referred to as network service subscribers. Remember that any domain can perform as a provider and a subscriber at the same time.

6.2. ADDRESS ALLOCATION

There are two requirements with regards to IPv6 unicast address allocation within the Internet.

- A set of administrative requirements for acquiring and allocating IPv6 addresses
- The technical manner of such assignments pertains to a great deal to routing (within a routing domain or between routing domains).

At present there are several routing domains including corporate and campus networks which are associated with transit networks in only one, or a reduced number of tightly controlled access points.

Addressing solutions that require a great deal of changes or must employ constraints on the current topology don't enter into the picture. In fact, it is the high-end IPv6 address allocation in the Internet, which provide benefits that involve encoding some topological information in IPv6 addresses to extensively decrease routing protocol overhead. The expected requirement for additional levels of structure within Internet addressing is important to handle network growth. The proposed mapping between Internet service providers, service subscribers, and IPv6 addressing and routing components is essential to managing all Internet entities. The segmentation of IPv6 address designation among service providers such as backbones, regionals, and service subscribers sites is just as important as the allocation of the IPv6 addresses by the Internet Registry.

Unicast Address

Local use includes Link-Local for addressing on a single link (physical network) or subnetwork, and Site-Local designed for local use that can later be integrated into global addressing.

Bits	3	n	m	o	p	125-n-m-o-p
	010	Registry ID	Provider ID	Subscriber ID	Subnet ID	Interface ID

Figure 6.1. Unicast Address

Link-Local Address

Bits	10	n	118-n
	1111111010	0	Interface ID

Figure 6.2. Link-Local Address

Site-Local Address

Bits	10	n	m	118-n-m
	1111111011	0	Subnet ID	Interface ID

Figure 6.3. Site-Local Address

An IPv4-compatible address provides compatibility between IPv4 and IPv6 until a complete transition is attained.

Bits	96	32
	0000 FFFF	IPv4 Address

Figure 6.4. IPv4-Compatible Address

The loopback address sends an IPv6 packet to itself. These packets are not sent outside a single node.

Bits	96	32
	0000 0000	0001

Figure 6.5. Loopback Address

6.3. BENEFITS

It is important to choose a high-order portion of the IPv6 addresses in leaf routing domains that are linked to more than one service provider such as a backbone or a regional network. However, there are several other aspects of IPv6 address allocation which include: address assignment and embedding address spaces from other network layer protocols (such as IPv4 in the IPv6 address space).

The addressing architecture for embedded addresses involves either multicast addressing, address allocation for mobile hosts, identification of particular administrative domains in the Internet, or mechanisms for creating registered information known to third parties (including an entity which has a specific IPv6 address or a section of the IPv6 address space has been allocated). It is important to point out: the method by which a routing domain or site needs to be organized within its internal topology or allocate a section of its IPv6 address space; the relationship between topology and addresses; the method of deciding on a specific topology or internal addressing plan; and the plan which is used for assigning host IPv6 addresses.

6.4. IPV6 ADDRESS ALLOCATION

Some of the points of information relevant to both address allocation and IPv6 routing include IPv6 partitions, the routing problem such as routing exchanges between end systems and routers, the routing exchanges between routers in the same routing domain, and the routing among routing domains.

IPv6 addressing and routing are crucial to understanding this protocol. An IPv6 address prefix is designated as an IPv6 address that has some idea of the leftmost contiguous significant bits which reside within this address portion.

When determining an administrative policy for IPv6 address assignment, the technical consequences must be considered. The goal is to use hierarchical routing to obtain some level of routing data abstraction, or summarization, to decrease the CPU, memory, and transmission bandwidth consumed in support of routing.

The idea of routing data abstraction can be used for different kinds of routing information. Reachability information determines the set of reachable destinations. Abstraction of reachability information determines that IPv6 addresses can be reserved according to topological routing structures. Administrative assignment, however, exists along organizational or political boundaries. These may not be congruent to topological boundaries so that the requirements of the both may conflict. Therefore, a middle ground is a necessity.

Reachability information abstraction exists at the limits within the hierarchically arranged topological routing structures. An element under in the hierarchy lists summary reachability information to its parents.

At routing domain boundaries, IPv6 address information is swapped with other routing domains. Should IPv6 addresses inside a routing domain be taken from non-contiguous IPv6 address spaces without permitting any abstraction occur, then the address information swapped at the boundary is composed of an explicit list of all the IPv6 addresses.

However, should the routing domain take IPv6 addresses for all the hosts inside of the domain from an individual IPv6 address prefix, boundary routing information can be summarized into one IPv6 address prefix. This allows substantial data reduction and permits better scaling.

Should the routing domains be interconnected in a non-hierarchical method, it is possible there can be no more abstraction of routing data. Due to the fact that routing domains would have no defined hierarchical relationship, administrators won't have the ability to designate IPv6 addresses within the domains out of some common prefix for the goal of data abstraction.

In the end, it would be flat inter-domain routing. All of the routing domains would require direct knowledge of all other routing domains which they route to, which can be equally applied to work well in small and medium sized Internets. Unfortunately, this does not scale to large Internets. As IPv6 grows exponentially across the world, it needs a greater degree of the reachability information abstraction above what can be obtained at the routing domain level.

When dealing with the Internet, it is possible to extensively constrain the volume and the complexity of routing information by employing the existing hierarchical interconnectivity. It therefore, presents an opportunity for a group of routing domains to each to be designated with an address prefix from a smaller prefix designated to another routing domain whose operation is to interconnect the group of routing domains. Each member of the group of routing domains has a longer prefix, from which it designates its addresses.

This can best be represented through a set of routing domains which are all linked to a single service provider domain and uses that provider for all external or inter-domain) traffic. A small prefix may be assigned to the provider. It yields a somewhat longer prefix to each of the routing domains to which it interconnects.

The provider is able, when communicating with the other routing domains of the addresses that it can reach, to abstract the reachability information for a large amount of routing domains into one prefix. This method permits a large amount of reduction for routing information, and can significantly increase the scalability of inter-domain routing.

Now we will observe that the amount of nodes at each lower level of a hierarchy will grow quite a bit. The most significant increase in the reachability information abstraction happens when the reachability information aggregation takes place close to the leaves of the hierarchy. The level of increase is significantly curtailed at each higher level. At a given time, the data abstraction stops to yield increasing benefits.

Locating the exact point at which the data abstraction stops to be of benefit needs to be specifically looked at with respect to the amount of routing domains. They are thought to occur at each level of the hierarchy as contrasted to the amount of routing domains and address prefixes which can conveniently and efficiently be supported through dynamic inter-domain routing protocols.

Efficiency and Control

Should the Internet work with a decentralized address administration, then the requirements need to be equally handled with regards to IPv6 addresses for efficient routing and the requirement for decentralized address administration. One steady addressing plan at any level within the Internet considers the options very carefully.

Administrative decentralization is best illustrated through the IPv6 address prefix which identifies part of the IPv6 address space allocated for North America. All addresses that reside within this prefix may be allocated along topological boundaries in support of heightened data abstraction. In this prefix, addresses may be allocated on a per-provider method that is founded on some relevant criteria.

Subscribers within North America employ parts of the IPv6 address space that is underneath the IPv6 address space of their service providers. Inside a routing domain addresses for subnetworks and hosts are allocated from the individual IPv6 prefix designated to the domain according to the addressing method for that domain.

6.5. ADDRESS ADMINISTRATION AND ROUTING

Internet routing components include service providers including backbones, regional networks, and service subscribers (including both sites and campuses). They are both set up hierarchically to a large extent. The standard method of mapping from these components to IPv6 routing components is for providers and subscribers to perform as routing domains.

Additionally, a subscriber can decide to act as a part of a domain created by a service provider. Some sites will decide to act as part of their provider's routing domain, substituting routing information directly with the provider. The site is designated with a prefix from the provider's address space, then the provider will advertise its own prefix through inter-domain routing.

This type of mapping allows for address administration and allocation to be carried out in such a way that it meets both administrative decentralization and data abstraction. However in order to accomplish that goal, you need to consider that some section within a routing domain, the leaf routing domain, the transit routing domain, and more widespread boundaries (e.g., continental boundary.)

There is a section within the routing domain that is associated with an arbitrary connected set of subnetworks. Should a domain be made up of several subnetworks, they are interconnected through routers. Leaf routing domains are associated with sites. The first goal is to yield intra-domain routing services. Transit routing domains are set up to convey transit or inter-domain traffic. Remember that backbones and providers are TRDs. There are more expansive boundaries which can be viewed as topologically extensive TRD groups.

The biggest difficulty involved when transmitting and operating on reachability information is at the highest point in the routing hierarchy. It is at this point where reachability information is inclined to collect. Internet providers are required to manage reachability information for all subscribers who are directly linked to the provider. Traffic which is meant for other providers is usually routed to the backbones. The backbones need to be aware of the reachability information for all associated providers and their subscribers.

The benefit involved when abstracting routing information at any specified level of the routing hierarchy is bigger at the higher levels of the hierarchy. There is a somewhat minimal benefit to the administration that acts as the abstraction, this is because it needs to sustain routing information separately on each linked topological routing structure.

Let's take an illustration of any specific site which is in the process of deciding whether or not to acquire an IPv6 address prefix directly from the IPv6 address space allocated for North America, or from the IPv6 address space allocated to its service provider. When it is looking over both alternatives, it takes into account its own interests when making this decision. The site needs to use one prefix or another, however the source of the prefix has a minimal effect on routing efficiency inside the site. The provider needs to sustain information regarding each linked site in order to route — but what doesn't matter is the similarity in the prefixes of the specified sites.

There is a difference when the provider distributes routing information to other providers. The provider is not able to aggregate the site's address into its own prefix since the address need to be specifically registered in routing exchanges. The answer is in an extra task for other providers which needs to exchange and support this data.

Other providers such as a backbone or TRD views an individual address prefix for the provider, which envelops the new site. This prevents the exchange of other routing information to determine the new site's address prefix. The benefits are a result of other providers that support routing information regarding both the site and provider.

6.6. IPV6 ADDRESSES ADMINISTRATION

When individual hosts reserve their IPv6 addresses from several unrelated IPv6 address spaces, there isn't any data abstraction outside what is established in existing intra-domain routing protocols. Inside a routing domain, it uses three independent prefixes designated from three different IPv6 address spaces linked with three different associated providers.

Inter-domain routing is effected poorly, specifically on those other domains that must support routes to the domain. There isn't any common prefix that can be employed to represent these IPv6 addresses, and as a result there is no summarization that can occur at the routing domain boundary. Once this routing domain to other routing domains advertises addresses, an expanded list of the three individual prefixes needs to be utilized.

The amount of IPv6 prefixes which leaf routing domains need to advertise measures out to be the amount of prefixes designated to the domain. The amount of prefixes a provider's routing domain needs to advertise is about the amount of prefixes associated with client leaf routing domains. In addition, for a backbone this would be summed across all linked providers.

This type of method is problematic in today's Internet, and is unruly for IPv6 Internet. There is a larger amount of hierarchical information that is critical in allowing for increased growth of the Internet.

Leaf Routing Domain

The largest amount of data abstraction occurs at the lowest levels of the hierarchy. This yields each leaf routing domain with a contiguous block of addresses from its provider's address block. The result is one of the largest increases in abstraction. When looking outside the leaf routing domain, the set of all addresses reachable in the domain can be illustrated by a single prefix. In addition, all destinations reachable inside the provider's prefix can be illustrated by a single prefix.

When you look at a single campus that is a leaf routing domain, it would need four separate IPv6 prefixes. However, they can be given a single prefix that yields the same amount of destination addresses. In addition, since the prefix is a subset of the provider's prefix, they don't inject any extra task on the higher levels of the routing hierarchy.

There is a tight coupling between hosts and routing domains. The routing domain is demonstrative of the only path between a host and the remainder of the Internetwork. This coupling also encompasses a common IPv6 addressing space. Therefore, the hosts which reside within the leaf routing domain needs to take their IPv6 addresses from the prefix designated to the leaf routing domain.

Transit Routing Domain

There are two different types of transit routing domains that include:

- Direct providers
- Indirect providers

The majority of subscribers of a direct provider are composed of domains that act only as service subscribers that don't convey any transit traffic. The majority of subscribers of an indirect provider include domains that act as service providers.

6.7. LOOKING TO THE FUTURE

Without a doubt, the Internet will continue or grow exponentially in the near future. Besides that, there is also an increased amount of growth with regards to internationalization of the Internet. The power of routing to scale relies upon the utilization of data abstraction based on hierarchical IPv6 addresses. It is important to select a hierarchical structure for IPv6 addresses carefully.

It is important to carefully look at the addressing structures to meet the disparate objectives of route optimality, routing algorithm efficiency, administrative efficiency of address registration, and what specific addressing authority designates considerations regarding which addresses. The internetworking community (requirement table shown in Figure 6.6) will best be served when the operations cost is minimized. When dealing with IPv6 address allocation, routing data abstraction is best supported.

The way in which data abstraction can occur is through the assignment of IPv6 addresses which needs to be accomplished in a method similar to the actual physical topology of the Internet. In the case where organizational and administrative boundaries are not related to the actual network topology, address assignment founded on this type of organization boundaries is not endorsed.

ADDRESSING	– Need IP addresses for the myriad of communicating devices in the internet – Simple and dynamic method of assigning IP addresses
MULTICAST	– Common Operational Picture to everyone – Distributed Collaborative Planning (DCP) – Both reliable and unreliable multicast delivery – Conserve bandwidth on tactical links
MOBILE NETWORKING	– Accomodate "roaming" of mobile users – Handle intermittent communications links – Mobile routers as well as mobile terminals
QUALITY OF SERVICE	– Support real-time multimedia like DCP – Support prioritization by data type as well as data source – Guarantee bandwidth available for critical applications
NETWORK SECURITY	– Ensure confidentiality, integrity, authenticity of data – Protect network infrastructure from attack

*Figure 6.6. Internetworking
Requirements*

Intra-domain routing protocols permit for greater information abstraction to be supported within a domain. In terms of zero-homed and single-homed routing domains you will find that the IPv6 addresses designated within a single routing domain employs one address prefix designated to that domain. In particular, this permits the set of all IPv6 addresses reachable inside a single domain to be completely described through a single prefix.

All of the routing domains which reside on a worldwide Internet is sufficient enough so that increased levels of hierarchical data abstraction besides the routing domain level will be needed. Network topology will have a tight coupling with national boundaries. The amount of network connectivity will usually be increased within a given country. Most dealing with IPv4 indicates that continental aggregation is advantageous and needs to be supported as a method of limiting the groundless distribution of routing exceptions.

Planning Address Allocation

Public interconnectivity between private routing domains is provided by a disparate set of TRDs, such as backbone networks, several regional or national networks, several commercial Public Data Networks.

These networks won't be interconnected in a formally hierarchical method. In fact, direct connectivity between regionals as well as all of these types of networks may have direct international connections. These TRDs can be employed for purposed of interconnecting several routing domains. These domains compose a corporation, campus, government agency, or other organizational entity. Besides that, private corporations may need to use dedicated private TRDs for the purposes of communication within their own corporation.

There are a large amount of routing domains that will be linked to only one of the TRDs, thereby allowing hierarchical address aggregation on a TRD. To solve this, addresses need to be assigned hierarchically which is based on address prefixes designated to single TRDs.

To handle continental aggregation of routes, all addresses for TRDs within a continent should be taken from the continental prefix. In terms of the proposed address allocation scheme, this calls for IPv6 address space sections to be designated for each TRD. This also includes the backbones and regionals. In terms of those leaf routing domains which are linked to a single TRD, they need to be designated with a prefix value from the address space associated to that TRD.

Multi-Homed Routing Domains

The routing domains that are linked to several TRDs within the same country, or to TRDs inside several different countries are called multi-homed routing domains. In effect, the strict hierarchical model does not effectively support such routing domains.

In fact, there are numerous method that the multi-homed routing domains can be handled. All of the methods are different with regards to the information which needs to be supported for inter-domain routing as well as inter-domain routes. The actual solutions are dependent upon resources used within routers within the TRDs, administrative cost on TRD personnel, and difficulty of configuration of policy-based inter-domain routing information within leaf routing domains. The solution that is employed can possibly affect the actual routes in which packets follow, besides altering the availability of backup routes when the primary route fails. This is why a one standard solution is not possible for all situations. Instead, cost will require several solutions for various routing domains, service providers, and backbones.

Link-Local Addressing/Name Resolution

IPv6 has the power to support its own version of PnP or plug and play. It allows a system to be interconnected with other IPv6 systems but without the necessity for a formal configuration. Specifically, using independently created Link-Local addresses are restricted to the physical link to where a system is connected.

The drawback however is the ability regarding the name to address as well as the inverse lookup function. This is an easy method of adding support to existing resolver routines to handle the lookup of IPv6 addresses from a local ASCII file. It is highly difficult to figure out the Link-Local addresses and names of all bordering systems. In addition, using a standard means which is inclined to data input errors, and the data itself may become out of data very quickly to detract from such methods.

When using an interface that handles the Link-Local model, it is prudent to advertise its name and associated Link-Local IPv6 address to a multi-cast group of Link-Local extent. In addition, it also permits a system to transmit a query for a specific name or address to the group, which may be responded to by the system which was the same as the given item. In this example, there is no central server, each system yields information regarding its own configuration.

6.8. IPV6 HOSTS

The objective in this section is to advertise and utilize names and link local addresses between IPv6 hosts. In addition, it is important also to maintain this addressing information out of the DNS/BIND server's data file. The reason for this is because it is highly unlikely for this type of server to know if providing such an address is appropriate, without the server verifying an improper amount of information regarding the comparative location of both the client system as well as the requested hostname.

Therefore it has some components that are similar to the Service Location protocol. In addition, it may be prudent to check the relationship between them due to the fact that the Service Location yields support for IPv6. In addition, the implementation of this method will assist other elements of IPv6 systems. Specifically, multicast support and the BSD API interface will benefit.

The two methods involved when implementing a simple name to address function includes:

- Providing local name and address information server
- Requesting and storing remote name or address information client

An IPv6 system needs to support server functionality, so as to distribute its own information to others. A system can choose to be a client, so as to learn and utilize the information of neighbors.

Advertisements

A system needs to advertise its system name as well as the associated Link-Local address throughout each of its interfaces. In addition, this is a sign regarding the length of information which needs to be considered valid. Furthermore, a system may transmit these packets only at discrete intervals, or with regards to particular requests. In fact, a combination of these two models would most likely be the most reasonable solution.

Client Processing

A system can function in a solely reactionary mode to user requests, so that it employs no caching of learned information. However, if it decides to record any advertised name/address bindings which are received. If information is recorded, then the values of the TTL field in responses must be respected.

When a Name is requested, then the address field needs to be set to a valid Link-Local address for the appropriate media type. The hostname field needs be empty. Should an address be requested, then the address field needs to be set to all 0, and the hostname field needs to contain a non-null entry. The Length field is indicative of the total length of the packet in octets.

6.9. DNS AND RESOLVER

The names and addresses need to be made available in order to be useful and available to applications and users. It must be integrated with the host's name resolving software. The best way to accomplish this goal is by using dynamic storage for link local addresses.

It is important to designate a specific category to this type of address, provided its restricted capabilities. There is a specific fake domain called ".link" which is a very useful method for both the unambiguous representation of these names as well as a system configuration mechanism.

For example, the resolving software can be configured to return address in the order BIND/LOCAL/LINK. Although this service returns naming information through the resolver software, the names are not BIND names even though they can be stated in a similar method using the same restrictions and conventions.

Trying to determine a fake TLD is also an interesting circumstance. This overall methodology involves requesting and supplying naming information. It should involve executing requests as generally as possible and yield specific answers. Furthermore, it is questionable to see if including the full DNS name may actually be providing too much information.

In addition, it involves making certain that inappropriate requests are not performed, as this would unnecessarily query local systems in an effort to endeavor to find a resolution of a name which is not locally available. It is prudent to use the resolver's configured default domain and search path into your overall goals when attempting lookups.

6.10. MULTILINK

It is important to consider two aspects when considering the multilink server as well as the client in a multilink environment. For the multilink server to correctly yield both name and addressing information, it is important to limit the advertisement of a specific address to the interface to which that address is designated.

Any client which has a multilink neighbor, needs to be able to work with a single name being resolved to several addresses. This may be supported similarly to any fully qualified hostname that returns several addresses. In addition, you can consider returning the address with the largest TTL or even the first received address. When a client is multilink itself, it may be required to store the received interface as well as the name/address pair.

Duplicates

When a system with several interfaces is linked to one link it may respond to requests for a single name with various addresses at various times. Optionally, a system can respond to requests for a given address with various names over a period of time, if it is configured with several aliases.

The detection of duplicate addresses will cause general interoperability difficulties. In addition, it is a function of Duplicate Address Detection.

6.11. OPTIONS

This utilization of IPv6 for methods involving a host's neighbors visible to the host's users is not defined in this specification. Furthermore, it is not known if Link-Local name servers need to be permitted, in which one system yields answers for another. This would necessitate a form of proxy bit in the Advertisement message.

The stateless approach is used when a site doesn't worry about the exact addresses hosts use, as long as they are unique and properly routable. The stateful approach is used when a site requires better control over exact address assignments. Both stateful and stateless address autoconfiguration can be used at the same time. The site administrator determines which type of autoconfiguration can be used through the setting of appropriate fields within the Router Advertisement messages. IPv6 addresses are leased to an interface for a certain amount of time. Each address has an associated lifetime that determines how long the address is bound to an interface. Once a lifetime expires, the binding and address are then invalid and the address can be reassigned to another interface elsewhere in the Internet. To take care of the expiration of address bindings effectively, an address goes through two individual phases while designated to an interface. First, an address is preferred, indicating that its use in arbitrary communication is not restricted. At a later point in time the address is then deprecated in anticipation that its current interface binding will become invalid. Inside of a deprecated state, using an address that is not acceptable. New communication such as the opening of a new TCP connection) should use a preferred address if possible. A deprecated address should be used only by applications that have been using it and would have problems in switching to another address without a service disruption.

Security

The standard ability to disable any particular function is always a simple but effective means of security. However, there does not seem to be any potential security risk in yielding a simple name associated with an easily acquired address.

6.12. CONCLUSION

In this chapter we examine unicast addressing and Link-Local addressing. It is important to note that there are various aspects involved in address allocation within the IPv6 protocol. Both requirements that involve both technical and administrative methods are needed to correctly allocate these addresses.

The solutions themselves are highly dependent on the allocation of IPv6 on the Internet. The benefits reduce routing protocol overhead and add levels within the hierarchy of Internet addressing. Furthermore, the benefits extent to both efficiency and control of this protocol. Address administration and routing are components important to both providers and subscribers. The ability for a subscriber to act as a part of a domain created by a service provider is crucial to proper allocation.

All in all, the technical material behind IPv6 illustrated here provides an addressing framework where IPv6 goes from here. The ability to work with the global Internet is no easy task as it is expanding on a daily basis, but IPv6 will work for the long term because of it expansive capabilities.

In this chapter we have dealt with address allocation, and the benefits involving both efficiency and control which are related to IPv6. We then move into address administration and routing as well as leaf, transit routing, and multi-homed routing domains. These chapters then discusses Link-Local addressing and name resolution, IPv6 hosts, and advertisements. We conclude with the all-important issue of security within IPv6 with a goal of looking toward the future of its capabilities and addressing architecture.

IPv6 Services

7

7.1. INTRODUCTION

This chapter illustrates an alternative to the addressing architecture for IPv6, which maintains global routing expansion. IPv6 demonstrates an important advancement in Internet technology. It yields bigger addresses and much needed functional capabilities, which is intended to be a platform for the growth of the Internet.

The existing IPv6 addressing still relies heavily upon CIDR-style aggregation for route growth control. Unlike IPv4, this IPv6 method is linked with support for simpler network renumbering as this makes it possible for provider-based addressing to happen.

For the most part, the existing IPv6 addressing model is not sufficient because CIDR-style aggregation decomposes as the multi-homed sites such as leaf sites or regional networks increasingly grow. The method of renumbering to achieve changing ISPs (e.g., topological rehoming) is a difficult problem that will only increase.

The bigger IPv6 addresses provide for huge growth in the amount of end systems which can be supported. In addition, it is predicted that there will be a large growth in the number of routes needed to reach them. Should

CIDR aggregation increase, as per existing models, this will present a critical problem due to the scaling actions of the global route computations.

This chapter looks at a new aspect of dealing with 16 byte IPv6 address that alleviates the route scaling problem as well as several other related matters. This model yields an aggressive topological aggregation while regulating the complexity of flat-routed regions. It utilizes and handles the dynamic address designation capabilities in IPv6. However, this causes the same capability to perform a local choice with reasonable costs and benefits as opposed to a force method for standard rehoming events.

This model analyzes the specific work completed by the world wide Internet foundation to handle multi-homed sites. This effectively isolates it into a particular method that can be traced to and contracted by just those sites who want to utilize this capability. It is now possible for sites to make informed cost-benefit choices regarding multi-homing.

7.2. THE MAIN IDEA

Routing Goop is fundamental term which has the following central concepts: The addressing model listed here is called "8+8" to individualize it from the existing proposals which are referred to as "Flat-16." The primary central concept in 8+8 involves the 16 byte IPv6 address is split into two 8-byte objects stored in the existing 16-byte container. The lower 8 bytes (least significant) form the *End System Designator,* or ESD. The upper 8 bytes that are most significant are called the Routing Goop, or RG. The ESD designates a computer system and the RG encodes information regarding its attachment to the global Internet. Just as with other methods which distinguish location from identity, the 8+8 model needs modifying of the upper level protocols to consider only the ESD when performing pseudo-header operations meant to identify the end system as opposed to its location.

The TCP checksum fake-header will employ only the ESDs instead of the Flat-16 addresses; TCP associations can be designated by ESD/Port instead of Flat-16/Port; IPSEC Authentication and ESP header calculations need only look at the ESD and not the RG of the address. In combination, these allow session-scale state like TCP connections to survive global topology changes without special considerations in the transport protocol.

The addressing model designated in this chapter is referred to as 8+8 in order to identify it from the present methods referred to as Flat-16. The primary illustration of 8+8 is that the 16-byte IPv6 address is segmented into two 8-byte objects recorded in an existing 16-byte box.

The lower 8 bytes compose the End System Designator-ESD. The upper 8 bytes are most important and are referred to as the Routing Goop (RG). The ESD indicates that a computer system and the RG encodes information regarding its link to the world-wide Internet topology.

Much like other methods that determine the location from identity, the 8+8 model needs to modify the upper level protocols in order to take into consideration just the ESD when operating on its pseudo header operations. These operations are designed to distinguish the end system instead of its location in the topology.

The TCP checksum pseudo header can illustrate this as it only employs ESDs as opposed to the Flat-16 addresses. TCP links would be distinguished by ESD/Port as opposed to the Flat-16/Port; IPSEC Authentication, and ESP header computations. However, they would only take into account the ESD but not the RG of the address. In combination, they both permit session-scale state like TCP connections to endure world wide topology alteration without distinct considerations in the transport protocol.

The second main idea reinforces the separation between Public and Private Topology. Public Topology is the foundation that must be realized by several other organizations. This definitely includes transit networks for the purpose of creating world-wide Internet connectivity. Private Topology is the foundation that is of no specific interest beyond the containing organization. Specifically, standard transit service is yielded by networks revealed in the Public Topology, while networks composed of only Private Topology are not able to yield standard transit service to the world-wide Internet.

In the existing IPv4 Internet, the separation between Public and Private Topology exists as a sidebar, but isn't used for any important advantage aside from CIDR-style aggregation. Private topology is the subnet structure employed by the topology within a site as used in the CIDR block for the complete site. Nobody beyond the site specifically deals with the internal foundation of the site. Therefore, there is no impending need to convey any routing information except for the CIDR block that described it.

In fact, the 8+8 form raises this perception to a significant structural component that yields a specific idea about a site. It is important to point out that a site is the easier link to the world wide Internet.

In addition, it is also a structural unit of Private Topology. Inside a site, the ESD of a system is adequate for attaining it via the Private Topology besides identifying the system outside the confines of the site to the world.

This site-internal reachability can be achieved by either flat-routing on the ESD with a site or by employing a structured ESD inside the site. Each of these solutions is handled by the foundation of the ESD, besides which each has discernible and comprehensible costs and advantages.

Public Topology is the transport foundation that conveys traffic from one site to another. Several carrier, reseller, and regional networks control it. The Routing Goop section of an 8+8 address is a locator that encodes data regarding the way a site that has Private Topology is linked to the Public Topology of the transit networks. Routing Goop densely encodes topology data with a large amount aggregation as it provides the opportunity to convey local detail for enhancing regional routes without offering worldwide aggregation.

7.3. ESD

End System Designators designate every computer system in the 8+8 Internet. It doesn't matter whether it is a host, router, or other network element. A system can have more than one ESD, each ESD is unique throughout the world.

It is important to point out that the ESD distinguishes a system, analogous to the XNS or Xerox Networking architecture. This distinction can also be similar to the interface as seen in the present IPv4 and IPv6 foundations. ESD chooses either a physical or virtual interface on a computer system. When processing an 8+8 address, a computer system needs only look at the ESD portion of the address to find out whether a packet is addressed to it.

There are cases where it is beneficial to an address for a computer system that is an individual of specific physical interface on that system. It is very common for IPv4 to form a distinctive virtual interface to yield a system which has an interface independent identity. This yields the same groundwork utility of XNS as it permits for the flexibility of the IPv4 addressed interface model. There is a logic to keeping the IPv4/IPv6 model.

ESD has unique characteristics that make it unique throughout the entire world. In addition, ESD distinguishes an interface on a computer system. An interface may have more than one ESD that is current. IPv6 currently needs implementations that support several addresses per interface.

An ESD can not determine a specific physical computer. Neighbor Discovery still yields a level of virtual address translation.

IEEE MAC addresses are unique throughout the world with regards to the delegation process where they are designated as interfaces by the manufacturers. Both XNS and IPX depend on this unique nature. IETF-NodeID values are unique by an analogous designation method. IPv4 addresses need to be unique around the world so that the global nature of the Internet can function with an effective designation method.

At times, an IPv4 prefix is not configured correctly, and it can be difficult to record. However, this difficulty can be handled appropriately. In fact, it is more common that two Ethernet interfaces possess the same MAC address.

7.4. SITE STRUCTURE

The 8+8 global routing architecture looks at a site as a leaf of the topology. It doesn't worry about the interior of this private topology. Instead, the internal topology of a site is very important to the management and operation of the site, therefore the ESD foundation yields an extensive set of organizational option with various cost benefit compromises.

ESDs are unique, but they also convey an internal structure. The global individuality is yielded by the Identity Token. The internal structure is taken in the *Private Topology Partition*. The ESD structure yields 32768 various Private Topology Partitions (PTPs) within a site. This is analogous to every site having been designated a CIDR block of 128 Class-B addresses subnetted down to a Class-C.

The distinction is that in an ESD, the subnet inhabitants are severely restricted by the link-level LAN technology as opposed to the 253 host limit of the Class-C subnet. This permits an a very fertile topology which is held within a site without it exporting complexity into the world wide routing foundation.

A company is not limited to being structured by a single site. The compromise is that the inter-site topology which must be a portion of the Public Topology. As the individual sites maintain their independence in topological structure and attachment to the Internet, they need to be knowledgeable about the changes between its component sites. Rehoming of constituent sites will possibly impact long-running sessions. This is the expense for exploiting the routing machinery which exists in the Public Topology.

Due to the flexibility for organizing a site, it is important to take into consideration that none of these corporate approaches is restricted. A large site can combine these methods to provide a positive effect and meet the goal of providing the designer of private site topology with several design options.

The easiest organization is to consider a site which employs all Mode-0 ESDs with each of the systems linked in a single Private Topology Partition. An example would be that all ESDs convey the same PTP value that is designated by the local network administration. The modern LAN-switching technology is powerful enough to provide a site that could be both big and internally complex. However, this complexity is digested into the LAN foundation and it looks as though it is the only partition from the 8+8 Private Topology view.

This foundation is advantageous in that rehoming a system inside this structure will not alter the ESD and TCP sessions and will persevere through arbitrary changes in the private topology. This works due to the fact that the single PTP is a virtual topology with the real topology concealed by the LAN Switching methodology.

There is another site model that has several PTPs that routes traffic between the segments. This is similar to the standard IPv4 structure of a CIDR block being subnetted to designate a prefix to each PTP. This proposal has the benefit of familiarity, however it has the distinct drawback that enduring TCP connections won't necessarily persevere through arbitrary changes to the private topology.

The IPv6 dynamic address designation methodology in place will act to make such internal changes easier than experienced with IPv4. It should also be noted that with several PTPs routed within a site, a Private Topology Partition does not compare to a physical LAN cable. The PTP values can be employed to label bigger organizational infrastructures or organizational departments as well. This effectively decreases the probability that standard internal topology alterations destroy enduring connections.

Another site model is called: Mode-2 ESDs. It is based upon IPv4 address designations in place. In this event, all the IPv4 Identity Tokens can be put in an individual PTP and then routed internally on the IPv4 address in the lowest 4 bytes of the Identity Token. The benefit seen here is that of extensive familiarity. However, it can also introduce externally-visible changes if ESDs need to be moved due to the needs of the private topology.

Remember, that IPv4 addresses employed in a Mode-2 ESD need to be officially registered.

When looking at all of the multi-segment cases, a Mode-1 ESD can be used to distinguish:

- any point-to-point link endpoint
- the loopback addresses in routers, or
- any other IP-accessible network elements which don't possess the IEEE MAC address for forming a Mode-0 ESD.

In each of these cases, the Mode-1 ESDs can be employed everywhere. However, it is more appropriate to employ Mode-0 whenever possible as this saves Identity Tokens from being wasted.

In the event where real topology is not totally virtualized by the LAN technology, there will be internal renumbering events precipitated by transferring systems between foundation segments. This will effectively destroy persisting off-site connections unless provisions are made to permit the systems to convey the previous ESDs as equivalent expressions. The biggest topology moves are composed of powering off the end system. However, the powerful renumbering support already created for IPv6 can make those other movements far less traumatic. External rehoming of a site to the global infrastructure can be performed silently in nearly every case.

7.5. ROUTING GOOP STRUCTURE

Routing Goop (RG) is the upper 8 bytes of an 8+8 address. Essentially, RG is a locator. It encodes the topological connectivity of the site which holds the computer system designated by the ESD in the lower 8 bytes. In the event of an individually homed site, rehoming to a new association to the Public Topology will alter just the RG in full 8+8 addresses for computer systems at that site.

This type of rehoming is best illustrated through a change of the site's Internet Service Provider. This change over can be silently created for users inside and outside the site. Even though it doesn't pertain to a practical restriction on the transition duration (relating to the length of the departing ISP) it is willing to expand transitional amenities. This type of alteration has new connections which are created through the new ISP connection.

This calls up the foundation of the topology information conveyed in RG as well as the way in which it is encoded. In particular, RG is a hierarchical locator that can be looked upon as a rooted path expression of flat-routed region which is tangent. Each element in the path expression has only sufficient detail to determine the flat-routed region.

It is advantageous to view the Routing Goop as moving down through the hierarchy of the topmost large structures, to the intervening levels of the Public Topology, and finally down to the site. When the RG travels down, the prefix moves to the right analogously to IPv4 CIDR. At this point each extension navigating the nested flat-routed areas, ultimately ceasing at the site, which then moves downward silently into the Private Topology of that site.

The nested flat-routed areas compare with the transit subnetworks of the Large Structure. An important aspect of these subnets is the reseller or wholesale transit customer of a Large Structure. The reseller network yields transit for sites, so it is a section of the Public Topology and looks much like a substring inside the Routing Goop.

7.6. DISTRIBUTION

There are two events when it is prudent to consider the way in which a Routing Goop is distributed:

- Source addresses
- Destination addresses

Each RG is part of the address, so we illustrate how a full 16-byte address with the right RG is established in these two types.

Source Addresses

RG of a source address is, for the most part, a site-local prefix. Should the destination address not be inside the site, the packet will leave the site through any available site boundary routers. The site Boundary Router injects the proper RG in the source address rooted on the trail the destination needs to use to send a packet back to the sender. With few exceptions this will be the RG which is associated with the attachment path of the site Boundary Router to the global Internet.

If the site is multi-homed through just one site Boundary Router, then the router is available to execute any local policy. Essentially, it must fill in a valid RG path which leads back to a site Boundary Router for that site. If the site is multi-homed through greater than one site Boundary Router, which router the packet leaves by and RG gets executed is local policy.

The dynamic insertion of RG at site exit can indicate that a computer system at a site must not worry about the exit topology policy matters which can be difficult in multi-homed sites. It may also indicate that computer systems are for the most part not impacted at all by topological rehoming of the site. It can also demonstrate that increasingly complex multi-homing scenarios with several site Boundary Routers each with several connections to the Internet can accomplish arbitrarily complex path recovery policy without worrying about the impact on a computer system doing source address selection.

In addition, while a computer system can produce the ESD in a source address, it is not able to produce the point of insertion into the Public Topology. This doesn't yield a strong authentication down to the specific computer system, however it is most likely a significant obstacle to some actions. This is due to the greatly enhanced traceability. There is also a first-hop attachment router in the Public Topology which can insert or override the RG at anytime if an errant packet leaves a site without it. This would effectively enforce tracability. The Public first-hop router may always just drop a packet carrying inappropriate source RG too. However, the brunt of injecting the proper RG in exiting source addresses is placed mainly on the site and site Border Router. All other locations of the task have poor performance scaling.

This method resolves several difficulties and can ease the operation and deployment of this structure, making it worth the ramification it has for site Border Routers. The site Border Router acquires the proper RG from the first-hop attachment router in the Public Topology. Optionally, as the initial method, the RG could be statically configured. However, the objective is to totally automate propagation allowing the entire complex structure to be rehomed without service disruption.

Destination Addresses

At the present time, the IPv6 address lookup for a DNS name sends back the information in a AAAA record — the full 16 bytes of the IPv6 address.

The 8+8 design suggests synthesizing the 16 bytes of information in a query response from two different sources:

- An "AA" record
- An "RG" record

The "AA" record conveys the 8-byte ESD for the DNS name as well as the "RG" record which conveys 8 bytes of the appropriate Routing Goop. It is interesting to note how the AA record is coupled with an RG record in any specified nameserver. One easy implementation is to pair an RG record with a zone. However, that proposes a problem of allowing all the systems in that zone to utilize the same Routing Goop which is in the same site.

It might be more effective to convey a RG name in the "AA" record. This would effectively permit a nameserver to concatenate an arbitrary RG prefix to the ESD yielding the complete 16 byte response. The RG name would be a complete DNS name that could be translated and cached. Formulated as an upward delegation with the correct Time-to-Live, a site can effectively import the Routing Goop information automatically from the service provider.

However, one specific event for an RG record may involve a delegation to a site Border Router that could support the proper RG automatically. This can work at least in single-homed cases as well as in multi-homed cases.

The end result of this groundwork is that individual zone entries for individual nodes are not altered when a site rehomes. The only item which logically gets changed involves the RG information which is made up of the nodes AA record to yield a complete 16-byte response. This effectively indicates that the standard Dynamic DNS machinery is not needed to support site rehoming.

Furthermore, it provides a notable potential for smart nameservers that inspect the source address of a query to yield a more topologically correct translation for any specified DNS query. This system provides much greater detail than existing nameservers have available without processing a complete BGP routing table to determine IPv4 prefix/AS correspondence.

7.7. SITE REHOMING

Once a site alters its area of attachment to the Internet, it rehomes. The most serious drawback to IPv4 CIDR and IPv6 is provider-based addressing.

It needs to renumber a site when it rehomes. The most direct goal of the 8+8 architecture is to lessen this impact.

Remember, Routing Goop of an 8+8 address is not simply a locator — it can encode a PATH from the top level of the hierarchy down to the site. Altering that path is what makes Rehoming and Multihoming have analogous operations.

Once a site decides to rehome, it needs to create a new attachment point to the Internet. It must, at the same time, create a new access path. At that time, it must start using that new path prior to the old path being removed. The way in which this action is accomplished is when a site creates a link with a new ISP and it is then able to convey the traffic. Now the site changes the upward delegation of the DNS RG records. Now, all new connections created with the new translations will adhere to the new path of the site. The new connection path is now the chosen exit path, while source addresses in packets exiting the site instantly start to be marked with the new return path. The previous connection needs to be sustained for an administratively specified grace period to permit DNS timeouts to transition new sessions to the new path so that long-running sessions cease.

It may initially look as though the exit path for the site switches over to the new path and the site Border Router begins marking packets with the new RG. Then the return path for long-running sessions would automatically switch over to the new path. However, a long-running session will be employing a destination address that holds all of the old RG acquired when the session began.

However, the site may ask for a Rehoming Courtesy from their previous ISP. This actually makes it a multi-homed site for a certain time period. Once multi-homing has been established, the previous connection can be removed and the long-running sessions would still persist so long as the site was multi-homed via Rehoming Courtesy.

It is important to note that the rehoming did not effect anything internal to the site's Private Topology. The only alteration was due to the attachment to the Public Topology and the Routing Goop that stores the attachment location.

7.8. MULTI-HOMING

When looking at the 8+8 model, multi-homing is a specific service that is executed for a site by the agents of the Public Topology that yield the access for the site. This device can be enhanced, however it is best illustrated through a site that is dual-homed by two different ISPs and as a result has two separate access paths as shown by two separate Routing Goop bodies.

The site is linked to each ISP through some link as we determine some kind of keep-alive protocol that specifies when reachability to the site's Border Router is lost. The ISP routers that operate as the dual-homed site are distinguished to each other through static configuration information in the easiest event or a dynamic protocol in the more general event. When a link to the site is lost, the ISP router keeping the inactive link just tunnels any traffic sent to the site through the other ISP router.

This method needs coordination between the two serving ISPs. While not a new restriction, multi-homing does need considerable coordination between the site and its providers. Establishing a new protocol for dynamically building a homing group is most likely useful but not necessary at the start.

Resellers Rehoming

Another important aspect is to look at rehoming a reseller. This is a somewhat more general example of the rehoming a site which was mostly determined by:

- Increased lead time
- A longer grace period
- Necessary coordination with customer sites to make certain that the Routing Goop reproduces accurately.

The Reseller can create a new connection resulting in a new path for the Reseller's topology. Once a Reseller changes the upward delegation of Routing Goop, it will cause an effect that spans downward to all associated customer sites by virtue of the upward delegations. The downward wave of Routing Goop through the upward delegations can reduce the site zone TTLs in order to make certain that the caches expire inside of the dual-homed transition grace period for the reseller.

The overall effect rehomes all the Reseller's customer sites and simultaneously the Reseller's infrastructure is rehoming and needs to be totally transparent with the exception of the long-lived sessions that do not end by the end of the grace period.

Reseller Multi-homing

There are two distinct sections that involve multi-homing a Reseller.
One section is analogous to the multi-homed site listed above, while the
other is not.

   When dealing with a Reseller which is dual-homed and has has two
distinct Routing Goop prefixes, the Reseller can seek multi-homed tunneling services from the two access point routers to yield alternate path service
much like a multi-homed site. The reason that traffic is coming to any specific router is affected by what routes are advertised for any specific connection through either BGP5 or IDRP. This example differs from the multi-
homed site case where the ESD is the main attraction and the RG just allows
the traffic reach the site boundary.

   It is important to point out which prefix is used for expanding downward to the customer sites. The solution is to choose one and use it. This
makes the sites normal in the selected prefix. The alternate prefix is able to
be advertised out the alternate path.

7.9. NAT BOXES

Network Address Translation (NAT) boxes have a two sided aspect. First,
8+8 model permits a NAT box to alter the Routing Goop during forwarding
without hampering end-to-end TCP checksums which depend upon the
ESDs. Second, it it is difficult to determine the direction of a NAT box
which would have given the 8+8 model.

   Under normal circumstances, a NAT box is referred to as a means to
have private topology inside a site which is then linked to the Public Topology through the NAT box by not showing anything about that private
topology. The inherent structure of the 8+8 model achieves this object. It
yields Private Topology within local purview while giving freedom of attachment point to the Public Topology. The basic result is that pure NAT boxes
can't grow with the given the 8+8 model. There are broader ranging application gateways which execute firewall functions or intranet bridges yielding crypto-tunnels between the protected interior of two sites.

7.10. IPV6 DIRECTIONS

Some aspects of 8+8 are significantly different from the IPv6 as it exists. For the most part it depends a great deal on the IPv6 groundwork which furnishes a great deal to what makes IPv6 so important. That aspect is Neighbor Discovery, where all the dynamic configuration machinery intended to make renumbering easier even using provider-based addressing. It also yields flexibility which makes tunneling and security attractive. The usual forwarding operations are based on longest-match-under-prefix-mask and the policy-based routing machinery of BGP5/IDRP are also easily understood.

What are routing protocols? Upper layer — a protocol layer immediately above IPv6. Examples are transport protocols such as TCP and UDP, control protocols such as ICMP, routing protocols such as OSPF, and internet or lower-layer protocols being tunneled over (e.g., encapsulated in) IPv6 such as IPX, AppleTalk, or IPv6 itself.

7.11. INTERNET HIERARCHY

It is important to first look at every connected entity having at least one labeling which creates a measurable tree that covers the nodes. The hierarchy is injected by a labeling function that segments the entity into regions and subregions. This operation is only globally visible at the top-level where an initial partitioning of the entity is utilized to create the first level of what will become the hierarchy. Inside each partition there is a local sub-partition function which designates labels where you can move forward in a repeated manner. The nested return directly brings about the hierarchy. This decay of the Internet yields anentity where each level is made up of a set of sub-entities that are directly connected.

It can be seen that the hierarchical segmentation can be brought about with an arbitrary selection of labeling function. However, the function needs to yield the minimum amount of partitioning. It is important to get the partitions to have various important properties, which effects the choice of labeling function.

The objective here is to yield a global labeling which represents the topology as efficiently as possible. However, it must permit for rich connectivity while bounding the complexity of the discrete regions that are flat-routed.

Inside of Large Structures, the sub-partition function is a compromise between the flat-routing complexity within a region and reducing total depth of the substructure. This is motivated by the internal topology of a Large Structure as well as the choices in various Large Structures that will not need to be similar. It is for this reason why Routing Goop only possesses one hard bit boundary. Large Structures have the ability to internally segment as they wish. However, they do need to condense a great deal of the Public Topology.

One participant in Large Structures includes large networks that already represent a great deal aggregation based on current CIDR deployment. Another participant may be Exchange Points. The 8+8 model can serve both of these at the same time, and permit IPv6-style Network-anchored Prefixes and Exchange-anchored Prefixes to live with and be comprised into a unified notion of Aggregator-anchored Prefixes.

Large Structures are designated to a Large Structure Identifier, called a LSID. The total number of LSIDs is purposely limited as we determine the paths between Large Structures are only flat-routed.

Routing between two interior points of two Large Structures is only permissable based on the LSID. This yields a final forwarding strategy for a router running default-free. In one case, the LSID partitions on the Internet are partitioned into a set of regions including that in the interior router, which only need to convey a per-LSID default. This indicates an appropriate Boundary Router which understands how to handle traffic bound beyond the Large Structure for a point in the other Large Structure.

7.12. CONCLUSION

The structure of IPv6 is very important is various addressing aspects. In looking at addresses it is important to determine exactly what is needed in various aspects of this next generation protocol.

In this chapter we discuss the IPv6 addressing model with concepts such as Routing Goop, End System Designators, and pseudo headers. We then proceed to detailing each site structure and Routing Goop structure. Routing Goop is further demonstrated through its means of distribution including the source address and destination address. This chapter proceeds with a discussion about site rehoming, multi-homing, and resellers rehoming and multi-homing. This chapter concludes with a discussion about the present and future of the Internet hierarchy.

Messaging Protocols

8

8.1. INTRODUCTION

This chapter looks into a set of Internet Control Message Protocol (ICMP) messages to be used with IPv6. IPv6 utilizes the Internet Control Message Protocol (ICMP) along with a several changes. The Internet Group Membership Protocol (IGMP) determined for IPv4 has been modified and absorbed into ICMP for IPv6. The end result was a protocol referred to as ICMPv6.

8.2. ICMPV6

IPv6 nodes list errors that are seen when operating on packets employ ICMPv6. In addition, they are used to execute other Internet-layer functions including diagnostics (e.g., ICMPv6 ping) and multicast membership reporting. ICMPv6 is a key component of IPv6 and needs to be completely instituted by every IPv6 node.

ICMPv6 messages are classified into two distinct groups:

- Error messages
- Informational messages

Error messages are distinguished by having a 0 in the high-order bit of the message Type field values. Therefore, error messages have message Types from 0 to 127. However, informational messages have message Types from 128 to 255.

The message formats for the ICMPv6 error messages include the destination unreachable, packet too big, time exceeded, and parameter problem. The ICMPv6 informational messages include:

- 128 Echo Request
- 129 Echo Reply
- 130 Group Membership Query
- 131 Group Membership Report
- 132 Group Membership Reduction

Each ICMPv6 message has an IPv6 header that precedes it, and 0 or more IPv6 extension headers. The ICMPv6 header is distinguished by a Next Header value (shown in Figure 8.1) of 58 in the header that it follows.

The Type field designates the type of the message. Its value specifies the format of the remaining data. The code field relies upon the message type. It is used for the purpose of creating an added level of message granularity. The checksum field is utilized to observe data corruption in the ICMPv6 message and sections of the IPv6 header.

8.3. THE MESSAGE SOURCE

A node that transmits an ICMPv6 message has to designate both the Source and Destination IPv6 Addresses in the IPv6 header prior to computing the checksum. Should the node have more than one unicast address, it needs to select the Source Address of the message by determining if the message is a reply to a message transmitted to one of the node's unicast addresses. Keep in mind that the Source Address of the response must be that same address.

Should the message be a reply to a message transmitted to a multicast or anycast group where the node is a member, the Source Address of the

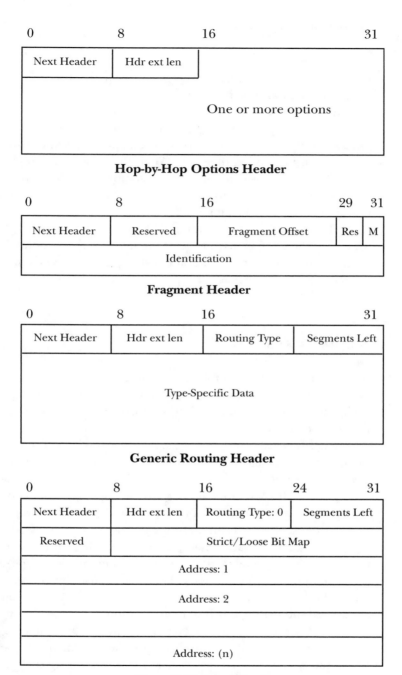

Hop-by-Hop Options Header

Fragment Header

Generic Routing Header

Type O Routing Header

*Figure 8.1. Generic Routing
Header*

reply needs to be a unicast address that is property of the interface in which the multicast or anycast packet was received.

Should the message be a reply to a message transmitted to an address which is not the property of the node, the Source Address needs to be the unicast address which is property of the node which will provide the most assistance in diagnosing the error. When the message is a reply to a packet forwarding action which can not be completed successfully, the Source Address needs to be a unicast address which is property of the interface where the packet forwarding broke.

However, the node's routing table needs to be inspected to find out which interface will be used to send the message to its destination. When a unicast address is property of that interface, it needs to be employed as the Source Address of the message.

8.4. MESSAGE PROCESSING

Implementations need to follow these rules when processing ICMPv6 messages: if an ICMPv6 error message is received, it needs to be passed to the upper layer. However, if an ICMPv6 informational message is received, it needs to be quietly discarded.

Each ICMPv6 error message has as much of the IPv6 packet causing the error packet that will fit without making the error message packet go beyond 576 octets. In the event where the Internet layer protocol is necessary to pass an ICMPv6 error message to the upper-layer protocol, the upper-layer protocol type is taken from the body of the ICMPv6 error message and used to choose the correct upper-layer protocol entity to resolve the error.

If the original packet had an abnormally high number of extension headers, it is conceivable that the upper-layer protocol type may not be available in the ICMPv6 message, because of packet truncation in order to satisfy the 576-octet restriction. In this event, the error message is quietly eliminated succeeding any IPv6 layer operations.

An ICMPv6 error message should not be transmitted as a result of receiving an ICMPv6 error message, or a packet which is to be sent to an IPv6 multicast address. However, there are the following exclusions:

- The Packet Too Big Message (which permits Path MTU discovery to operate for IPv6 multicast)

- The Parameter Problem Message (which lists an unrecognized IPv6 option)
- A packet sent as a link-layer multicast
- A packet sent as a link-layer broadcast
- A packet whose source address does not individually distinguish a single node (i.e., the IPv6 Unspecified Address)
- An IPv6 multicast address, or
- An address known by the ICMP message sender to be an IPv6 anycast address, and to the sender of an incorrect data packet.

IPv6 nodes need to restrict the rate of ICMPv6 error messages sent so as to conserve the bandwidth and forwarding expenses caused by the error messages. This occurs when a generator of error packets doesn't reply to those error messages by terminating its transmissions.

8.5. RATE LIMITING

There are quite a few methods that can institute rate-limiting function including a timer and bandwidth based example. A time-based method restricts the rate of transmission of error messages to a any given source to a maximum of once every T milliseconds. A bandwidth-based method restricts the rate that error messages are transmitted from a specific interface to some fraction F of the associated link's bandwidth. The restriction measurements for the time and bandwidth based examples above need to be configured for the node, with a reasonably default value in order to best illustrate proper values.

When dealing with a Destination Unreachable message it needs to be created by a router, or by the IPv6 layer in the initiating node. It is a reply to a packet that is unable to be delivered to its destination address. An ICMPv6 message can not be created if a packet is eliminated due to congestion however.

8.6. THE UPPER LAYER

When a node receives the ICMPv6 Destination Unreachable message it is required to notify the upper-layer protocol. When dealing with a Packet Too Big it needs to be sent by a router as a reply to a packet which it is unable to forward due to the fact that the packet is bigger than the MTU of the outgoing link.

Transmitting a Packet Too Big Message is an exception to one of the rules regarding when to transmit an ICMPv6 error message. As opposed to other messages, it is transmitted as a reply to a packet received with an IPv6 multicast destination address, or a link-layer multicast or link-layer broadcast address. When dealing with upper-layer notification, any received Packet Too Big messages need to be passed to the upper-layer protocol.

When a router receives a packet with a Hop Limit of zero, or if the router reduces a packet's Hop Limit to zero it needs to eliminate the packet and transmit an ICMPv6 Time Exceeded message to the source of the packet. This indicates either a routing loop or too small an original Hop Limit value that was too small.

The router that transmits an ICMPv6 Time Exceeded message needs to take into account the receiving interface of the packet. This is because the interface where the packet forwarding failed had chosen the Source Address of the message. In terms of upper layer notification, an incoming Time Exceeded message needs to be sent to the upper-layer protocol.

When an IPv6 node operating on a packet locates a problem with a field in the IPv6 header or extension headers it finds that it is not able to finish processing the packet. Instead, it needs to eliminate the packet and is required to transmit an ICMPv6 Parameter Problem message to the packet's source. This illustrates both the type and location of the difficulty.

8.7. ECHO REQUESTS

When a node receives this ICMPv6 message, it is required to notify the upper-layer protocol. Each node is required to institute an ICMPv6 Echo responder function that obtains Echo Requests and then transmits associated Echo Replies. A node must also institute an application-layer interface for transmitting Echo Requests and receiving Echo Replies — useful for diagnostic methods.

The source address of an Echo Reply is transmitted in reply to a unicast Echo Request message. It needs to be the same as the destination address of that Echo Request message. An Echo Reply needs to be sent as a reply to an Echo Request message transmitted to an IPv6 multicast address. The source address of the response needs to be a unicast address that is property of the interface where the multicast Echo Request message was received.

The data received in the ICMPv6 Echo Request message needs to be returned completely and unmodified in the ICMPv6 Echo Reply message, with the exception that the Echo Reply would surpass the MTU of the path back to the Echo requester. In this event, the data is truncated to fit the path MTU. In upper layer notification, the Echo Reply messages are required to be sent to the ICMPv6 user interface, except if the associated Echo Request started in the IP layer.

8.8. PATH MTU DISCOVERY

At the time when an IPv6 node has a big amount of data to transmit to another node, the data is sent in a series of IPv6 packets. It is often favorable that these packets be of the biggest size that can correctly go across the path from the source node to the destination node. The packet size is designated as the Path MTU (PMTU). In addition, it is equivalent to the minimum link MTU of all the links within a path. IPv6 designates a standard method for a node to determine the PMTU of an arbitrary path.

IPv6 nodes are required to implement Path MTU Discovery so as to discover and take advantage of paths with PMTU more than the IPv6 minimum link MTU. A minimum IPv6 implementation can decide to eliminate implementation of Path MTU Discovery.

Nodes that do not implement Path MTU Discovery employ the IPv6 minimal link MTU as the largest packet size. Most of the time, this results in the utilization of shorter packets than needed. This is because the majority of paths have a PMTU greater than the IPv6 minimum link MTU. A node transmitting packets much shorter than the Path MTU permits is wasting network resources and most likely getting poor throughput.

8.9. THE PROTOCOL

This primary focus in this section is on a method to dynamically discover the PMTU of a path. The central concept is that a source node originally believes that the PMTU of a path is the known MTU of the primary hop in the path. Should any of the packets be transmitted on that path be too big to be forwarded by a node along the path, the node will eliminate them and return

ICMPv6 Packet Too Big messages [ICMPv6]. When it receives this type of message, the source node decreased its designated PMTU for the path rooted on the MTU of the limiting hop as illustrated in the Packet Too Big message.

The Path MTU Discovery process is completed when the node's determination of the PMTU is smaller than or equivalent to the real PMTU. There are numerous repetitions of the packet-sent/Packet-Too-Big-message-received method that can occur prior to the Path MTU Discovery process being finished, as there may be several links with shorter MTUs farther along the path.

Optionally, the node may choose to finish the discovery process by not sending packets bigger than the IPv6 smallest link MTU. The PMTU of a path may alter over time, this is to effect alterations in the routing topology. Reductions of the PMTU are realized by Packet Too Big messages. In order to observe growth in a path's PMTU, a node must occasionally extend its PMTU. This action commonly results in packets that are eliminated and Packet Too Big messages are created. This is due to the fact that in most cases the PMTU of the path will not have been altered. The effort to find growth in a path's PMTU should be done now and then.

Path MTU Discovery handles multicast as well as unicast target. When dealing with a multicast destination, duplicates of a packet may go through several paths to various nodes. Individual paths may have various PMTU, and an individual multicast packet may end up in several Packet Too Big messages. Each message indicates a different next-hop MTU. The smallest PMTU number via the set of paths in use indicates the size of future packets transmitted to the multicast destination.

Path MTU Discovery needs to be executed in the event where a node believes a destination is associated with the same link as itself. In a situation similar to a neighboring router performing as proxy for some destination, the destination can to look as though they are directly connected; however, in reality they are only more than one hop away.

Requirements

IPv6 nodes do not need to employ Path MTU Discovery. The requirements operate only for implementations that possess Path MTU Discovery.

Once a node obtains a Packet Too Big message, it needs to decrease its determination of the PMTU for the appropriate path that is founded on the value of the MTU field in the message. The exact manner in which a node operates in this circumstance is not designated, because various applications may have different requirements. Due to the fact that there are numerous implementation architectures, this may accommodate various strategies.

Once a Packet Too Big message is received, a node is required to try and avoid obtaining similar messages in the future. The node needs to decrease the size of the packets it is transmitting along the path. The utilization of PMTU to determine a bigger than the IPv6 minimum link MTU may proceed to bring about Packet Too Big messages. When each of these messages eat up network resources, the node needs to make the Path MTU Discovery process come to completion.

Nodes can find growth in PMTU, however doing so makes transmitting packets bigger than the existing estimated PMTU, due to the probability that the PMTU will not have grown. This must be done at sporadic intervals. Trying to determine growth by transmitting a packet bigger than the current estimate cannot be accomplished in less than five minutes following a Packet Too Big message which has been received for the designated path. In fact, the recommended setting for this timer is double the minimum value that is 10 minutes.

A node needs to decrease its estimate of the Path MTU underneath the IPv6 minimum link MTU. A node may receive a Packet Too Big message indicating a next-hop MTU that is shorter than the IPv6 minimum link MTU. In this event, the node does not have to curtail the size of subsequent packets transmitted on the path to less than the IPv6 minimum link MTU. Instead, it does have to include a Fragment header (shown in Figure 8.2) in those packets.

A node can not expand its estimate of the Path MTU with regards to the contents of a Packet Too Big message. A message indicating an increase in the Path MTU may be a stale packet that has been moving around in the network. While a false packet that is part of a denial-of-service attack (essentially shutting you out of your network) the result of having several paths to the destination each which has a different PMTU.

Implementation

There are several pertinent issues relating to the implementation of Path MTU Discovery. These issues involve the particular layer or layers which implement Path MTU Discovery, the way in which PMTU information is cached, how old PMTU information is removed, and mechanics behind transport and higher layers do.

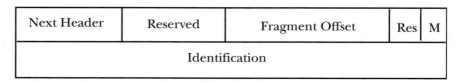

Figure 8.2. Fragment Header

8.10. LAYERING

The IP structure involves a selection of the transmitted packet to be performed by a protocol at a layer above IP. This section looks at packetization protocol. Packetization protocols are normally transport protocols (TCP/IP) shown in Figure 8.3, however they can also be higher-layer protocols built on top of UDP.

Instituting Path MTU Discovery in the packetization layers eases many of the inter-layer issues, however they have numerous problems:

- The implementation may need to be performed for each packetization protocol
- It is difficult to share PMTU information between various packetization layers
- The connection-oriented state sustained by some packetization layers does not easily grow to save PMTU information for extended periods.

Therefore, the IP layer needs to record PMTU information, and the ICMP layer needs to operate on received Packet Too Big messages. The packetization layers may reply to alterations in the PMTU, by altering the size of the messages they transmit.

Furthermore, the packetization layer (i.e., UDP application outside the kernel) is not able to alter the size of messages it transmits. This may cause a packet size that is bigger than the Path MTU. In order to handle this type of event, IPv6 designated a method that permits bigger payloads to be segmented into fragments. Each fragment transmits a separate packet. However, packetization layers are motivated to stop transmitting messages that will need fragmentation.

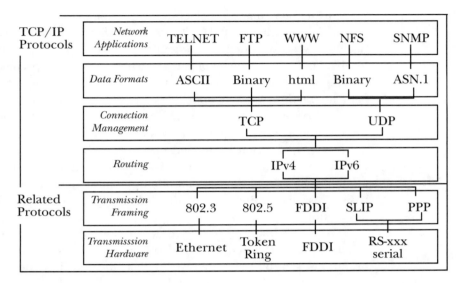

Figure 8.3. TCP/IP Protocols

8.11. RECORDING PMTU DATA

PMTU values need to be linked with a distinct path covered by packets sent between the source and destination nodes. In the majority of cases, a node will not have sufficient data to totally and correctly determine this type of path. Instead, a node needs to link a PMTU value with a type of local representation of a path. It is then left to the implementation to choose the local depiction of a path.

When dealing with a multicast destination address, duplicate of a packet may go across several different paths to reach various nodes. The local representation of the path to a multicast destination needs to portray a possibly big set of paths.

At least, an implementation needs to sustain a single PMTU value to be employed for all packets that started from the node. The PMTU value needs to be the smallest PMTU accomplished via the set of all paths that are used by the node. This approach will probably result in the utilization of shorter packets than is needed for a majority of paths.

An implementation may employ the destination address as the local portrayal of a path. The PMTU value linked with a destination could be the smallest PMTU obtained throughout the set of all paths which are utilized for that destination. The set of paths which are used for a specific destination is thought to be little, however in the majority of cases composed of a single path, this method will yield optimally sized packets on a per-destination basis.

If flows are being used, an implementation may employ the flow ID as the local depiction of a path. Packets transmitted to a specific destination are property of various flows and may utilize different paths. This occurs with the selection of a path that is dependent upon the flow ID. This method will result in the utilization of optimally sized packets on a per-flow basis. This yields a finer granularity than PMTU values sustained on a per-destination basis.

When dealing with source routed packets, the source route may also suit the local depiction of a path. However, some paths may be more refined by various security classifications. At first, the PMTU value for a path is thought to be the known MTU of the first-hop link.

When a Packet Too Big message is received, the node decides which path the message applies to, this decision is based upon the contents of the Packet Too Big message. If the destination address is utilized as the local representation of a path, the destination address from the initial packet (shown in Figure 8.4) would be utilized to determine which path the message operates on.

When the initial packet hold a Routing header, the Routing header needs to be used to designate the location of the destination address inside the original packet. When Segments Left is equal to zero, the destination address is in the Destination Address field in the IPv6 header. When Segments Left is bigger than zero, the destination address is the last address in the Routing header.

The node then employs the value in the MTU field in the Packet Too Big message as a conditional PMTU value, and contrasts the conditional PMTU to the present PMTU. Should the conditional PMTU be smaller than the present PMTU estimate, the conditional PMTU substitutes for the existing PMTU as the PMTU value for the path.

The packetization layers need to be informed about reductions in the PMTU. Any packetization layer TCP connection that is actively utilizing the path needs to be notified if the PMTU estimate is shortened.

Should the Packet Too Big message hold an Original Packet Header which refers to a UDP packet, the TCP layer need to be informed of any of

Figure 8.4. Initial Packet

its connections using the given path. The event that sent the packet which obtained the Packet Too Big message needs to be informed that its packet has been eliminated, even if the PMTU estimate has not been altered, so that it may retransmit the eliminated data.

Any implementation can avoid using an asynchronous notification method for PMTU reductions by delaying notification involved in transmitting a packet bigger than the PMTU estimate. Employing this method involves trying to transmit a packet that is bigger than the PMTU estimate. The SEND (transmit) function should stop and yield an appropriate error indication. This method may be more appropriate to a connectionless packetization layer that can be difficult to notify from the ICMP layer. In this event, the normal timeout-based retransmission method would be employed to recover from the eliminated or dropped packets. Notification of the packetization layer occurrences utilizing a path in the PMTU which is different from the notification of a distinct event in which a packet has been eliminated.

Killing Outdated (Stale) PMTU Data

Internetwork topology is powerful because it can route changes over time. When the local representation of a path may stay the same, the actual paths that are used may change. Therefore, PMTU information cached by a node can end up being stale.

When a stale PMTU value is too big, is will be determined instantly once a sufficiently large packet is transmitted along the path. There is no method that exists for deterring that a stale PMTU value is too small. Therefore, an implementation should have a life span for cached values. When a PMTU value has not been shortened for a period of time, the PMTU estimate needs to be set to the MTU of the first-hop link, while the packetization layers need to be informed of the change. This will make the complete Path MTU Discovery operation occur once more.

Any implementation needs to yield a method to alter the timeout duration, this also deals with setting it to infinity. When dealing with nodes attached to an FDDI link which are linked to the rest of the Internet through a small MTU serial line, where they are not going to discover a new non-local PMTU — they do not need to cope with packets which are eliminated every so often.

An upper layer should not resent data as a reply to an expansion in the PMTU estimate. The growth never comes in reply to an indication of an eliminated packet.

One method to institute PMTU aging is to link a timestamp field to a PMTU value. This field is initialized to a reserved value. This indicates that the PMTU is the same as the MTU of the initial hop link. When the PMTU is reduced in reply to a Packet Too Big message, the timestamp is set to the current time.

Each minute a timer-driven operation goes through all cached PMTU values. Then, for each PMTU whose timestamp is not reserved and is older than the timeout interval, the PMTU estimate is set to the MTU of the first hop link, the timestamp is set to the reserved value, and packetization layers employing this path is informed of the expansion.

8.12. T C P

The TCP layer needs to trace the PMTU for the paths that are used by a connection. It doesn't need to transmit a section which would end up in packets bigger than the PMTU. An easy implementation may query the IP layer for this value each time it a new segment is established. However, this could be insufficient. In addition, TCP implementations that adhere to the slow-start congestion-avoidance algorithm usually compute and cache numerous other values take from the PMTU. It may be easier to retrieve asynchronous notification once the PMTU changes, there these variables may be updated.

The time in which a Packet Too Big message is received indicates that the node that sent the ICMP message eliminated a packet. If the Path MTU

Discovery operation needs numerous procedure to locate the PMTU of the full path, this could delay the connection by numerous round-trip times.

However, the retransmission could be completed with an instant response to a notification that the Path MTU has been altered. However, this is only valid for the particular connection designated by the Packet Too Big message. The packet size employed in the retransmission should be no larger than the new PMTU. This indicates that the TCP layer must have the ability to understand when a Packet Too Big notification is reducing the PMTU which is used to send a packet on the specified connection, and should summarily ignore any other notifications.

The majority of TCP implementations merge congestion avoidance and slow-start algorithms to increase performance. As opposed to a retransmission brought about by a TCP retransmission timeout, a retransmission brought about by a Packet Too Big message need not alter the congestion window. However, it should prompt the slow-start mechanism.

TCP performance can be decreased if the sender's maximum window size is not a precise multiple of the segment size in use. In several systems the segment size is usually set to 1024 octets, while the maximum window size is often a multiple of 1024 octets. Therefore, the correct relationship is standard. If Path MTU Discovery is utilized, the segment size does not have to be a sub-multiple of the send space, yet it may alter during a connection. This indicates that the TCP layer may be required to alter the transmission window size when Path MTU Discovery changes the PMTU value. The maximum window size should be set to the highest multiple of the segment size which is smaller than or equivalent to the sender's buffer space size.

Transport Protocols

Some transport protocols are not permitted to repacketize when executing a retransmission. When an attempt is made to send a segment of a certain size, the transport is not able to segment the contents of the segment into shorter segments for retransmission. In this event, the IP layer during retransmission can fragment the initial segment. All further segments that are transmitted for the first time shouldn't be bigger than permitted by the Path MTU.

Management

An implementation should yield a method for a system utility program to determine that Path MTU Discovery should neither be done on a given path nor should it alter the PMTU value comparable to a given path. This type of implementation can be achieved by associating a flag with the path. Once a packet is transmitted on a path with this flag set, the IP layer won't transmit packets bigger than the IPv6 minimum link MTU.

These features can be employed around an anomalous situation, or by a routing protocol implementation which has the ability to acquire Path MTU values. This type of implementation should also yield a way to alter the timeout period for aging stale PMTU information.

8.13. SECURITY

The Path MTU Discovery method allows two denial-of-service assaults, both founded on a malevolent party transmitting false Packet Too Big messages to a node. In the first type of assault, the false message illustrates a PMTU much shorter than it really is. This need not completely terminate data flow, because the victim node should not set its PMTU estimate underneath the IPv6 minimum link MTU. But the ultimate effect is poor performance.

In the second type of assault, the false message illustrates a PMTU bigger than it really is. If this is taken at face value, it may cause a temporary blockage as the victim transmits packets that will be eliminated or dropped by some router. In the period of one round-trip, the node would realize the mistake of receiving Packet Too Big messages from that router, however frequent repetition of this assault would cause a great deal of packets to be eliminated. A node should not ever increase its estimate of the PMTU based on a Packet Too Big message so it won't be as vulnerable to an attack. If the node receives a Packet Too Big message then it could not possible increase the size of the PMTU.

However, a hacker could also cause problems if he or she terminates a victim from having the ability to receive legitimate Packet Too Big messages. However, there are simpler denial-of-service attacks available so it is important to protect yourself and your network.

8.14. CONCLUSION

In this chapter we have seen implementations of ICMPv6 that are used by IPv6. These control message used in ICMPv6 to list errors which are seen when operating on packets. Besides, that there are various messages which allow for executing Internet layer functions such as diagnostics. The error and informational messages add value to allow for different message formats to inform you of various system aspects.

Path MTU Discovery is also another key topic this chapter which designates packet size as the Path MTU. IPv6 nodes need to implement Path MTU Discovery to benefit from paths with Path MTU. In fact, only in minimal implementations of IPv6 is Path MTU Discovery eliminated.

IPv6 nodes list errors that are observed when packets are operated on under ICMPv6. This chapter goes into further detail to list their error and informational messages. These messages are further dissected by examining the message source and how each message is processed. We examine both rate and the upper layer protocol involved when a node receives an ICMPv6 destination unreachable message. We expand further on this topic with echo requests and detail in Path MTU Discovery. Implementation considerations are then used along with the concept of recording PMTU data and then killing outdated PMTU data if need be. Our discussion then turns to transport protocols such as TCP and management involved in them. Finally, we conclude with the issue of security involved in these transport protocols to demonstrate the sound nature of IPv6.

Header Compression

9

9.1. INTRODUCTION

Header compression is advantageous on low or medium speed links. Header compression can work to increase interactive response time. In addition, low speed links can benefit. However, echoing of characters may consume as much time as 100–200 ms due to the time needed to send large headers. That time frame is the maximum that users can normally withstand without giving up on the overall computer response time.

It permits small packets to be used for bulk data with sufficient line efficiency. This is crucial when telnet and ftp traffic are combined due to the fact that the heavy ftp data needs to be conveyed in small packets to lessen the waiting time when a packet with interactive (telnet) data is caught behind a heavy or unwieldy ftp data packet.

The main idea of any network design is to always reduce the load as much as possible. When you utilize shorter packet sizes for the ftp traffic, you effectively provide a visionary solution to a shortsighted problem. It will expand the load on the network as it has to work with many small packets. A better solution may be to fragment the big packets locally over the slow link.

It is important to permit the utilization of small packets for delay sensitive low data-rate traffic. In applications such as voice, the time required to fill a packet with data is significant if packets are big. In order to achieve low end-to-end delay short packets are favored. In the absence of header compression, the shortest possible IPv6/UDP headers (48 octets) utilize 19.2 kbit/s, with a packet rate of 50 packets/s which is the same as having 20 ms worth of voice samples in each packet. Tunneling or routing headers (i.e., supporting mobility) will expand the bandwidth used up by headers by at least 10-20 kbit/s. Header compression can decrease the bandwidth required for headers greatly. This would effectively enable higher quality voice transmission over 14.4 and 28.8 kbit/s modems.

It can also decrease header overhead. Since a common size of TCP segments for heavy transfers over medium-speed links is 512 octets now. When TCP segments are tunneled because of Mobile IP is used, the header is 100 octets. IPv6 specifications detail path MTU discovery, therefore with IPv6 heavy TCP transfers should employ segments bigger than 512 bytes when possible.

One of the benefits is the reduction of packet loss rate over poor links. Since there are less bits transmitted per packet, the packet loss rate will be less for a specified bit-error rate. This actually translates into increased throughput for TCP as the transmitting window can open up more between losses, and result in fewer lost packets for UDP. Furthermore, UDP has neither windowing nor sequencing capabilities. These methods are meant for a point-to-point link. However, great care has been given to allow extensions for multi-access links and multicast.

Headers that can be compressed include TCP, UDP, IPv4, and IPv6 base/extension headers. Header compression depends upon several fields that remain constant or changing infrequently in consecutive packets that are property of the same packet stream. Fields that do not change between packets are not even required to be sent at all. Fields that change frequently with small values include TCP sequence numbers. They can be encoded progressively so that the amount of bits required for these fields decrease considerably. The fields that change frequently include checksums or authentication data, which must be transmitted in every header.

The basic idea behind header compression is to sporadically transmit a packet with a full header. Then all succeeding compressed headers designate the full header and can hold successive changes to the full header.

9.2. COMPRESSION

A great deal of the header information remains the same over the life of a packet stream. When dealing with non-TCP packet streams nearly all fields of the headers are constant. However, for several fields, TCP is constant while others change with small and predictable values.

To bring about compression of the headers of a packet stream, a complete header that holds a compression identifier, CID, is sent over the link. The compressor and decompressor record the majority of fields of this full header as Compression State. The Compression State is composed of the header fields whose values are the same and neither need to be sent over the link at all nor be changed between consecutive headers. In this way it employs fewer bits to transmit the difference from the former value as compared to transmitting the absolute value.

Any field changes that are expected to be the same in a packet stream will make the compressor transmit a full header again to update the Compression State at the decompressor. As long as the Compression State is analogous to the compressor and decompressor, headers can be decompressed to be the same as they were prior to compression. Should a full header or compressed header be absent during transmission, the compression state of the decompressor may be obsolete due to the fact that it is not updated properly. Compressed headers will then be decompressed incorrectly.

IPv6 isn't supposed to be used over links that can send a meaningful fraction of spoiled packets to the IPv6 module. This indicates that links need to have a very low bit-error rate or that link-level frames which need to be protected by checksums or forward error correction. The link-layer will throw spoiled frames away.

The link-layer execution may have the ability to inform you if a frame header compression module has been ruined, but it will not tell you what packet stream it is property of. This is because it may be the CID that was damaged. In addition, frames may vanish without the link-layer implementation's knowledge. The type of link errors that a header compression module should work with and protect will involve packet loss. A header compression method requires mechanisms to update the Compression State at the decompressor in addition to detecting or avoiding incorrect decompression. The compression methods in this chapter depend upon the fact that packets are not reordered between the compressor and decompressor.

9.3. PACKET

This compression method uses four packet types besides the IPv4 and IPv6 packet types. The association of link-level packet type and the value of the first four bits of the packet individually determine the packet type.

A full header is indicative of a packet with an uncompressed header. This incorporates both a CID and a generation (if not a TCP packet). It creates the Compression State for the packet stream identified by the CID.

Compressed non-TCP is a non-TCP packet with a compressed header. The compressed header is composed of a CID determining what compression state is used for decompression as well as a generation to determine inconsistent Compression State and the varying fields of the header.

Compressed TCP illustrates a packet with a compressed TCP header which is composed of a CID, a flag byte determining what fields have been altered, and the altered fields encoded as the difference from the former value.

Besides the regular packet types employed for compression, standard IPv4 and IPv6 packets will be employed whenever a compressor chooses to not compress a packet.

Lost Packets

Because TCP headers are compressed by employing the difference from the former TCP header, loss of a packet with a compressed or full header will bring about further compressed headers which will be incorrectly decompressed due to the compression state employed for decompression was not incremented correctly.

The loss of a compressed TCP header will bring about the TCP sequence numbers of further decompressed TCP headers to be off by k. The value k is the size of the lost segment. This type of incorrectly decompressed TCP header will be discarded by the TCP receiver as the TCP checksum finds errors that are off by the amount of k within the sequence numbers for k.

TCP's repair method will ultimately resend the discarded segment and the compressor moves into the TCP headers to determine when TCP resend. At this occurrence, the compressor transmits a complete header believing that the resend was because of mismatching Compression State at the decompressor.

Lost Packets in UDP/Non-TCP Packet Streams

The UDP checksum is not calculated and the checksum is actually optional. Erroneously decompressed headers of UDP packets as well as other non-TCP packets are protected well by checksums as TCP packets due to the fact that differential coding isn't employed because there no sequence numbers. The UDP checksum only covers payload, UDP header, and fake headers. The fake header (shown in Figure 9.1) incorporates the source and destination addresses, the transport protocol type and the length of the transport packet. With the exception of these fields, large parts of the IPv6 header are not protected by the UDP checksum.

To effectively avoid erroneous decompression of non-TCP headers, each version of the compression state for non-TCP packet streams is distinguished by a generation, a short amount is conveyed by the full headers which create and renew the compression state. Compressed headers convey the generation value of the Compression State, which were employed to compress them. When a decompressor views a compressed header it conveys a generation value besides that of the generation of its compression state for that packet stream. The Compression State is not up to date and the packet needs to either be eliminated or stored until a full header creates a correct compression state.

Differential coding is not employed for non-TCP streams, therefore compressed non-TCP headers do not change the compression state. The elimination of a compressed header does not void subsequent packets with compressed headers. Instead, the generation field is altered only when the Compression State of a full header is unlike the Compression State of the previous full header. This indicates that relinquishing a full header will make the Compression State of the decompressor outmoded only when the full header would actually have altered the Compression State.

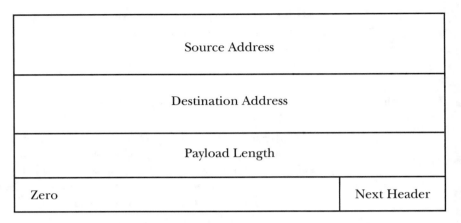

Figure 9.1. Fake Header

Slow-Start

To allow the decompressor to recover quickly from losing a complete header that would have changed the Compression State, full headers are sent at periodic intervals with an extensively increasing period after an alteration in the Compression State. This method prevents an exchange of messages between compressor and decompressor utilized by other compression methods. This type of exchange can be costly for wireless mobiles, due to the fact that as more power is eaten by the transmitter. In addition, delay can be injected by switching from the sender to the receiver. In addition, techniques which require an exchange of messages can not be employed over simplex links, including direct-broadcast satellite channels or cable TV systems, as they are difficult to adapt to multicast over multi-access links.

Header Refreshes

To stop losing too many packets when a receiver has lost its compression state, there is an upper limit on the amount of non-TCP packets with compressed headers which can be sent between header refreshes. To stop excessive periods of disconnection for low data rate packet streams, there is also an upper limit on the time between full headers in a non-TCP packet stream. When a packet is to be transmitted and too much time has elapsed since the last full header was sent for this packet stream, a full header needs to be transmitted.

Full Headers

The expense involved in header refreshes with regards to bandwidth are above similar costs for hard state methods. This is illustrated where full headers need to be acknowledged by the decompressor prior to sending compressed headers. This type of method usually transmits one full header in addition to a few control messages when the Compression State changes. Hard state methods need more types of protocol messages, while an exchange of messages is essential. Hard state methods require the need to explicitly deal with several error conditions which soft state methods automatically support. One example is when one party disappears unexpectedly. This proves to be a common situation on wireless links where mobiles operate beyond the range of the base.

The distinct advantage of the soft state method is that no handshakes are required between compressor and decompressor, so the method can be employed over simplex links. The expense of bandwidth is for more than hard state methods. However, the ease of the decom-pressor protocol besides the lack of handshakes between compressor and decompressor excuses this small cost. In addition, soft state methods are more easily extended to multicast over multi-access links (e.g., radio.)

9.4. GROUPING PACKETS

To determine how packets may be grouped together into packet streams for compression, we need to achieve the best compression rates. Packets need to be grouped together so those within the same packet stream have similar headers. When this grouping doesn't work, the header compression operation will be poor due to the fact that the compression algorithm hardly uses the existing Compression State for the packet stream and full headers need to be sent frequently.

The compressor accomplishes grouping. A compressor may use any methods to locate the appropriate means by which to group packets into packet streams. To find out what packet stream a packet belongs to, a compressor may inspect the compressible chain of subheaders, inspect the contents of an upper layer protocol header which follows the compressible chain of subheaders (e.g., ICMP headers, DVMRP headers, or tunneled IPX headers).

In addition, it may use data acquired from a resource manager. Once example deals with the resource manager who requests compression for a specific packet stream and yields a method of determining where packets are part of the packet stream. A compressor also can choose not to group packets into packet streams for compression. This allows some packets to keep their normal headers and passing them through unmodified. Adhering to the methods and rules regarding a packet stream are followed and as long as subheaders are compressed as outlined here, the decompressor has the ability to rebuild a compressed header correctly regardless of how packets are grouped into packet streams.

Fragmented Packets

Fragmented and unfragmented packets are never grouped together within the same packet stream. The Identification field of the Fragment header or IPv4 header is not employed to determine the packet stream. If it were, the initial fragment (shown in Figure 9.2) of a new packet would make a compression slow-start.

Priority Field

It is possible that a Priority field of the IPv6 header can change between packets with identical DEF fields when the Flow Label is zero. When IP packets are tunneled, they are encapsulated with an extra IP header at the tunnel entry point and then transmitted to the tunnel endpoint. To group such packets into packet streams, the inner headers must be inspected to determine the packet stream. When this is not accomplished, the complete headers will be transmitted each time the headers of the inner IP packet change. Therefore, when a packet is tunneled, the identifying fields of the

IPv6 Header Next Header: Routing	Routing Header Next Header: Fragment	Fragment Header Next Header: TCP	Fragment of TCP Header + Data

Figure 9.2. Fragment of TCP

inner subheaders need to be taken into account besides identifying fields of the first IP header.

An implementation can employ other fields for identification as well. If too many fields are utilized for identification, performance may decrease because more CIDs will be employed and the wrong CIDs may be reused when new flows need CIDs. If too few fields are utilized for identification, performance can decrease because there are too many changes in the Compression State.

9.5. COMPRESSION IDENTIFIERS

Compression identifiers can be 8 or 16 bits in length. Their size is not pertinent for locating the Compression State. An 8-bit CID with value two and a 16-bit CID with value two are the same.

The CID spaces for TCP and non-TCP are different, therefore a TCP CID and a non-TCP CID do not distinguish the same compression state, even when they have the same value. This also acts as the available CID space while employing the same amount of bits for CIDs. It is possible to determine if a complete or compressed header is for a TCP or non-TCP packet — this effectively eliminates confusion.

Non-TCP compressed headers encode the amount of the CID by employing one bit in the first byte of the compressed header. The 8-bit CID permits a minimum compressed header size of 2 octets for non-TCP packets, the size bit and the 6-bit Generation value are appropriate in the first octet and the CID uses the second octet.

In terms of TCP the only permissible CID amounts is 8 bits. Eight bits is most likely sufficient, as TCP connections are often point-to-point.

The 16 bit CID amount is most likely not required for point-to-point links. However, it is meant for use on multi-access links where a bigger CID space may be required for effective CID choice.

The major problem with multi-access links is that most compressors share the CID space of a decompressor. CIDs are not chosen independently by the compressors as collisions occur. Allowing the decompressors to maintain an individual CID space for each compressor can solve this difficulty. While maintaining individual CID spaces you must have decompressors which can distinguish which compressor transmitted the compressed packet. This may occur by employing link-layer information regarding who transmitted the link-layer frame. If this type of data is unavailable, all compressors on the multi-access link may be specified. This can happen by automatic means or by providing the number as a section of the CID.

Compression State Size

The size of the Compression State needs to be restricted to ease the implementation of compressor and decompressor, and place a restriction on the memory requirements. Yet, there is no upper limit on the amount of an IPv6 header as the chain of extension headers can have an arbitrary length. This is a difficulty as the Compression State is basically a stored header.

9.6. HEADERS SIZE

It is preferable to avoid expanding the packet size with full headers above their original size. This is because their size may be optimized for the MTU of the link. It is likely that the link-layer implementation yields the length of packets, it is possible to employ the length fields in full headers to pass the values of the CID and the generation to the decompressor.

IPv6/UDP or IPv4/UDP packet will possess four octets accessible to pass the generation and the CID, so all CID sizes can be employed. Fragmented or encrypted packet streams may possess only two octets to pass the generation and CID. Therefore, the 8-bit CIDs may be the only CID magnitude that can be used for such packet streams. At a time which IPv6/IPv4 or IPv4/IPv6 tunneling is employed, there will be a minimum of four octets, and both CID sizes can be utilized.

The generation value is sent in the higher order octet of the initial length field in the full header. At a time in which only one length field is available, the 8-bit CID is sent in the low order octet. When two length fields are accessible, the lowest two octets of the CID are sent in the second length field and that the low order octet of the first length field conveys the highest octet of the CID.

In terms of the rules governing the compressibility of a chain of subheaders that are compressed and can be compressed to incorporate IPv6 base and extension headers, TCP headers, UDP headers, and IPv4 headers. The compressible chain of subheaders stretch out from the beginning of the header and up to the first header which isn't an IPv4 header, an IPv6 base or extension header, a TCP header, or a UDP header. Alternatively, this can stretch out to include the first TCP header, UDP header, Fragment Header, Encapsulating Security Payload Header (payload format shown in Figure 9.3), or IPv4 header for a fragment. However, this depends on which provides the smaller chain.

9.7. IPV6 HEADER

The Payload Length field of encapsulated headers needs to be the same as the length value of the encapsulating header. If it doesn't, the header chain will not be compressed. This distinction indicates that the complete IPv6 base header can be compressed away.

The initial fragment of a packet has Fragment Offset = 0 and the chain of subheaders reaches beyond its Fragment Header. If a fragment is not the initial one which has a fragment offset that is not 0, there are no further

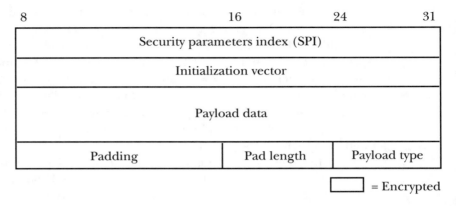

Figure 9.3. Payload Format

subheaders. There is the exception, however, that the chain of subheaders in the initial fragment doesn't fit completely in the first fragment.

Due to the fact that packets may be reordered prior to attaining the compression point, there are some fragments which can observe other routes through the network, a compressor is not able to depend upon viewing the first fragment prior to other fragments. This indicates that information in subheaders succeeding the Fragment Header of the first fragment cannot be examined to decide the proper packet stream for other fragments.

Design compression methods can compress subheaders after the Fragment Header. This neither complicates the rules for transmitting full headers nor those governing compression and decompression. In addition, the chain of subheaders that come after a Fragment Header should not be compressed.

Encapsulating the Header

Encapsulating a header indicates that the some parts of the packet are encrypted. Therefore, no more header compression is feasible on further headers. This is because encryption is usually performed when the compressor sees the packet.

When the ESP Header is used in tunnel mode the whole IP packet is encrypted. In addition, the headers of that packet may be compressed prior to the packet being encrypted at the entry point of the tunnel. This indicates that it is possible to supply an IP packet as well as its length to the decompressor, as if it had come from the link-layer. When dealing with a point to point link, the compressor has a complete understanding of what CIDs are currently in use at the decompressor and can alter what CID a packet stream uses or reuse CIDs.

9.8. DROPPING PACKETS

When a decompressor retrieves a packet with a compressed TCP header with CID C, it needs to be dropped when the compression state for C has not been initialized by a full header. Once a decompressor retrieves a packet with a compressed non-TCP header with CID C and generation G, the header can not be decompressed via the current compression state when the decompressor has been disconnected from the compressor for more than a minimum amount of time. This is due to the fact that the Compression State can be obsolete even if it has generation G. It is important to note that the Compression State for C has a generation other than G.

In either of the above events, a packet can either be dropped instantly or stored for a short time until the compression state is updated by a packet with complete non-TCP header with CID C and generation G, after which the header can be decompressed. Packets recorded through this method must be dropped when it received complete or compressed non-TCP headers with CID C and a generation besides G.

When full or complete headers are lost, a decompressor may receive compressed non-TCP headers with a generation value besides that of the generation of its compression state. Therefore, the decompressor is allowed to store these type of headers until they can be decompressed using the correct compression state.

9.9. LOW-LOSS HEADER COMPRESSION

Because fewer bits are sent per packet with header compression, the packet loss rate is less than with header compression than without. When dealing with a fixed bit-error rate. This method is advantageous for links with high bit-error rates including wireless links.

Since TCP headers are compressed with differential encoding, one single lost TCP segment can destroy an entire TCP sending window due to the fact that the Compression State is not incremented correctly at the decompressor. All further headers will then be decompressed to be different than prior to compression and then eliminated by the TCP receiver because the TCP checksum fails.

When a TCP connection in the wide area which has last hop over a medium speed poor link which experiences loss (e.g., wireless LAN) it will then have poor performance with conventional header compression. This is due to the fact that the delay-bandwidth product is reasonably big and the bit-error rate relatively large.

There are two simple mechanisms which provide fast repair of the Compression State. These methods offer header compression that will increase TCP throughput throughout links which experience loss in addition to links with low bit-error rates.

9.10. REQUESTS FOR HEADERS

When the decompressor ceases to repair the Compression State after a loss, the decompressor asks for a full header from the compressor. The easiest and most widely chosen configuration is more than likely to be that the TCP acknowledgment and data streams that pass through the same nodes on each side of a high loss link. There will then be a compressor/decompressor pair on each side of the link.

If you were to think that an acknowledgement has been destroyed on the high loss link from node X to node Y. The link-level checksum find the ruined frame and eliminates it. Imagine that the decompressor in node Y is not able to repair its compression state when the next compressed acknowledgment arrives. Then the decompressor in node Y will then query the compressor in node Y to establish a bit in a full header in the associated TCP stream moving in the other direction. When the decompressor in node X views the bit, it inquires about its companion compressor in order to transmit a full header in the packet stream with the associated IP addresses and port numbers. The full header revises the Compression State for the decompressor in node Y and acknowledgments begin to flow once more.

The TCP acknowledgment stream in this method is repaired after a roundtrip-time over the high loss link, then the majority of the window will traverse the distance unharmed. The lower packet loss rate is due to the fact that shorter packets will result in higher throughput due to the fact that the TCP window can increase between losses.

The header request method will not operate when routes are not symmetric. In addition, the TCP streams don't visit the same nodes. There are some situations that are somewhat normal. The method of transmitting a header request is a clue that it is prudent to transmit a full header in the associated TCP packet stream. However, header requests is only a performance improving method and it is acceptable to ignore these indications so long as there isn't any associated TCP packet stream which can be found. Compressors need to quietly ignore requests for full headers in TCP streams for which they are not compressing. Decompressors need to ignore inquiries for full headers when they are not able to contact an appropriate compressor.

9.11. REORDERING PACKETS

There are some links that reorder packets, such as multi-hop radio links that use deflection routing to route around congested nodes. Packets routed various ways can then reach a destination in a different order than the way in which they were transmitted.

Compressed non-TCP headers don't alter their compression state. In addition full headers don't refresh them. When a full header changes the Compression State comes out of order some difficulties can arise.

A compressor can forego sending compressed TCP headers and only transmit compressed TCP headers when reordering is involved over the link. Compressed headers will usually be 17 bytes when employing this method, a number that is considerably bigger than the standard byte size which is between four to seven.

Full TCP headers will only have sufficient space for one byte of sequence number when there is no tunneling. It is not possible to expand the size of full headers due to the fact that the packet size may be optimized for the MTU of the link. In essence, only the least important byte of the packet sequence number can be arranged in this type of full headers.

However, when dealing with compressed TCP headers the two-byte packet sequence number is put just after the TCP Checksum.

To achieve increased compression rates, the method of adding only two bytes to the compressed header for a total of 6–9 bytes is employed. A packet sequence number, incremented by one for every packet in the TCP stream, is linked with each compressed and full header. This permits the decompressor to place the packets in the correct sequence and utilize their deltas to the compression state in the proper sequence. An easy sliding window method can be employed to place the packets in the proper sequence.

Two bytes are required for the packet sequence numbers. One byte yields just 256 sequence numbers. In a sliding window method, the window need not be bigger than half of the sequence number space. Therefore, packets can not get more than 127 positions out of sequence. This is the same as a delay of 260 ms on 2 Mbit/s links with 512 byte segments. Delays of that magnitude are not unusual over wide area Internet connections.

Added Header Compression

In order to permit added header compression methods for headers of protocols layered above UDP, you need to look at the initial chain of subheaders. They are compressed while the other header compression method is used to the header above the UDP header. Enabling some error detection, these types of methods usually require a sequence number that may need to be sent in full headers in addition to compressed UDP headers.

Demultiplexing

It is important have the ability to distinguish packets in the following ways:

- IPv4 headers
- Regular IPv6 headers
- Full IPv6 packets
- Full IPv4 packets
- Compressed TCP packets
- Compressed non-TCP packets.

It is important to note that link-layers need to be able to verify that a packet is in fact an IPv6 packet.

Precautions

It should be noted that you shouldn't identify packet streams with the help of information that is encrypted, even if this type of information is available to the compressor. Otherwise, traffic patterns would be easily intercepted.

9.12. CONCLUSION

Header compression is an important aspect when exploring IPv6. When dealing with low to medium speed links, there is a beneficial effect by allowing small packets to be used for bulk data with sufficient line efficiency. If any users employ either telnet or bulk ftp — the data must be sent in small packets so that there is a minimal amount of delay when small telnet data is caught behind large ftp packets of data.

Compression is also a useful aspect within this chapter to illustrate that both TCP and non-TCP packet streams can be used. Even when any field change, they are expected to be the same in a packet stream in order to make the compressor send a full header again in an effort to update the compression state at the decompressor. The dealings with packets and headers can effectively meet requirements and provide a meaningful relationship for headers, packets, and compression under IPv6.

Packet Tunneling

10

10.1. INTRODUCTION

This chapter looks at the method by which IPv6 encapsulation of Internet packets involve both IPv6 and IPv4. This method can be also used with other protocol packets such as AppleTalk, IPX, CLNP, or others.

The specific method in which a packet is encapsulated and conveyed as payload within an IPv6 packet is the focus of this section. The resultant packet is referred to as an IPv6 tunnel packet. The forwarding path between the source and destination of the tunnel packet is referred to as IPv6 tunnel. The mechanism is referred to as IPv6 tunneling.

A sample illustration of IPv6 tunneling is an event where an intermediate node exerts specific routing control by determining specific forwarding paths for chosen packets. This control is acquired by looking at each initially chosen original packets or IPv6 headers which distinguish the forwarding path. Besides the overall portrayal of IPv6 tunneling mechanisms, certain methods involved for tunneling IPv6 and IPv4 packets is a main focus within this section.

10.2. TUNNELING

IPv6 tunneling is a method which creates a virtual link between two IPv6 nodes for sending data packets as payloads of IPv6 packets. When looking at this from the perspective of the two nodes, the virtual link is referred to as an IPv6 tunnel. It emerges as a point to point link whereby IPv6 performs like a link-layer protocol. The two IPv6 nodes have very specific duties.

One node encapsulates the original packets retrieved from other nodes or itself and then sends the resultant packets through the tunnel. The second node decapsulates the retrieved tunnel packets and sends the resultant first packets to their destinations. The encapsulator node is referred to as the tunnel entry-point node, and it is the source of the tunnel packets. The decapsulator node is referred to as the tunnel exit-point, and is the destination of the tunnel packets.

The discussion here primarily deals with tunnels between two nodes distinguished by unicast addresses. These tunnels look a great deal like virtual point to point links. The methods also work towards tunnels where other types of addresses (e.g., anycast or multicast) determine the exit-point nodes.

An IPv6 tunnel is a unidirectional device where tunnel packet flow occurs in one direction between the IPv6 tunnel entry-point and exit-point nodes. Bi-directional tunneling is acquired by merging two unidirectional mechanisms which involves the configuration of two tunnels. Each has opposite direction to the other, where the entry-point node of one tunnel is the exit-point node of the other tunnel.

10.3. ENCAPSULATION

IPv6 encapsulation is composed of the initial packet, an IPv6 header, and possibly a set of IPv6 extension. They are altogether referred to as tunnel IPv6 headers. The encapsulation occurs in an IPv6 tunnel entry-point node, as the result of an original packet sent to the virtual link depicted by the tunnel. The initial packet is operated on during forwarding with respect to the forwarding rules of the protocol of that packet. Should the initial packet be an IPv6 packet, the IPv6 original header hop limit is decreased by one. In an IPv4 packet, the IPv4 original header time to live field (TTL) is decreased by one.

During encapsulation, the source field of the tunnel IPv6 header is occupied with an IPv6 address of the tunnel entry-point node, while the destination field is occupied with an IPv6 address of the tunnel exit-point. Afterward, the tunnel packet that results from encapsulation is transmitted to the tunnel exit-point node.

Packet Processing

A tunnel Hop by Hop Options extension header is operated on by each receiving node in the tunnel. Then, a tunnel Routing extension header determines the intermediate operating nodes and also controls (with a finer granularity) the forwarding path of the tunnel packet through the tunnel. The tunnel Destination Options extension header is operated on at the tunnel exit-point node.

10.4. DECAPSULATION

After receiving an IPv6 packet that is meant for an IPv6 address of a tunnel exit-point node, its IPv6 protocol layer operates on the tunnel headers. The exacting left-to-right processing rules for extension headers are used. When processing is finished, the control is sent to the next protocol engine, which is classified by the Next Header field value in the last header processed.

When this is set to a tunnel protocol value, the tunnel protocol engine throws away the tunnel headers and sends the resultant initial packet to the Internet or lower layer protocol determined by that value for more processing. When dealing with the Next Header field that has the IPv6 Tunnel Protocol value, the resultant initial packet is sent to the IPv6 protocol layer. The tunnel exit-point node (which decapsulates the tunnel packets) and the destination node (that receives the resulting original packets) can actually be the same node.

During implementation, a tunnel upper-layer input and output can be instituted in the same way as the input and output of the other upper-layer protocols. In addition, the tunnel link-layer input and output can be instituted in the same way as the input and output of the other link-layer protocols. For example, associating an interface or fake interface with the

IPv6 tunnel may apply here. Remember, choosing the IPv6 tunnel link over other links is a result from the packet forwarding choice that was observed based on the content of the node's routing table.

10.5. NESTED ENCAPSULATION

Nested IPv6 encapsulation is defined as the encapsulation of a tunnel packet. It occurs when a hop of an IPv6 tunnel is a tunnel. The tunnel that holds a tunnel is referred to as an outer tunnel. The tunnel held in the outer tunnel is referred to as an inner tunnel. Note that, inner tunnel and their associated outer tunnels are nested tunnels.

The entry-point node of an inner IPv6 tunnel retrieves tunnel IPv6 packets encapsulated by the outer IPv6 tunnel entry-point node. The inner tunnel entry-point node considers the receiving tunnel packets as initial packets and executes encapsulation. The resulting packets are tunnel packets for the inner IPv6 tunnel and nested tunnel packets for the outer IPv6 tunnel.

In the event of a forwarding path that has several levels of nested tunnels, a routing-loop from an inner tunnel to an outer tunnel is specifically troublesome when packets from the inner tunnels re-enter an outer tunnel from which they have not yet emerged. In this situation, the nested encapsulation turns into a recursive encapsulation that has negative repercussions. Due to the fact that each nested encapsulation increases a tunnel header by adding a new hop limit value, the IPv6 hop limit method is not able to control the amount of times the packet reaches the outer tunnel entry-point node. Furthermore, it is unable to control the amount of recursive encapsulations.

Once the packet path from source to final destination incorporates tunnels, the largest number of hops that the packet can go across needs to be controlled by two methods employed at the same time. This effectively cancels the negative effects of recursive encapsulation in routing loops.

First, the initial packet hop limit is decreased as each forwarding operation is executed on an initial packet. This contains each encapsulation of the initial packet. However, it does not include nested encapsulations of the initial packet. The tunnel IPv6 packet encapsulation limit is decreased at each nested encapsulation of the packet.

10.6. NESTED ENCAPSULATION RESTRICTIONS

The tunnel IPv6 packet size is restricted to the highest IPv6 datagram size. Each encapsulation expands the size of a tunnel packet as well as the size of the tunnel IPv6 headers. As a result, the amount of tunnel headers, nested encapsulations, and inner IPv6 tunnels with an outer IPv6 tunnel is restricted by the maximum packet size.

The expansion in the size of a tunnel IPv6 packet is primarily due to nested encapsulations that may need fragmentation. In addition, each fragmentation as a result of nested encapsulation regarding a fragmented tunnel packet that results in a twofold increase in the number of fragments. In addition, it is very likely that when this fragmentation starts, each new nested encapsulation results in additional fragmentation. It is prudent, therefore, to limit nested encapsulation. The method that involves restricting extravagant nested encapsulation is a tunnel encapsulation limit that is conveyed within an IPv6 Destination Option.

10.7. TUNNEL ENCAPSULATION RESTRICTIONS

The Tunnel Encapsulation Limit is an effective restriction destination alternative that is provided only by tunnel entry-point nodes. It is eliminated only by tunnel exit-point nodes, and then is employed to convey optional information that must be examined only by tunnel entry-point nodes.

Tunnel Encapsulation Limit destination alternatives are defined by the highest-order two bits (value 00) which indicative of hopping over this option if it is not recognized. Then, the third-highest-order bit (value 0) is indicative of the fact that the option information in this alternative does not alter in route to the packet's destination.

In order to curtail unneeded nested encapsulation, an IPv6 tunnel entry-point node can work towards a packet going through encapsulation a Tunnel Encapsulation Limit Destination Option. The OptData Value field of the option is set to a pre-configured value. Value results from an amount recorded in the IPv6 destination options header, or if such a header exists and if it has a Tunnel Encapsulation Limit option, the OptData Value of the existing option is duplicated into a new Tunnel Encapsulation Limit option and then decreased by one.

Tunnel encapsulation limit destination option is the maximum amount of nested encapsulations of a packet. The Tunnel Encapsulation Limit destination option is provided only by tunnel entry-point nodes and is discarded only by tunnel exit point nodes. It is used to carry optional information that must be examined only by tunnel entry-point nodes. The OptData Value is used to avoid excessive nested encapsulation. An IPv6 tunnel entry-point node may prepend a packet undergoing encapsulation. The OptData Value field of the option is set to a pre-configured value should the packet being encapsulated and has neither a IPv6 destination options header or Tunnel Encapsulation Limit option in such a header. A value that results from an amount is stored in the IPv6 destination options header. When such a header exist and contains a Tunnel Encapsulation Limit option, the OptData Value of the extant option is duplicated into a newly prepended Tunnel Encapsulation Limit option and then decremented by one.

Exceptions

There is an exception involving the processing of destination options extension header. During encapsulation the IPv6 tunneling protocol engine looks forward to an IPv6 destination header which has a Tunnel Encapsulation Limit option just after following the existing IPv6 main header.

Should the Tunnel Encapsulation Limit be decreased to zero, the packet enduring encapsulation is thrown away. When the packet is dropped, a Parameter Problem ICMP message is sent back to the packet originator. This is the former tunnel entry-point. The message specifies the Opt Data Value field within the Tunnel Encapsulation Limit destination header of the packet. The field designates a value of one.

10.8. LOOPBACK ENCAPSULATION

Loopback encapsulation is a specific case of encapsulation which needs be avoided. Loopback encapsulation occurs when a tunnel IPv6 entry-point node encapsulates tunnel IPv6 packets initiated from itself, and sent to itself. This can create an infinite processing loop within the entry-point node.

To avoid this problem, you need to have an implementation method which both inspects and gets rid of the configuration of a tunnel where both the entry-point and exit-point node addresses are property of the same node. Furthermore, the encapsulating engine checks for and rejects the encapsulation of a packet that has the pair of tunnel entry-point and exit-point addresses which are the same as the pair of the initial packet source as well as the final destination addresses.

10.9. NESTED ENCAPSULATION RISK

Nested encapsulations of a packet turn into a recursive encapsulation when the packet re-enters an outer tunnel prior to emerging from it. The circumstance under which it has the highest risk of recursive encapsulation exists in the cases where a tunnel entry-point node is not able to conclude whether a packet undergoes encapsulation re-enters the tunnel prior to emerging from it. Routing loops that make tunnel packets re-enter a tunnel prior to emerging from it is a significant cause of the problem. However, since routing loops do occur, it is necessary realizes the cases in which the recursive encapsulation risk is highest.

There are two factors which determine the risk factor of routing loop recursive encapsulation. The first involves the type of tunnel. The second is a type of route to the tunnel exit-point which determines how the specifics of packet forwarding through the tunnel or over the tunnel virtual-link.

The kind of tunnels that are designated as a high risk factors for recursive encapsulation in routing loops include inner tunnels with analogous exit-points. These tunnels can be fixed-end inner tunnels with unique entry-points. However, it may instead be free-end inner tunnels with unique entry-points. Remember that the free-end inner tunnels are grouped with identical exit-point tunnels.

Due to the fact that the source and destination of an original packet incorporates the main information employed to determine whether to forward a packet through a tunnel or not — a recursive encapsulation is averted in case of a single (non inner) tunnel. However, you may also determine that the packet that is to be encapsulated is not initiated on the entry-point node.

This level of protection doesn't perform well in the event of inner tunnels with unique entry-points, and analogous exit-points. Inner tunnels that have unique entry-points and analogous exit-points inject a level of uncertainty in determining whether to encapsulate a packet. At the point in which a packet is encapsulated in an inner tunnel extends to the entry-point node of an outer tunnel by using a method involving a routing loop.

This is because the source of the tunnel packet is the inner tunnel entry-point node and is unique from any entry-point node of the outer tunnel. The source address checking is not able to detect invalid encapsulations. Therefore, as a result the tunnel packet becomes encapsulated at the outer tunnel every time it reaches it through the routing loop.

The type of route to a tunnel exit-point node also has been distinguished as a high risk factor of recursive encapsulation in routing loops. One route type to a tunnel exit-point node is a route to a specified destination node. The destination is a valid designated IPv6 address pertaining to route to node. This type of route can be chosen based on the more distant peer of an initial packet destination address with the destination address recorded in the tunnel entry-point node routing table entry for that route. The packet forwarded on this type of route is primarily encapsulated and then forwarded towards the tunnel exit-point node.

There is also another type of route to a tunnel exit-point node, it is a route to a designated prefix-net. Essentially, the destination is a valid designated IPv6 prefix pertaining to route to net. This type of route can be chosen based on the more distant path equivalent of an initial packet destination address with the prefix destination recorded in the tunnel entry-point node routing table entry for that route. The packet forwarded on this type of a route is primarily encapsulated and then forwarded towards the tunnel exit-point node.

An alternate route to a tunnel exit-point is a default route or a route to an undesignated destination. This route is chosen when no-other match for the destination of the initial packet has been located within the routing table. A tunnel that is the primary hop of a default route is referred to as a default tunnel.

If the route to a tunnel exit-point is a route to node, the risk factor for recursive encapsulation is minimal. However, if the route to a tunnel exit-point is a route to net, the risk for recursive encapsulation is moderate. There exists a range of destination addresses that will match the prefix the route it is linked to. When there is at least one inner tunnel with various tunnel entry-points that have exit-point node addresses that match the route to net of an outer tunnel exit-point. At this point a recursive encapsulation can occur if a tunnel packet is deflected from inside such an inner tunnel to the entry-point of the outer tunnel which has a route to its exit-point that matches the exit-point of an inner tunnel.

When the route to a tunnel exit-point is a default route, the risk for recursive encapsulation is maximal. Packets are forwarded through a default tunnel because there isn't a more effective route. In the majority of situations, forwarding through a default tunnel can occur for a wide extent of destination addresses, which at the maximum limit is the entire Internet less the node's link. As a result, it is likely that in a routing loop case the packet will be encapsulated again because the default routing method will not be able to know differently which based on the destina-tion. This situation involves a tunnel packet that gets deflected from an inner tunnel to an outer tunnel entry-point in which the tunnel is the default tunnel.

When dealing with the IPv6 node configuration parameters, a tunnel entry-point node may add to the tunnel IPv6 main header at least one IPv6 extension header (e.g., routing).

Tunnel Exit-Point Node Address

The tunnel exit-point node address is employed as IPv6 destination address for the tunnel IPv6 header. The tunnel exit-point node address can be con-figured with a distinct IPv6 address. In this event the tunnel is called a fixed-exit tunnel. This type of tunnel performs the same as would a virtual point to point link between the entry-point node and exit-point node. However, a tunnel exit-point address can be configured with no particular address. In this case, the tunnel is referred to as a free-exit tunnel. This type of tunnel performs like a virtual point to point link between the entry-point node and an exit-point node distinguished by the destination address from the initial packet header.

The tunnel exit-point node address is duplicated to the destination address field in the tunnel IPv6 header while packet encapsulation occurs. The configuration of the tunnel entry-point and exit-point addresses is nei-ther dependent to IPv6 Autoconfiguration nor IPv6 Neighbor Discovery.

Tunnel Hop Limit

An IPv6 tunnel is patterned after a single-hop virtual link tunnel which involves sending the initial packet through the tunnel. This is like sending the initial packet over a one hop link. The actual amount of hops in the IPv6 tunnel doesn't matter.

The single-hop method needs to be instituted by maintaining the tunnel entry point node so that it is set to a tunnel IPv6 header hop limit separately from the hop limit of the original header. The single-hop method is concealed from the initial IPv6 packets the amount of IPv6 hops of the tunnel. The tunnel hop limit needs to be configured with a value which makes certain that a tunnel IPv6 packets can reach the tunnel exit-point node. It must also provide a fast expiration of the tunnel packet when a routing loop happens within the IPv6 tunnel.

The tunnel hop limit default value for hosts involves the IPv6 Neighbor Discovery advertised hop limit. The tunnel hop limit is duplicated into the hop limit field of the tunnel IPv6 header of each packet encapsulated by the tunnel entry-point node.

Tunnel Packets

The IPv6 Tunnel Packet Priority illustrates the value that a tunnel entry-point node establishes in the priority field of a tunnel header. The default value is zero. The configured Packet Priority determines if the value of the priority field in the tunnel header is duplicated from the original header, or it is set to the pre-configured value.

The IPv6 Tunnel Flow Label illustrates value that a tunnel entry-point node establishes in the flow label of a tunnel header. This has a default value of zero.

The Tunnel Encapsulation Limit value is indicative of whether the entry-point node is configured to restrict the amount of encapsulations of tunnel packets that are conceived on that node. The IPv6 Tunnel Encapsulation Limit is the most number of encapsulations allowed for packets which always undergo encapsulation at that entry-point node.

Tunnel MTU

The tunnel MTU is set to the Path MTU between the tunnel entry-point and the tunnel exit-point nodes less the size of the tunnel headers — this is the maximum size of a tunnel packet payload which can be transmitted through the tunnel without fragmentation. The tunnel entry-point node acts like Path MTU discovery on the path between the tunnel entry-point and exit-point nodes. The tunnel MTU of a nested tunnel is the tunnel MTU of the outer tunnel less the size of the tunnel headers.

Even though it should be able to transmit a tunnel IPv6 packet of any valid size, the tunnel entry-point node tries to avert the fragmentation of tunnel packets. It accomplishes this goal by declaring to source nodes of the initial packets that the MTU can be employed in sizing initial packets transmitted towards the tunnel entry-point node.

Size Issues

A tunnel packet that results from the encapsulation of an IPv6 original packet may need to be fragmented. A tunnel IPv6 packet that is the result of the encapsulation of an initial packet is believed to be an IPv6 packet starting from the tunnel entry-point node. Essentially, like any source of an IPv6 packet, a tunnel entry-point node needs to support fragmentations of tunnel IPv6 packets.

A tunnel intermediate node (which forwards a tunnel packet to another node in the tunnel) adheres to the IPv6 rule that it should not fragment a packet enduring forwarding. A tunnel exit-point node receives tunnel packets at the end of the tunnel for decapsulation that administers the precise left-to-right operating rules for extension headers. During the case of fragmentation headers, the fragments are reassembled into a tunnel packet prior to deciding that an embedded IP packet is there.

Tunnel Packet Fragmentation

Tunnel packets that go beyond the tunnel MTU are contestants for fragmentation. The fragmentation of tunnel packets that hold IPv6 original packets is operated on by the initial IPv6 packet with a size greater than 576 octets. The entry-point node drops the packet and it gives back an ICMPv6 Packet Too Big message to the source node of the initial packet with the suggested MTU size field set to the maximum between 576 as well as the tunnel MTU. The tunnel MTU is the Path MTU between the tunnel entry-point and the tunnel exit-point nodes less the size of the tunnel headers.

If the initial IPv6 packet is the same or smaller than 576 octets, the tunnel entry-point node encapsulates the original packet. The next step involves fragmentation of the resultant IPv6 tunnel packet into IPv6 fragments that do not surpass the tunnel MTU.

Tunnel packets that surpass the tunnel MTU are contestants for fragmentation. The fragmentation of tunnel packets which contain IPv4 original packets is performed if the initial IPv4 packet header with the "Don't Fragment" or DF bit flag is SET. The entry-point node drops the packet and gives back an ICMP message.

In the initial packet header the Don't Fragment bit flag is CLEAR, the tunnel entry-point node encapsulates the initial packet. The next involves fragmenting the resultant IPv6 tunnel packet into IPv6 fragments which do not surpass the tunnel MTU.

Error Reporting

IPv6 tunneling adheres to the standard rule regarding an error discovered during the operation of an IPv6 packet. It is then reported through an ICMP message to the source of the packet.

When dealing with forwarding path that incorporates IPv6 tunnels, an error detected by a node that doesn't exist in any tunnel is instantly reported to the source of the initial IPv6 packet.

An error detected by a node within a tunnel is reported to the source of the tunnel packet. In essence, it is the tunnel entry-point node. The ICMP message transmitted to the tunnel entry-point node has (as ICMP payload) the tunnel IPv6 packet (which has the initial packet as its payload.)

The basis of a packet error discovered within a tunnel can be problematic with both a tunnel header, or the tunnel packet. Both the tunnel header and tunnel packet difficulties are reported to the tunnel entry-point node.

When a tunnel packet problem is the result of a problem with the initial packet (which is the payload of the tunnel packet) then the problem is also reported to the source of the initial packet. To report a problem detected within the tunnel to the source of an original packet, the tunnel entry point node needs to relay the ICMP message retrieved from within the tunnel to the source of that initial IPv6 packet.

10.10.   ICMP MESSAGES

The tunnel ICMP messages that are reported to the source of the initial packet include:

- Hop limit exceeded: This is where the tunnel has a incorrectly configured hop limit, or holds a routing loop. Furthermore, packets do not get to the tunnel exit-point node. This difficulty is reported to the tunnel entry-point node, it is at this point where the tunnel hop limit can be reconfigured to a higher value.
- Unreachable node: One of the nodes in the tunnel is not reachable. This difficulty is reported to the tunnel entry-point node, which needs to be reconfigured with a valid and active path between the entry and exit-point of the tunnel.
- Parameter problem: This involves a Parameter Problem ICMP message indicating that a valid Tunnel Encapsulation Limit Destination header with a Tun Encap Lim field value is set to one which is an sign that the tunnel packet exceeded the maximum amount of encapsulations allowed.

The above difficulties are detected within the tunnel configuration and tunnel topology. Furthermore, it is reported to the source of the initial IPv6 packet as a tunnel generic unreachable problem brought about by a link problem.

The packet too big indicates that a tunnel packet surpasses the tunnel Path MTU. The data conveyed by this type of ICMP message employed by receiving a tunnel entry-point node to adjust the tunnel MTU. This is accomplished by transmitting tunnel entry-point node to indicate to the source of an original packet the MTU size which needs to be employed in transmitting IPv6 packets towards the tunnel entry-point node.

ICMP Messages for IPv6 Initial Packets

The tunnel entry-point node creates the ICMP and IPv6 headers of the ICMP message. They are, in turn, sent to the source of the initial packet. The IPv6 fields includes the Source Address which is a valid unicast IPv6 address of the outgoing interface. In addition, the Destination Address is duplicated from the Source Address field of the initial IPv6 header. It is also very possible that you will be dealing with tunnel ICMP error messages such as:

- hop limit exceeded
- unreachable node
- parameter problem: This indicates a valid Tunnel Encapsulation Limit destination header with the Tun Encap Lim field set to a value one.

Values include:

- Type 1 — unreachable node
- Code 3 — address unreachable

ICMP Messages Destined For IPv4 Original Packets

The tunnel entry-point node creates the ICMP and IPv4 header of the ICMP message that is transmitted to the source of the initial packet by using IPv4 fields such as:

- Source Address: which is valid unicast IPv4 address of the outgoing interface.
- Destination Address: this is duplicated from the Source Address field of the initial IPv4 header.

ICMP Messages Destined For Nested Tunnels Packets

When dealing with an error uncovered with a nested tunnels packet, the inner tunnel entry-point (which receives the ICMP error message from the inner tunnel reporting node) relays the ICMP message to the outer tunnel entry-point. Also, the outer tunnel entry-point relays the ICMP message to the source of the initial packet.

10.11. SECURITY

The IPv6 tunnel can be secured, however to accomplish that goal the IPv6 path between the tunnel entry-point and exit-point node needs to be secured. A secure IPv6 tunnel may perform much like a gateway-to-gateway secure path.

The exit-point node of a secure IPv6 tunnel executes security algorithms and operates on the tunnel security headers as part of the tunnel headers processing listed in the previous section of this chapter. The exit-point node drops the tunnel security headers with the remainder of the tunnel headers after tunnel headers operations are finished.

The level of integrity, authentication, confidentiality, and the security processing executed on a tunnel packet at the entry-point and exit-point node of a secure IPv6 tunnel rely upon the type of security header:

- Authentication (AH)
- Encryption (ESP)

Also, there are several parameters configured in the Security Association for the tunnel. There is no inter-dependency or interaction between the security level and mechanisms used for the tunnel packets and the security applied to the initial packets that are the payloads of the tunnel packets. In the event of nested tunnels, each inner tunnel may possess its own set of security services, separately from those of the outer tunnels or of those between the source and destination of the initial packet.

10.12. CONCLUSION

Packet tunneling is an integral part of IPv6. The method by which IPv6 encapsulation of Internet protocol versions 4 and 6 occurs is crucial to the understanding of IPv6. In this chapter we have dealt with tunneling packets and have traced the forwarding paths outlined in the preceding section from its source to its destination in an attempt to more carefully illustrate the mechanism involved in packet tunneling.

Tunneling is an effective way of creating a virtual link between two IPv6 nodes. This allows for the transmission of data packets as payloads of IPv6 packets.

Encapsulation is also examined in this section as it deals with the initial packet, header, and extensions. Encapsulation is a method that happens in an IPv6 tunnel entry-point node as the result of the initial packet transmitted to the virtual link portrayed by the tunnel. The successive packet processing explains the forwarding rules governing the packet.

Even nested encapsulation explains that the size of the tunnel packet and the size of the tunnel IPv6 headers are expanded. The results in the amount of tunnel headers, nested encapsulations, and inner IPv6 tunnel with an outer IPv6 can be limited by the overall maximum packet size. All in all we see a method which brings the packet and its associated transmission to life where we can see it clearly in the actual application of packet tunneling within IPv6.

Compatibility

11

11.1. INTRODUCTION

In this chapter we will look at the changes which are required to make the Domain Name System support hosts operating IPv6. These changes incorporate a new resource record type to record an IPv6 address, a new domain to support lookups founded on an IPv6 address, and revised definitions of existing query types that return Internet addresses as a component of additional section processing. The extensions are intended to be compatible with existing applications as well as DNS implementations.

11.2. DNS EXTENSIONS

Existing support for Internet address storage in the Domain Name System (DNS) is not expanded to support IPv6 addresses. This is due to the fact that applications presume that address queries only return 32-bit IPv4 addresses.

To support IPv6 address storage, it is necessary to designate extensions such as a new resource record type — which is defined to map a domain name to an IPv6 address. Also, a new domain is designated to support lookups based on these addresses.

In addition, Present queries which execute additional section processing to find IPv4 addresses are designated to execute further section processing on both IPv4 and IPv6 addresses. These alterations are intended to be compatible with existing software. The present support for IPv4 addresses is maintained.

11.3. RESOURCE RECORDS

New record types are defined to record a host's IPv6 address, and a host that has greater than one IPv6 address needs to have greater than one such record. The AAAA resource record type is a new record distinct to the Internet class that records an individual IPv6 address. The AAAA data format involves a 128 bit IPv6 address that is embedded (IPv6 Address with Embedded IPv4 Addresses depicted in Figure 11.1) in the data section of an AAAA resource record in network byte order.

An AAAA query for a particular domain name in the Internet class sends back all associated AAAA resource records in the answer portion of a response. A type AAAA query does not execute additional section processing.

Special Domain

A special domain is designated to locate a record given its address. The intention behind this domain is to yield a method of mapping an IPv6 address to a host name. However, it may be employed for other purposes too. The domain is grounded at IP6.INT.

An IPv6 address is portrayed as a name within the IP6.INT domain by a sequence of nibbles detached by dots with the suffix. The sequence of nibbles is encoded in reverse order, where the low-order nibble is encoded first, then the next low-order nibble is encoded. A hexadecimal digit depicts each nibble.

Bits	80	16	32
	0000..............................0000	FFFF	IPv4 Address

Bits	80	16	32
	0000..............................0000	0000	IPv4 Address

Figure 11.1. IPv6 Address with
Embedded IPv4 Addresses

Query Types

All present query types which execute type A additional section processing such as name server (NS), mail exchange (MX), and mailbox (MB) query types — need to be designated to execute both type A and type AAAA additional section operations.

11.4. LIMITING THE ROLE OF IPV4 COMPATIBLE ADDRESSES IN IPV6

This section deals with the way in which you can limit IPv4-compatible IPv6 addresses to tunneling interfaces within the transition from IPv4 to IPv6. The reasons and context for limiting the usage in this method are listed below.

IPv4 compatible addresses are created to simplify the transition of IPv4 to IPv6 by employing the freely available IPv4 address space and protocols to yield IPv6 connectivity. They currently serve two uses pertaining to tunneling. The first permits you to have isolated IPv6 nodes to emerge on the Internet and talk with other IPv6 nodes through automatic tunneling. This does, however, require a small amount of configuration. The second aspect involves identifying an IPv6 router's next-hop interface address throughout a manually configured tunnel.

In this example, all IPv4-compatible addresses are on-link to the tunnel interface, while the IPv4 Internet forms one large link-layer. At this time, address resolution is an insignificant function. However, manually configured tunnels are utilized with static routes to IPv6 prefixes, where the next-hop is an IPv4 compatible address on the link. Ideally, then it can be shown that IPv6 packets is utilizing IPv4 compatible addresses need to be considered as employing a specific type of link-local address. Then the Hop Limit needs to be set with a value of one, without any abnormal end results.

The Transition Mechanisms in place also incorporate a condition to permit an IPv4-compatible address to be designated to an interface for native IPv6 communications. It has all the conditions of Neighbor Discovery, and this usage should be ceased to simplify the overall structure and increase the total interoperability.

The Structure

Even though both IPv4 and IPv6 illustrate various network protocols, IPv4 addresses can be depicted as IPv6 addresses. These addresses still outline the IPv4 endpoint — that is an interface on a link coupled to an IPv4 network that employs IPv4 protocols. It is possible to use them in several methods for both IPv4 and IPv6 packets on a particular interface besides that for tunneling, as this can lend to interoperability difficulties. This dual usage also lends to needless implementation complications. The source address selection algorithm need not allow the use of an IPv4 compatible address as either a source or destination with an IPv6 global address.

The encapsulation of IPv6 packets within IPv4 packets basically employs the IPv4 network as a special media type. The Generic Packet Tunneling in IPv6 specification provides the mechanics where one protocol can run over another. In order to maintain the standard IP philosophy of an address that is linked with a specific interface, it is important to realize that a tunnel interface is not just an abstraction, but instead a real interface to a particular media type, with its own rules and manners.

Limiting the usage of IPv4 compatible addresses will remove a great deal of the complexity of the definition, implementation, and usage of this specific address form. It will also serve to level the IPv4 to IPv6 transition.

11.5. ISOLATED HOSTS

There are two definitions of the Isolated Host term which have been intended with regards to IPv4 compatible address usage.

Class 1 Isolated Nodes

The primary definition of an isolated host is a host that does not have an on-link IPv6 router. In addition, it must encapsulate all packets to off-link destinations. However, this node is linked to an IPv6-capable Internet Service Provider (ISP). In addition, it has a Provider Based Address (PBA) for IPv6. This PBA is reserved to the tunnel interface and is employed as the source address in outgoing packets. The node has a manually configured tunnel to an ISP router. This PBA is founded upon the ISP's prefix as well as the IPv4 address of the IPv4 interface whereby the encapsulated packets get forwarded to the ISP. Remember that the IPv4-compatible address can, at some point, be employed as the link-local address in a routing protocol.

Class 2 Isolated Nodes

Another type of isolated nodes includes nodes that are not linked to an IPv6-capable ISP- and as a result don't have a PBA. They do possess an IPv4 compatible address and they talk with other IPv6 nodes that have IPv4 compatible addresses through end-to-end automatic tunneling. This requires the destination node to also have an IPv4-compatible address. Furthermore, it indicates that the packet will make a single hop or that the IPv6 packet won't be forwarded.

For these nodes to talk with other IPv6 nodes on the Internet, the remote IPv6 system needs to have automatic tunneling approved on every IPv6 node on the Internet. During the transition when the IPv4 address space is exhausted, IPv6 nodes won't be able to obtain IPv4 compatible addresses to perform automatic tunneling. These nodes will only possess PBAs, but they will not have the ability to communicate with class 2 isolated nodes. Therefore, while this class of system illustrates a simple configuration, it is obvious from the start that these nodes may only have the ability to communicate with a subset of the IPv6 network.

The amount of unreachable hosts will more than likely expand over time. Therefore, the heavy use of IPv4 compatible addresses for communications between IPv6 systems will illustrate the IPv4 routing foundation, without advertising the use of IPv6 hierarchical routing.

It is important to determine if an IPv4-compatible address needs to be designated for all physical interfaces that have IPv4 addresses. There is also a problem involved with the IPv4-compatible addresses as they are considered to be special with regards to name services such as DNS and DHCP, with data duplication and possible operational confusion resulting.

11.6. THE HOST

Hosts may need to work with several method involved with acquiring addresses. In addition, it needs to support dual address lifetime constructs. DHCP is often used to obtaining IPv4 addresses, DHCPv6 doesn't support the designation of IPv4-compatible addresses, as a result the server will not identify these types of addresses as property of any given client.

SLIP is an acronym for serial line Internet protocol, while point-to-point protocol. These are primarily the two types of Internet connections, but PPP is more commonly used. These protocols allow the dialer to connect to the Internet via standard Internet protocols (TCP/IP) via a network connection or analog telephone line.

In addition, designating an IPv4-compatible address to the interface where IPv4 is running may not be possible. An IPv4 host employing SLIP can support an IPv6 implementation through tunneling, however it may not be a native interface.

11.7. THE ROUTER

A great deal of this chapter deals with the impact to IPv6 hosts, however there are several concerns pertaining to dual IPv6/IPv4 routers. Dual protocol routers at the borders of IPv6 islands can be employed to execute packet routing using IPv4 compatible source and destination addresses. This presents to be an excellent solution when you consider that the encapsulation of IPv6 packets in IPv4 tunnels will be a needed functionality of dual IPv4/IPv6 routers.

11.8. SIMPLE NETWORK TIME PROTOCOL (SNTP)

This section details the Simple Network Time Protocol (SNTP) Version 4. This version is a conversion of the Network Time Protocol (NTP) employed to synchronize computer clocks in the Internet. SNTP can also be used when the supreme performance of the total NTP implementation is not necessary. When working with existing and previous NTP and SNTP versions, SNTP Version 4 doesn't have any specification changes to NTP nor does it have any known implementations. However, it does have clear design functions of NTP which permit for the operation in a simple, stateless Remote Procedure Call (RPC) mode which has both accuracy and reliability expectations that are the same as the UDP/TIME protocol.

There is one extensive protocol change in SNTP Version 4 that did not exist in earlier versions of NTP and SNTP. This involves an adjusted header interpretation to work with IPv6 and OSI addressing. SNTP Version 4 incorporates several optional extensions in addition to the basic Version 3 model. This includes an anycast mode as well as an authentication method created particularly for multicast and anycast modes.

11.9. NETWORK TIME PROTOCOL

The Network Time Protocol (NTP) Version 3 is used in several implementations to synchronize computer clocks on the Internet. It yields extensive methods for access to national time and frequency publication services. It also can organize the time synchronization subnet as well as adjust the local clock within each participating subnet peer. In the majority of places of the Internet, NTP yields an accuracy of 1-50 ms however; this number relies upon the specifics of the synchronization source and network paths.

Application Layer
Presentation Layer
Session Layer
Transport Layer
Network Layer
Data Link Layer
Physical Layer

Figure 11.2. OSI Layer Architecture

Version 3

The NTP Version 3 protocol machine states, transition functions and actions, and has engineered algorithms to increase its timekeeping ability and lighten the load among several synchronization sources, this can be especially useful if some are not working correctly. In order to obtain accuracy in the low milliseconds over paths reaching across major portions of the Internet, these intricate algorithms as well as their functional duplicates are important. In several cases an accuracy in the order of important fractions of a second are acceptable.

There are much simpler protocols including the Time Protocol that can also be used. These protocols often involve an RPC exchange where the client requests the time of day and the server transmits it back in seconds past some known reference time.

NTP must be used by clients and servers with a wide set of capabilities and over a large amount of network delays. The majority of users employing Internet NTP synchronization subnet employ a software package that incorporates several NTP options and algorithms, which are somewhat complex and have real-time applications. Although the software has been sent to several hardware platforms dealing with anything from personal computers to supercomputers, the size and complexity is not correct for many applications. It is beneficial to look at optional access methods that employ easier software needed for less strict accuracy expectations.

Version 4

The Simple Network Time Protocol (SNTP) Version 4 is a simpler access method involved for servers and clients employing NTP Version 3 which is not in use on the Internet. The access model is analogous to the UDP/ TIME Protocol and, can easily adapt to a UDP/TIME client implementation (e.g., PC). This allows it to operate using SNTP. Also, the SNTP is meant to operate in a dedicated server configuration (e.g., integrated radio clock). When dealing with a specific design and control method involving various latencies in the system, it is possible to create time accuracy on the microsecond scale.

SNTP Version 4 is created to work with present NTP and SNTP Version 3 clients and servers, but when operating with existing and previous versions of NTP and SNTP, it neither requires any changes to the protocol nor implementations that will be implemented particularly for NTP or SNTP Version 4. When dealing with a NTP or SNTP server, NTP and SNTP clients are indiscernible. However, when dealing with a NTP or SNTP client, NTP and SNTP servers are also indiscernible. Similar to NTP servers working in non-symmetric modes, SNTP servers are stateless and can handle large amounts of clients. Unlike the majority of NTP clients, SNTP clients usually operate with only just one server.

NTP and SNTP Version 3 servers can perform in unicast and multicast modes, while SNTP Version 4 clients and servers can institute extensions to work in anycast mode. In fact, SNTP should only be employed at the borders of the synchronization subnet. SNTP clients only need perform at the leaves of the subnet and in configurations where no NTP or SNTP client relies upon another SNTP client for synchronization. SNTP servers only need perform at the root of the subnet. It will then only work in configurations where there is no other source of synchronization besides that of a reliable radio or modem time service that is available. The basic function of reliability is usually expected of primary servers only employing the redundant sources, diverse subnet paths and crafted algorithms of a full NTP implementation.

This also applies to the primary source of synchronization itself in the form of several radio or modem sources as well as backup paths to other primary servers in the event that all of the sources fail or if many of them send the wrong time. Be careful when using SNTP as opposed to using NTP in primary servers.

11.10. OPERATING MODES

SNTP Version 4 can work in either unicast — point to point, multicast — point to multipoint, or anycast — multipoint to point modes. The unicast client transmits a request to a specified server at its unicast address and looks for a reply that it can use to determine the time. In may also use this information to calculate the roundtrip delay and local clock offset with respect to the server. A multicast server will transmit a unsolicited message to a specified IPv4 or IPv6 local broadcast address or multicast group address from time to time. It usually expects that there are no requests from clients. A multicast client waits to hear this address and usually doesn't transmit any requests. An anycast client transmits a request to a specified IPv4 or IPv6 local broadcast address or multicast group address. At least one anycast server responds with their distinct unicast addresses (a provider based unicast address is shown in Figure 11.3). The client attaches to the first one received, then continues operation in unicast mode.

Multicast servers need to reply to client unicast requests, in addition to transmitting unsolicited multicast messages. Multicast clients may transmit unicast requests so as to figure out if the network propagation delay

Bits	3	n	m	o	p	$125\text{-}n\text{-}m\text{-}o\text{-}p$
	010	Registry ID	Provider ID	Subscriber ID	Subnet ID	Interface ID

Bits	10	n	$118\text{-}n$
	1111111010	000...0	Interface ID

Bits	10	n	$118\text{-}n$
	1111111010	000...0	Interface ID

Figure 11.3. Provider-Based Unicast Addresses

between the server and client. It may then continue operation in multicast mode.

When dealing with the unicast mode, the client and server end-system addresses are designated after the standard IPv4, Ipv6, or OSI conventions (Open System Interconnect shown in Figure 11.4). When dealing with multicast mode, the server employs a specified local broadcast address or multicast group address. An IP local broadcast address has its field of interest restricted to one IP subnet, due to the fact that routers do not reproduce IP broadcast datagrams.

Alternatively, an IP multicast group address has its interest extended to perhaps the entire Internet. The extent, routing, and group membership operations are designated by other factors as well.

Multicast clients look for the specified local broadcast address or multicast group address. In the event of local broadcast addresses, no other provisions are needed. In the event of IP multicast addresses, the multicast client and anycast server need to implement the Internet Group Management Protocol (IGMP) so that the local router links the multicast group and relays messages to the IPv4 or IPv6 multicast group addresses. Besides IP addressing conventions and IGMP, there is no difference in the server or client operations with either the local broadcast address or multicast group address.

Layer	Functionality
7	Application
6	Presentation
5	Session
4	Transport
3	Network
2	Data Link
1	Physical

Figure 11.4. Open System Interconnect (OSI) seven-layer reference model

It is very important to configure the time-to-live (TTL) field in the IP header of multicast messages to a fair value. This effectively limits the network resources employed by the multicast service. Just the multicast clients in this involvement will receive multicast server messages. Furthermore, only cooperating anycast servers in this extent will respond to a client request.

Anycast mode is used with a set of cooperating servers whose addresses are not known previously by the client. An anycast client transmits a request to the specified local broadcast or multicast group addresses and expects a reply from at least one anycast server. At least one anycast server observes the specified local broadcast address or multicast group address. After receiving a request, the anycast server transmits a unicast response message to the initial client. The client then links to the first message received and proceeds with the operation in unicast mode. All further responses from other anycast servers are disregarded.

When dealing with SNTP as indicated here, there are specific problems in which the SNTP multicast clients can be disrupted by behaving poorly or having hostile SNTP or NTP multicast servers somewhere else on the Internet. When appropriate, access control routed on the server source address can be employed to choose just the specific server known to and trusted by the client.

Although not essential to SNTP, IP broadcast addresses must be used just in IP subnets and LAN segments including a completely functional NTP server with several dependent SNTP multicast clients on the same subnet. At the same time, the IP multicast group addresses will be employed only in the event where the TTL is managed particularly for each service domain.

When dealing with NTP Version 3, the reference identifier is frequently utilized to walk-back the synchronization subnet to the root or primary server for management expectations. When dealing with NTP Version 4, this functionality is unavailable. This is due to the fact that addresses are bigger than 32 bits. The intent in creating this protocol was to yield a method of detecting and avoiding loops. A peer would be able to decide if a loop was possible by contrasting the contents of this field with the IPv4 destination address within the same packet. A NTP Version 4 server can achieve the same goal by contrasting the components of this field with the low order 32 bits of the initial timestamp within the same packet. There is a small likelihood of false alarm in this method. However, the false alarm rate can be shortened by randomizing the low order unused bits of the transmit timestamp.

NTP Timestamp Format

To meet with the standard Internet customs, NTP data is designated as integer or fixed-point amounts. Due to the fact that NTP timestamps are cherished data and because they portray the main product of the protocol — a special timestamp format has been created.

NTP Message Format

The NTP and SNTP are clients of the User Datagram Protocol in which it is itself a client of the Internet Protocol (IP). The UDP port number designated to NTP is 123, and this needs to be used in both the Source Port and Destination Port fields in the UDP header.

Definitions

Leap Indicator (LI) is a two-bit code cautioning the imminent leap second to be inserted/deleted in the last minute of the current day, with bit 0 and bit 1, respectively. Version Number (VN) is a three-bit integer which illustrates the NTP/SNTP version number. In IPv4, the version number is 3 for Version 3. It is 4 for Version 4 (IPv4, IPv6 and OSI). It may be necessary to make a distinction between IPv4, IPv6, and OSI, and the encapsulating context needs to be examined.

In either unicast and anycast modes, the client sets this field to 3 for client in the request, and the server sets it to 4 for the server in the response. In multicast mode, the server sets this field to 5 for broadcast.

Stratum is a eight-bit unsigned integer determining the stratum level of the local clock. Poll Interval is an eight-bit signed integer illustrating the maximum interval between consecutive messages. This is expressed in seconds to the nearest power of two. Precision is an eight-bit signed integer illustrating the precision of the local clock. It is expressed in seconds to the nearest power of two. The values that usually appear in this field range from –6 for main-frequency clocks to –20 for microsecond clocks found in some workstations.

Root Delay is a 32-bit signed fixed-point number illustrating the total roundtrip delay to the primary reference source. It is expressed in seconds with fraction point between bits 15 and 16. It is important to note that this variable can take on both positive and negative values with respect to the relative time and frequency offsets. The values that usually appear in this field range from negative values of a few milliseconds to positive values of several hundred milliseconds. Root Dispersion is a 32-bit unsigned fixed-point number illustrating the minimal error comparative to the primary reference source. It measures in seconds with fraction points between bits 15 and 16. The values that usually appear in this field range from zero to several hundred milliseconds.

11.11. THE SNTP CLIENT

The SNTP client can perform in multicast mode, unicast mode, or anycast mode. In multicast mode, the client doesn't transmit any requests, instead it waits for a broadcast from a specified multicast server. In unicast mode, the client transmits a request to a specified unicast server and waits for a reply from that server. In anycast mode, the client transmits a request to a specified local broadcast or multicast group address and waits for a reply from at least one anycast servers. The client utilizes the first response received to create the specific server for all future unicast procedure. The latest responses from this server including duplicates as well as any other server are ignored. Besides the address choice in the request, the anycast and unicast procedure clients are the same. Requests are usually transmitted in time periods ranging from 64 seconds to 1024 seconds. This number relies upon the frequency tolerance of the client clock as well as the needed accuracy.

A unicast or anycast client originates the NTP message header, transmits the request to the server and removes the time of day from the Transmit Timestamp field of the response. All of the NTP header fields can be set to zero, with the exception of the first octet and possibly the Transmit Timestamp fields.

There will most likely continue to be NTP and SNTP servers of all four versions interoperating in the Internet, specific consideration needs to be given to the version used by SNTP Version 4 clients. Clients use the latest version known to be supported by the chosen server with respect to the highest accuracy and reliability. SNTP Version 4 clients can interoperate with all former version NTP and SNTP servers, due to the fact that the header fields used by SNTP clients are unchanged. Version 4 servers need to reply in the same version as the request. Therefore, the VN field of the request also determines the version of the reply.

In conforming client implementation, a unicast, and anycast mode is not necessary but advantageous in that they transmit timestamps. The request is set to the time of day with respect to the client clock in NTP timestamp format. This permits a simple calculation to conclude what the propagation delay between the server and client will be and to straighten the local clock within a few milliseconds relative to the server. Furthermore, it yields a simple way to determine that the server reply is in fact a legitimate reply to the particular client request and avoid replays. In multicast mode, the client has no data to calculate the propagation delay or figure out the validity of the server, unless the NTP authentication method is employed.

In order to determine the roundtrip delay d and local clock offset t relative to the server, the client sets the transmit timestamp in the request to the time of day with respect to the client clock in NTP timestamp format. The server duplicates this field to the initial timestamp in the reply and sets the receive timestamp and transmit timestamp to the time of day with respect to the server clock in NTP timestamp format.

Once the server response is received, the client decides a Destination Timestamp variable as the time of arrival with respect to its clock in NTP timestamp format.

11.12. THE SNTP SERVER

The SNTP Version 4 server working with either a NTP or SNTP client of similar or former versions doesn't have any persistent state. Due to the fact that a SNTP server usually doesn't implement the full set of NTP algorithms meant to handle redundant peers and diverse network paths, a SNTP server needs to be operated only in conjunction with a source of external synchronization. This may include a reliable radio clock or telephone modem. A SNTP server can function in unicast mode, anycast mode, multicast mode, or any association of these modes. In unicast and anycast modes, the server obtains specific fields in the NTP header and transmits a response through the same message buffer as the request. In anycast mode, the server observes a specific local broadcast or multicast group address, however it employs its own unicast address in the source address field of the reply. Besides the selection of address in the reply, the operations of anycast and unicast servers are the same. Multicast messages are usually sent at poll intervals from 64 seconds to 1024 seconds. This value relies upon the expected frequency tolerance of the client clocks and the required accuracy.

It is very advantageous for a server to support a multicast mode as well as a unicast mode. If the server supports anycast mode, then it also needs to support unicast mode. There does not appear to be a large advantage to operate both multicast and anycast modes at the same time, although the protocol specification doesn't prohibit it.

In unicast and anycast modes, the server may respond if it is not synchronized to a proper operating radio clock, but the favored option is to respond as this permits reachability to be specified despite synchronization state. In multicast mode, the server transmits broadcasts only if synchronized to a proper operating reference clock.

The leftover fields of the NTP header are set so that we should presume the server is synchronized to a radio clock or other primary reference source and operating in the correct way. The Precision field is set to illustrate the maximum reading error for the local clock. In terms of the majority of events, it is computed as the negative of the number of significant bits to the right of the decimal point in the NTP timestamp format. The Reference Identifier is set to indicate the primary reference source.

The timestamp fields are set so that if a server is unsynchronized or first coming up, all timestamp fields are set to zero. When it is synchronized, the Reference Timestamp is set to the time the last update was received from the radio clock or modem. When dealing with either unicast and anycast modes, the Receive Timestamp and Transmit Timestamp fields are set to the time of day when the message is sent as well as to the initial Timestamp field is duplicated, unchanged from the Transmit Timestamp field of the request. It is important that this field be copied completely, as a NTP client utilizes it to avoid replays. In multicast mode, the initial Timestamp and Receive Timestamp fields are set to 0 while the Transmit Timestamp field is set to the time of day when the message is transmitted.

There is a degree of flexibility on the part of most clients to pardon invalid timestamps. This can happen when first coming up or during time periods when the primary reference source is not functional.

11.13. MANAGEMENT CONFIGURATION

The first setup for SNTP servers and clients can be accomplished using a configuration file if a file system is available, or a serial port if it is not. It is meant that in-service management of NTP and SNTP Version 4 servers and clients be operated on using SNMP and a suitable MIB to be published at a future time. Usually, SNTP servers and clients are believed to operate with little or no site-specific configuration, other than determining the IP address and subnet mask or OSI NSAP address.

Unicast clients need to be configured with a specific server name or address. When a server name is used, the address of at least one DNS server needs to be provided. Multicast servers and anycast clients need to be provided with the TTL and local broadcast or multicast group address. Anycast servers and multicast clients can be configured with a list of address-mask pairs for access control, so that only those clients or servers known to be trusted will be employed. These servers and clients need to implement the IGMP protocol and be given the local broadcast or multicast group address too.

There are numerous events that yield automatic server discovery and selection for SNTP clients with no pre-determined configuration, besides that of the IP address and subnet mask or OSI NSAP address. When dealing with an IP subnet or LAN segment as well as a fully functional NTP server, the clients can be configured for multicast mode by employing the local broadcast address. This same method can be used with other servers employing the multicast group address. In both events, the provision of an access control list is an excellent means of making certain that only trusted sources can be employed to set the local clock.

In another situation available for an extended network with a great deal of propagation delay, clients can be configured for anycast mode. This can occur for initial startup and after some time when the existing unicast source has not been observed. Succeeding the defined protocol, the client attaches to the first reply observed and continues operation in unicast mode. In this mode the local clock can be automatically adjusted to make up for the propagation delay.

11.14. CONCLUSION

The main themes covered in this chapter include DNS extensions, limiting the role of IPv4 compatible addresses in Ipv6, and the simple network time protocol. In each of these situations we see another aspect of the way in which IPv6 function in situations that include connections with its predecessor, IPv4, and the aspect of time involved throughout the global Internet.

IPv6 in an IPv4 World

IN THIS CHAPTER:

Transmission of IPv6 Packets over IPv4 Networks without Tunnels

RIPng for IPv6

12

12.1. INTRODUCTION

The chapter examines the frame format with respect to the transmission of IPv6 packets and the method of creating IPv6 link-local addresses over IPv4 networks. Then we will designate the content of the Source/Target Link-layer Address option used for Router Solicitation, Router Advertisement, Neighbor Solicitation, and Neighbor Advertisement messages. These events occur when the above messages are sent on an IPv4 network.

This chapter designates the frame format for transmission of IPv6 packets as well as the method of creating IPv6 link-local addresses over IPv4 networks. In addition it also determines the specific information regarding the Source/Target Link-layer Address option employed.

The mechanism for this method permits isolated IPv6 hosts, which exist on a physical link and have no directly connected IPv6 router, to be completely functional IPv6 hosts by employing an IPv4 network as its virtual local link. One or more IPv6 routers utilize the same method that needs to be linked to the same IPv4 network if IPv6 routing to other links is needed.

IPv6 hosts linked in this manner don't need IPv4 compatible addresses or configured tunnels. This allows IPv6 to gain a great deal of independence in the underlying links which can move over many hops of IPv4 subnets.

12.2. MAXIMUM TRANSMISSION

The default MTU size for IPv6 packets on an IPv4 network is 1480 octets. This size can be decreased by a Router Advertisement that has an MTU option that defines either a smaller MTU or by a manual configuration of each node.

12.3. FRAME FORMAT

IPv6 packets are sent in IPv4 packets with TBD1 (IPv4 protocol type). The IPv4 header has the Destination and Source IPv4 addresses. The IPv4 packet body has the IPv6 header succeeded instantly by the payload.

In addition, we consider stateless Autoconfiguration and Link-Local Addresses. The address token for an IPv4 interface is the interface's 32-bit IPv4 address that has the octets in the same sequence in which they would appear in the header of an IPv4 packet. They are padded at the left with zeros with a total of 48 bits. When the host has greater than one IPv4 address in use on the physical interface involved, an administrative choice of one of these addresses is executed.

If IPv4 multicast is available, an IPv6 packet which has DST (multicast destination address) is required to be transmitted to the IPv4 multicast address whose first byte is the value TBD2 and has the last three bytes which are the last three bytes of DST, sequenced from most to least significant. The extent of all multicast groups whose first address byte is TBD2, MUST be administratively restricted to the IPv4 network having a desired procedure of IPv6 over IPv4.

12.4. IPV4 MULTICAST MECHANISM

It is important to use IPv4 multicast, but if the IPv4 network does not support this feature, its purpose must be simulated. The answer is to employ the IPv4 global broadcast address of 255.255.255.255 as the destination IPv4 address for all IPv6 multicast packets. In this event, the extent of such IPv4 broadcasts needs to be administratively restricted to the IPv4 network in which operation of IPv6 over IPv4 is chosen.

Non-IPv6 IPv4 hosts receiving these types of broadcasts with protocol type TBD1 need to be quietly eliminated. This solution needs to be implemented as an option that uses IPv4 multicast. Unfortunately, it carries an inherent risk of broadcast storms and cannot be the default configuration. This answer cannot be employed in an IPv4 topology, as it has alternate paths because there is no certain method to contain broadcast storms in this event. Furthermore, you can treat the IPv4 network as an Non-Broadcast Multiple Access (NBMA) network, however this solution is too complex and may yield more problems than it solves.

Security

There is always a risk of your security being breached on the Internet. However, anyone who implements this protocol needs to be aware of the fact that besides possible attacks against IPv6, security attacks against IPv4 must also be taken into account.

The utilization of security at both IPv4 and IPv6 levels needs to be avoided, for efficiency reasons. In an example when IPv6 is operating in an encrypted mode, you would see that IPv4 threats would be rare unless there was a threat to traffic breakdown. If IPv6 is operating authenticated, then authentication of IPv4 will add little more precautions. In the same way, IPv4 security will not protect IPv6 traffic when it leaves the IPv6 over IPv4 domain. In essence, implementing IPv6 security is necessary even if IPv4 security is available. This topic is discussed in more detail in Chapter 14.

RIPng

This section looks into one protocol within a series of routing protocols founded on an algorithm which has been used for routing computations in computer for a great deal of time. The specific packet formats and protocols listed here are based on the program *routed*.

In an international Internet, it is most unlikely that an individual routing protocol is actually utilized for the complete network. Instead of the network being organized as an aggregate of Autonomous Systems (AS) where each one is administered by an individual entity, each AS will possess its own routing technology, which can be different among other ASs. The routing protocol utilized within an AS is designated as an Interior Gateway Protocol (IGP). An independent protocol is referred to as an Exterior Gateway Protocol (EGP), which is employed for the purpose of transfer routing information among the AS's. RIPng was created to work as an IGP in moderate-size ASs. It is not meant to be used in more complex environments.

12.5. PROTOCOL LIMITATIONS

This protocol doesn't fix every possible routing problem. It must be used as an IGP in networks of moderate size. There are certain limitations involved in this network. This protocol is restricted to networks that have the longest path involving the network's diameter of fifteen hops. The basic protocol design is not acceptable for larger networks. These limitations expressed here presume a cost of one that is utilized for each network. This is the method in which RIPng is usually configured. When the system administrator decides to use larger costs, the upper bound of fifteen can readily be a problem.

This protocol relies upon counting to infinity to determine how it is used for certain non-standard events. If the system of networks has several hundred networks, and a routing loop was created which involves all of them, the solution of the loop would need either a great deal of time when the routing frequency updates are limited or bandwidth when updates were transmitted whenever changes were detected. This type of loop would consume an enormous amount of network bandwidth just prior to the loop being fixed. This may only be a problem with slow lines. This difficulty is somewhat strange due to the fact that various precautions are taken which should prevent these problems in the majority of cases.

This protocol employs fixed metrics to contrast optional routes. It is not suitable for situations where routes are required to be chosen based on real-time parameters (e.g., measured delay, reliability, or load.) The apparent extensions which permit metrics of this level will inject certain instabilities that the protocol is not able to utilize.

12.6. RIPNG SPECIFICATIONS

RIPng is meant to permit routers to exchange information for computing routes via an IPv6-based network. RIPng is a distance vector protocol and need only be implemented in routers. IPv6 yields additional methods for router discovery. Any router that employs RIPng is thought to have interfaces to at least one network. If not, it isn't truly a router. These are then

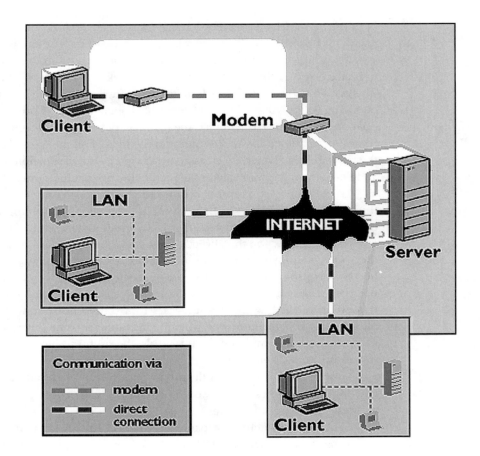

*Figure 12.1. Modem vs. Direct
Connection*

designated as its directly connected networks (shown in Figure 12.1). This
protocol depends upon access to certain information regarding each of
these networks.

The most significant part of the protocol is that which pertains to its
metric. The RIPng metric of a network is an integer which measures
between one and fifteen, inclusive and is set in a method which is not specified in this protocol. When dealing with the maximum path limit of fifteen,
a value of one is commonly employed. Implementations need to permit the
system administrator to establish the metric of each network. Furthermore,

besides the metric, each network may possess an IPv6 destination address prefix and prefix length linked with it. These are to be established by the system administrator in a method that is not designated in this protocol.

Each router that implements RIPng is believed to have a routing table. This table has one entry for each destination that is reachable across the system operating RIPng. Aligned to each entry that contains the IPv6 prefix of the destination, is a metric which depicts the total cost of sending a datagram from the router to that destination. This metric is the total of all the costs attached with the networks that would be crossed over to get to the destination, or the IPv6 address of the next router along the path to the destination or next hop.

When the destination is on one of the directly connected networks, this item is not necessary. A flag is used to verify that information regarding the route has changed recently. This is designated as the route change flag.

The records for the directly connected networks are established by the router employing information collected by means which are not specified in this protocol. The metric for a directly connected network is set to the cost of that network. As you know, the value 1 is the standard cost. In this event, the RIPng metric decreases to a simple hop-count. More complex metrics may be employed when it is advantageous to illustrate partiality for some networks over others. It may also be useful to indicate differences in bandwidth or reliability.

Implementors may also decide to permit the system administrator to add additional routes. These would probably include routing systems. They are designated as static routes.

The way in which a protocol is to yield complete information on routing, is that every router in the AS needs to share in the protocol. In the event where several IGPs are used, there needs to be at least one router which can leak routing information between the protocols, and while they are not directly involved in the routing process — RIPng will advertise them.

Format

RIPng is a UDP-based protocol. Each router which employs RIPng has a routing process which transmits and acquires datagrams on UDP port number 521 (the RIPng port) as opposed to port 520 (for RIP). All communications that are intended for another router's RIPng process is transmitted to the RIPng port. All routing update messages are transmitted from the RIPng port. Unsolicited routing update messages have both the source and destination port the same as the RIPng port. Those transmitted as a reply to a request are transmitted to the port where the request originated. Distinct queries may be transmitted from ports besides that of the RIPng port, however they must be directed to the RIPng port on the target device.

12.7. FIELD SIZES

Field sizes are listed in octets. For the most part, fields contain binary integers, in network byte order, with the most-significant octet first. Each tick mark depicts one bit.

Every message possesses a RIPng header that is composed of a command and a version number. The command field is used to designate the purpose of this message. Version 1 commands a request for the responding system to transmit either all or part of its routing table. The second command details the response A message that contains either all or part of the sender's routing table. This message can be transmitted in response to a request, or it may be an unsolicited routing update created by the sender.

With respect to each of these message types, the remainder of the datagram holds a list of several Route Table Entries (RTE). Each RTE in this list holds:

- A destination prefix
- The number of significant bits in the prefix
- The cost to reach that destination in metric terms, and
- The route tag.

The destination prefix is the standard 128-bit, IPv6 address prefix recorded as 16 octets in network byte order. The route tag field is an attribute attached to a route that needs to be preserved and re-advertised with a route. This must be used as the route tag so it can yield a mechanism for separating internal RIPng routes. This may involve routes for networks within the RIPng routing domain from external RIPng routes. They may have been imported from an EGP or another IGP.

Routers that support protocols besides that of RIPng need to be configurable to permit the route tag to be set up for routes imported from various sources. When dealing with routes imported from an EGP, you need to be able to have their route tag set to an arbitrary value or set to at least a number of the Autonomous System from which the routes were obtained.

There are also other uses of the route tag that are valid, this is acceptable as long as all routers in the RIPng domain use it regularly.

The prefix length field is the length (bits) of the important section of the prefix that starts from the left of the prefix and has a comprehensive value between 0 and 128. The metric field holds a comprehensive value between one and fifteen which determines either the current metric for the destination or the value sixteen (referring to infinity) that points to the fact that the destination is not reachable.

The largest datagram size is restricted by the MTU of the conditions by which the protocol is implemented. Since an unsolicited RIPng update is never reproduced across a router, there is possibility of an MTU mismatch. The decision regarding the number of RTEs that can be placed into a message, is a service of the environments MTU, the amount of octets of header information that comes before the RIPng message, the size of the RIPng header, and the size of an RTE.

RIPng also yields the ability to determine the immediate next hop IPv6 address in which packets sent to a destination are designated by a route table entry (RTE). The forwarding mechanism must be similar to RIP-2 where each route table entry has a next hop field. This incorporates a next hop field for each RTE in RIPng that would nearly increase the size of the RTE twofold. In RIPng, the next hop is determined by a special RTE and is employed on all of the address RTEs after the next hop RTE. This occurs until the end of the message or until another next hop RTE is reached.

A next hop RTE is designated by a value: 0xFF within the metric field of an RTE. The prefix field determines the IPv6 address of the next hop. The route tag and prefix length in the next hop RTE needs to be set to zero on transmission but ignored on reception.

The purpose of the next hop RTE is to drop packets that are routed through extra hops in the system. It is especially useful when RIPng is not being operated on all of the routers on a network. Remember that the next hop RTE is advisory, meaning that if the provided information is ignored — a poor but valid route may be taken.

12.8. ADDRESSING

The separation between network, subnet, and host routes (node and router on link shown in Figure 12.2) doesn't need to be set for RIPng due to the

End Node Address Type	End Node on Link?	IPv4 Router on Link?	IPv6 Router on Link?
IPv4	Yes	N/A	N/A
IPv4	No	Yes	N/A
IPv4	No	No	N/A
IPv4-compatible	Yes	N/A	N/A
IPv4-compatible	No	Yes	N/A
IPv4-compatible	No	No	Yes
IPv4-compatible	No	No	No
IPv6-only	Yes	N/A	N/A
IPv6-only	No	N/A	Yes
IPv6-only	No	Yes	No
IPv6-only	No	No	No

Figure 12.2. IPv4 and IPv6 Node and Router on Link

fact that an IPv6 address prefix is unmistakable. Any prefix that has a prefix length of zero is employed to determine a default route.

A default route is employed when it is not advantageous to detail each possible network in the RIPng updates. When at least one of the routers in the system is ready to support traffic to the networks which are not explicitly listed, the default routers utilize the default route as a path for all datagrams in which they have no specific route. The determination as to the method in which a router is a default router or how a default route entry is established is the responsibility of the person who implements it. For the most part, the system administrator will be given a method to determine which routers need to create and advertise default route entries.

If this method was employed, the implementation needs to permit the system administrator to determine the metric linked with the default route advertisement. This will allow you to establish priority across several default routers. The default route entries are supported by RIPng in the same method, as would any other destination prefix. System administrators need to be careful when decide what default routes do not proliferate further than is needed. In most cases, each AS has its own favored default router. In essence, the default routes should not leave the boundary of an AS.

12.9. INPUT

It is important to discuss the handling of datagrams that are received on the RIPng port. Any operations will rely upon the value in the command field. Version 1 supports two commands:

- Request
- Response

12.10. REQUEST

The Request message is employed for the purpose of asking for a response that has all or a section of a router's routing table. Under normal conditions, Requests are transmitted as multicasts from the RIPng port by routers that have recently emerged and are looking to fill in their routing tables as soon as it can be done. There are certain events including router monitoring in which the routing table of only an individual router is required. In this event, the Request needs to be sent directly to that router from a UDP port besides that of the RIPng port. When this type of Request is received, the router answers directly to the requestor's address and port with a globally valid source address. This is because the requestor may not exist on the directly attached network.

The Request is operated on by each RTE entry. When there aren't any entries, no response is provided. When there is only one entry in the request which has a destination prefix of zero, a prefix length of zero, and a metric of infinity — then this is a request to transmit the entire routing table. In this event, a call is made to the output process to transmit the routing table to the requesting address/port. With this one exception, the operation is reasonably simple. It is important to inspect the list of RTEs in the Request individually. For each entry, examine the destination in the router's routing database and when there is a route you need to place that route's metric into the metric field of the RTE. When there is no explicit route to the designated destination, insert infinity into the metric field. When all the entries have been completed, modify the command from Request to Response and transmit the datagram back to the requestor.

It is important to point out that there is a difference in metric handling for specific and whole-table requests. When the request pertains to a complete routing table, normal output processing is completed. Should the request be for specific entries, they are inspected in the routing table and the information is then returned without any changes.

When a router first emerges, it multicasts a Request on each connected network appealing for a complete routing table. It is believed that these complete routing tables will be used to update the requestor's routing table. Furthermore, it is important to point out that it is believed that a Request for any particular network is created only by diagnostic software, and is not employed for routing. In this event, the requester would wish to know the exact composition of the routing table, but wouldn't need any information that has been hidden or modified.

12.11. RESPONSE

The Response message can be received for reasons such as the fact that there is a response to a particular query, regular update, or triggered update brought about by a route change. It is important to point out that processing is always same regardless of the reason why the Response was created.

Due to the fact that processing of a Response may update the router's routing table, the Response needs to be checked cautiously for validity. The Response has to be ignored if it is not from the RIPng port. The datagram's IPv6 source address also needs to be checked to determine whether the datagram is from a valid neighbor. The source of the datagram needs to be a link-local address. It is also important to check to see if the response is from one of the router's own addresses as well.

Interfaces that reside on broadcast networks may receive duplicates of their own multicasts right away. If a router processes its own output as new input, the result will be problematic, because datagrams need to be ignored. One further method involves checking periodic advertisements that need to have their hop counts set to 255, and inbound multicast packets transmitted from the RIPng port. This may involve a timely advertisement or triggered update packets that needs to be inspected to make certain that the hop count is 255. This will make certain that a packet is from a neighbor, this is due to the fact that any intermediate node would have decreased the hop count. Queries as well as their responses may still intersect intermediate nodes and as a result may not require the hop count test to be completed.

When the complete datagram has been validated, then processing of the RTEs in the Response is accomplished individually. This entire procedure begins with validation. Any incorrect metrics or other format errors often indicate neighbors which behave poorly and should most likely be brought to the administrator's attention. This can be best illustrated when the metric is greater than infinity, it is necessary to ignore the entry but log the event.

Output

It is important to point out the type of processing used to create response messages that contain the complete routing table or a portion thereof. This processing may be stimulated by input processing, or when a Request is received. When this happens, the Response is transmitted to only one destination such as the unicast address of the requestor.

Processing may also be brought about by the regular routing update. Every 30 seconds, a Response that has the whole routing table is transmitted to every neighboring router. In addition, when a metric for a route is changed, an update occurs.

Response Messages

When dealing with IPv6, you need to know how a Response message is created for a specific directly connected network. First, the IPv6 source address needs to be a link-local address of the possible addresses of the sending router's interface. This is true for all cases except when responding to a unicast Request Message from a port besides that of the RIPng port. When an incorrect source address is employed, other routers may not be able to route datagrams. Most of the time, routers are set up with several IPv6 addresses on one physical interface. Under normal circumstances, this indicates that several logical IPv6 networks are conveyed over one physical medium. Furthermore, it is possible that a router may have several link-local addresses for one interface. In this event, the router must only initiate one Response message with a source address of the specified link-local address for a specific interface.

The determination of the specific link-local address to employ need only change when the current choice is no longer valid. This is important because nodes receiving Response messages utilize the source address to determine the sender. When multiple packets from the same router hold various source addresses, nodes will believe they come from different routers. This, however, brings about unattractive conduct.

In order to fill in the RTEs, inspect each route in the routing table. Routes to link-local addresses cannot ever be incorporated in an RTE. If a stimulated type update is created, only entries whose route change flags are set must be included. After Split Horizon processing, if the route doesn't need to be included — don't include it. If the route is to be included, then the destination prefix, prefix length, and metric are placed into the RTE.

Split Horizon

A Split Horizon is an algorithm for avoiding difficulties brought about by incorporating routes in updates transmitted to the gateway where they are obtained. The most common split horizon algorithm excludes routes acquired from one neighbor in updates transmitted to that neighbor. In the event of a broadcast network, all routes acquired from any neighbor on that network are excluded from updates transmitted on that network.

A Split Horizon with Poisoned Reverse does incorporate these types of routes in updates. However, it sets their metrics to infinity. It basically broadcasts the fact that there are routes that are not reachable. This is the favored method of operation, however, implementations need to yield a per-interface control which does not permit horizoning, split horizoning, or poisoned reverse to be chosen.

12.12. CONTROL

It is important to call some attention to administrative controls. These are a segment of the protocol, however experience with existing networks tells us that they are important. Since this is not an essential ingredient of the protocol, they are thought to be optional. Depending upon your specific situation, some of them really should be integrated into every implementation. These controls are meant to permit RIPng to be connected to networks whose routing may be unstable or subject to errors.

These controls can best be illustrated in situations where it is sometimes preferable to limit the routers where updates will be accepted or where updates will be transmitted. This is primarily useful for administrative and routing policy reasons.

Furthermore, there are several sites that limit the set of networks that they permit in Response messages. One company may have a connection to another that they employ for direct communication. In terms of security or performance reasons, the first company may not be willing to provide other organizations access to that connection. In this event, the first company should not include the second company's networks in updates that the first company transmits to any other organizations.

Although the RIPng protocol doesn't need these or any other controls, some controls are illustrated by a neighbor list that permits the network administrator to have the ability to designate a list of neighbors for each router. A router will take response messages only from routers on its list of neighbors. An analogous list for target routers needs to be accessible to the administrator. However, no restrictions are defined by default.

In addition, a filter for particular destinations would allow the system administrator to have the ability to determine a list of destination prefixes to accept or reject. The list can be linked with a specific interface in the incoming or outgoing directions. Just the accepted networks can be listed in Response messages going out or processed in Response messages coming in. When a list of accepted prefixes is designated, all other prefixes are rejected. If a list of rejected prefixes are designated, all other prefixes are accepted. The default, however, is that no filters are applied.

12.13. CONCLUSION

In this chapter we see the methods by which IPv6 packets are transmitted over IPv4 networks without tunnels. As the preceding chapters discuss the implementation of tunnels, this section provides an alternative for the transmission of packets over this Internet protocol.

This chapter deals with RIPng for IPv6. In this section we see a broadside view into one protocol in a series of routing protocols. We examine the limitations of this protocol, its specifications, format, and parameters to provide perspective on the RIPng routes involved for its own routing domain.

Routing Issues

13

13.1. INTRODUCTION

This chapter reviews a routing protocol for an IPv6 Internet. It is rooted in both the protocols and algorithms that are extensively used in the IPv4 Internet. This specification depicts a new version of the Inter-Gateway Routing Protocol (IGRP) which will be used with IPv6 as well as other protocols.

When dealing with a very large network like the Internet, it is improbable that one routing protocol will be employed for the whole network. Instead, the network is organized as an aggregate of Autonomous Systems (AS) administered by one individual; it has its own routing technology that may vary with each AS. The routing protocol employed within an AS is called an Interior Gateway is referred to as an Exterior Gateway Protocol (EGP) used to transfer routing information among the ASs. IGRPng is created to work as an IGP in moderate to large size ASs operating IPv6. IGRPng is not appropriate for very large complex networks. In this event, OSPF is a superior routing protocol.

IGRPng integrates many of the useful features of IGRP. This is particularly intended to yield stable routing in large networks. This stability is accomplished by preventing routing loops from happening. IGRPng employs a vector of metrics to distinguish how good a path to a destination really is. This allows physical characteristics to be integrated into the routing decision regarding what path to choose for any given destination. The ability to associate physical characteristics with routing data assists in managing complex configurations in large corporate networks. IGRPng handles several paths to a single destination. In addition, IGRPng permits designated routes to be taken into account as participants for the default route. This permits the best exterior route to be employed as the default route. This feature is important when there are several exit points in an AS.

13.2. RIPNG DIFFERENCES

IGRPng must be used as an IGP in networks. IGRPng does not have problems experienced from some of the restriction of RIPng. These restrictions include the fact that the protocol is not restricted to networks whose diameter is 15 hops. RIPng may only be employed in networks of moderate size. As opposed to RIPng, IGRPng employs a vector of metrics with a large range of values. Networks are configured with metric values that depict the unloaded physical delay and bandwidth attributes of the network. The vector of metrics employed by IGRPng provides increased accuracy in calculating routes as opposed to the hop-count metric of RIPng. This is because most distance vector protocols possess one metric that usually represents delay.

This specific protocol doesn't rely upon counting to infinity in order to eliminate routing loops. Due to the larger range of the metrics as compared with RIPng, IGRPng cannot depend on counting to infinity to split routing loops. However, stability measures are integrated into the protocol to stop routing loops on a small or large scale from being created. Yet, the loop prevention actions make the protocol ignore new data for a period of time subsequent to certain changes.

IGRPng is different from RIPng in the way in which it supports the default route. RIPng expressly reproduces the default route in the same way as any other route, while IGRPng permits the actual network routes to be designated as candidate routes for the default. IGRPng can then better accommodate several exit points in a given AS.

IGRPng packets are transmitted instantly over IPv6's network layer, while RIPng encapsulates its packets in UDP. IGRPng also has a per packet address family identifier which permits IGRPng to operate with protocols besides that of IPv6.

13.3. IGRP DIFFERENCES

IGRP has been in wide deployment for a number of years and there is a large amount of operational experience with it. Some features of the protocol are not advantageous while others inject instability in the routing tables. IGRPng has eliminated IGRP features such as variance that is not supported. Variance yielded the power to have multiple equivalent cost paths. When implemented, it is too easy to configure permanent routing loops.

The analogous idea of IPv4 Type of Service (TOS) was not brough forward to IPv6. Furthermore, TOS routing wasn't a feature of IGRP which was commonly utilized in practice. IGRPng has no support for TOS types of routing.

Both the load and reliability metrics are no longer available. These metrics were measured values and could cause a route's metrics to change repeatedly. When implemented, they were usually eliminated too from the composite metric computation. The IGRP and IGRPng trigger update packets when changes in the network topology are observed. As opposed to IGRP, the update packet that IGRPng transmits only has those entries that have changed since the last update packet was transmitted.

The default value for the update timer is changed from 90 seconds to 30 seconds. The other timer default values are still designated as multiples of the update timer. While timer values need to be configurable, the higher frequency update interval is merited by bigger link bandwidth and brought about by the requirement for faster convergence.

The individual packets convey an address family identifier. This permits IGRPng to convey routing information for several network protocols.

IGRP is a classful routing protocol which only conveys three bytes of the IPv4 address. However, the fourth byte is indicated by the route type. IGRP designates three types of routes

- Interior
- System
- Exterior

The difference between network, subnet, and host routes is not determined for IGRPng due to the fact that an IPv6 address prefix is apparent. Therefore, IGRPng links the IGRP route types of interior and system to the interior type. In addition, IGRP designates an edition number for the routing table. This field is usually ignored and is not brought forward to IGRPng. Both the delay and bandwidth metrics have been expanded from 24-bit quantities to 32-bit quantities.

13.4. PROTOCOL SPECS

IGRPng is meant to permit routers to exchange information for calculating routes through an IPv6-based network. IGRPng is a distance vector protocol that needs to be implemented only in routers. IPv6 yields other mechanisms for hosts to discover routers. Any router that employs IGRPng is thought to have interfaces to two or more networks. These are designated as directly connected networks. The protocol relies on access to certain information about each of these networks.

The most significant aspect is its various metrics. The IGRPng metrics of a network incorporates the topological delay time and the bandwidth of the smallest bandwidth segment of the path. These metrics need to be rooted in the delay and bandwidth mechanics of the directly connected networks. These networks include:

- Ethernet
- Fast Ethernet
- FDDI
- ATM

Implementations need to permit the system administrator to establish these metrics for each network. Besides the metrics, each network has at least one IPv6 destination address prefix.

Each router that implements IGRPng is believed to have a routing table. This table has one entry for each destination that is reachable throughout the autonomous system operating IGRPng. Each entry has at least the IPv6 prefix of the destination, and a vector of metrics that is indicative of the total cost of transmitting a datagram from the router to that destination. These metrics also incorporate a delay, bandwidth, hop-count, and MTU. The delay is the total of the delays associated with the networks that would be traveled to get to the destination. The bandwidth is the smallest bandwidth of all the network segments that would be crossed. The hop-count is the total of the hop-counts of all the networks that would be traveled. The MTU is the smallest MTU of all the networks that would be traveled.

In addition, this also includes the IPv6 address of the next router along the path to the destination or next-hop. When the destination is on one of the directly connected networks, this item is not required. In addition, a flag is used to designate that the metrics for the route have been altered recently. This is called the route change flag. A flag is used to determine if the route is an exterior route. It is also used to determine if the route can be updated and used for route hold-downs. IGRPng route hold downs prevent routing update information from being accepted for a route for a given length of time once a route is determined as being unreachable. This makes certain that the update is not an echo of the route that persists in the network. The route hold down must be of sufficient time for triggered updates to reproduce across the IGRPng autonomous system as well as at least two update cycles to make up for dropped updates. Once a triggered update is lost, the following regular update cycle will restart the triggered update wave. Some of the reasons that make routes unreachable include: the originator of the route designates the route as unreachable in a received update packet, or the route timeout expires.

The metrics involved for directly connected networks are set to the cost of that network. The default cost for each metric is actually the physical characteristic comparable with the directly connected network — this includes the delay and bandwidth.

The person who implements the protocol can decide to permit the system administrator to enter additional routes. These are routes to hosts or networks beyond the routing system. They are designated as static routes. Similarly to RIPng, static routing doesn't pertain to adaptive routing supplied through routing protocols. These records for destinations along with the initial static routes are added and updated by specific algorithms in the latter portion of this chapter.

The way in which the protocol can yield total information on routing, every router in the AS needs to share a responsibility in the protocol. In the event where several IGPs are being used, there needs to one or more routers which can reproduce routing information between the protocols. IGRPng also conveys an AS number in each routing protocol packet which can permit numerous routing systems to participate on one given link without interfering with each other.

13.5. MESSAGE STRUCTURE

IGRPng transmits its packets immediately over the IPv6 network layer. It is encapsulated in at least one IPv6 header with the Next Header field. IGRPng protocol packets need to be given priority over regular IPv6 data traffic — this is important to both transmission and reception. It is important to note that field sizes are stated in octets. Fields possess binary integers unless stated otherwise in network byte order — with the most important octet listed first. Each message has an IGRPng header which is composed of the following:

- Version number
- Operation code
- Autonomous system number
- Number of interior routes
- Number of exterior routes
- Checksum covering the total contents of the IGRPng packet.

The OPCODE field is used to designate the purpose of this message. The opcodes which are used in version 1 include:

- Request: which is a call for the responding system to transmit all or part of its routing table.
- Update: which is a message which is composed of all or part of the transmitter's routing table. This message can be transmitted as a reply to a request, or it may be an unsolicited routing update created by the transmitter itself.

The autonomous system number is employed to affiliate the routing information in a packet with a given occurrence of IGRPng. Routes for an AS are transmitted only in updates for that AS. When a router obtain a request or an update with an AS which is dissimilar than the configured one, the update doesn't count.

The route counts for both the interior and exterior routes designate the amount of routes in each section of the update message. RTEs are not determined by any other means. The first portion includes the interior routes succeeded by the exterior routes. Exterior routes can be selected as the route of last resort. The exterior route with the best composite metric will be employed in choosing the next-hop for the default route. This is the only method in which exterior and interior routes are different.

Since each packet has an address family identifier, IGRPng can convey routing information for several network protocols. Therefore, each packet has an address family identifier that is used to determine the type of address that is designated in that packet. However, RIP differs in that the address family is pertinent for all RTEs for a given packet.

In order to permit future enhancements, implementations need to ignore packets which are not supported. IGRPng is only appropriate protocol which possess contiguous network masks.

The checksum is actually an IP checksum that is calculated through the usual IP checksum algorithm. The checksum work on the IGRPng header as well as all RTEs which exist within it. The checksum field is set to zero when calculating the checksum.

When dealing with each of these message types, the remaining sections of the datagram are composed a list of RTEs. The RTEs in this group are composed of a destination prefix, the amount of significant bits in the prefix, the delay, bandwidth, hop count, MTU costs to reach that destination, and a route tag.

The destination prefix is the standard 128-bit, IPv6 address prefix are recorded as 16 octets in network byte order. Bits outside the prefix length are ignored or set to zero. The prefix length field is the size in bits of the important part of the prefix beginning from the left of the prefix.

The hop-count field determines the current hop-count for the destination. The bandwidth field determines the current bandwidth for the destination. This yields a range of values from 2 bps to 10 Gbps. The bandwidth is utilized in determining the minimum bandwidth of any given network portion from the router to the destination.

The MTU field determines the current MTU for the destination. The MTU is utilized in determining the smallest MTU of any network segment from the router to the destination along a path without being fragmented. The MTU is not currently utilized by the protocol.

The route tag field is an attribute designated to a route that needs be reserved and advertised again with a route. It must be used as a route tag in order to yield a method of dividing internal IGRPng routes from external IGRPng routes that could have been imported from an EGP or another IGP.

Routers that handle protocols besides that of IGRPng need to permit the route tag to be configured for routes imported from various sources. When routes are imported from an EGP they need to be able to have their route tag either set to an arbitrary value, or to the number of the Autonomous System from which the routes were acquired. In addition, there are other uses of the route tag, which are valid, as long as all routers in the IGRPng autonomous system utilize it on a regular basis.

The largest datagram size is restricted by the MTU of the environment over which the protocol is utilized. Due to the fact that an unsolicited IGRPng update is never reproduced through a router, there is no possibility of MTU mismatch. Deciding on the number of RTEs that may be put into a message through a function of the environment's MTU.

Updating Messages

IGRPng employs the link-local source address of an update message as the next-hop address for RTEs that are imported as routes. IGRPng also yields the power to determine the next-hop IPv6 address to where packets of a destination which are designated by a route table entry.

The next-hop RTE is designated by a value of 0xFF in the hop-count field of an RTE. The prefix field determines the IPv6 address of the next hop. The prefix length, delay, bandwidth, MTU, and route tag in the next-hop RTE need to be set to zero on transmitting and ignored on reception.

RTE designates that the next-hop address needs to be the initiator of the IGRPng advertisement. Besides this special address, an address designated as a next-hop must be a link-local address.

Routing Table Size

IPv6 replaces the current IPv4. With regards to IPv6 a set of IPv4-compatible IPv6 addresses have been designated. The addresses are 128 bits in length and are composed of a fixed 96 bit prefix and then has an embedded 32-bit IPv4 address in the low-order portion of the address.

When dealing with an existing IPv4 backbone, the size of the IPv4 routing table is a large operational procedure. A backbone router is specified as a router that is made up of all IPv4 routes with the exception of the default route.

IPv6 deployment within a backbone will expand the amount of total routes that backbone routers need to convey. In order for IPv6 addresses to be grouped more effectively than IPv4 routes have been, the procedures involved for deployment of a second network-layer protocol needs to be alleviated. With each IPv6 routing prefix 128 bits are required as opposed to the 32 bits for an IPv4 routing prefix. The overall size of a routing table entry differs greatly in various implementations of IPv6 routing. At times when an IPv6 route entry were the same size as an IPv4 route entry, the router would require double the memory for the routing table. This has proven to be an important operational issue in default-less routers.

Security

It is possible to remove an operational network through improper injection of inaccurate routes. In addition, it is also possible to remove an operational network by injecting increased routes than that network's routing systems are able to support. These can happen even through operator error in addition to a hacker attack.

Router Alert Option

IPv6 employs daisy-chained optional headers to expand the versatility and eliminate the IPv4 restriction on how big options actually are. Due to the fact that numerous optional headers can be present between the base IPv6 header and the final payload, an increased parsing effort is required in order to decide what type of upper layer information is available in a specified IPv6 packet. The object is to provide a means where routers can seize packets that are not addressed to them directly without contracting any notable performance problems.

Routers that handle this type of processing in the fast path can demultiplex processing based on the Hop-by-Hop header options. When all Hop-by-Hop option types are handled in the fast path, then the addition of an extra option type to process is not likely to degrade performance. If some Hop-by-Hop option types are not supported in the fast path, this new option type will be unrecognized and make packets which convey it to be pushed down into the slow path. Therefore, if no change to the fast path is needed, then no performance degradation will occur for regular data packets.

Routers which do not support option processing in the fast path will make packets conveying this new option be forwarded through the slow path. Furthermore, no change to the fast path is needed and no performance degradation will happen for standard data packets. When nodes do not recognize this option, they need to hop over this option and continue operating on the header. This option can not change while en-route.

13.6. PROTOCOL IMPACT

In order for this procedure to work, it needs to have legitimate status protocols which believe that routers will execute important processing on packets which are not directly addressed to them. All IPv6 packets that have an ICMPv6 Group Membership message need to possess this option within the

IPv6 Hop by Hop Options Header of this type of packets. In addition, all of the IPv6 packets which have a Resource ReSerVation Protocol (RSVP) message needs to have this option within the IPv6 Hop by Hop Options Header of this type of packets shown in Figure 13.1.

When dealing with an extended IPv4 to IPv6 transition duration, IPv6-based systems need to live with the installed base of IPv4 systems. In this type of dual internetworking protocol environment, both IPv4 and IPv6 routing infrastructure will be available. At first, deployed IPv6-capable domains may not be interconnected around the world through an IPv6-capable Internet infrastructure and as a result may need to have the ability to communicate across IPv4 only routing regions. To obtain dynamic routing in this type of mixed environment requires a method of globally issuing IPv6 network layer reachability information between dispersed IPv6 routing regions. Analogous methods can be employed in future stages of IPv4 to IPv6 transition to route IPv4 packets between isolated IPv4 only routing areas over IPv6 foundations.

The IPng transition yields a dual-IP-layer transition, expanded by implementation of encapsulation when it is needed. Routing issues pertaining to this transition incorporate routing for IPv4 packets, routing for IPv6 packets that include IPv6 packets with IPv6 native addresses and IPv6 packets with IPv4 compatible addresses. This also deals with the mechanics of manually configured static tunnels, the mechanics of automatic encapsulation which are involved in finding encapsulators and making certain that routing is the same with encapsulation.

The standard means available to achieve these goals include: include the Dual IP layer Route Computation, manual configuration of point to point tunnels, and route leaking to handle automatic encapsulation. The basic means for routing of IPv4 and IPv6 incorporates dual IP layer routing. This indicates that routes are individually computed for IPv4 addresses and for IPv6 addressing.

IPv6 Addressing

IPv6 employs a 128-bit addressing scheme. This increases address space by a factor of 296 which effectively provides for suffcient addressing capability for any network. In using 128 bits rather than 32 bits as IPv4 does, IPv6

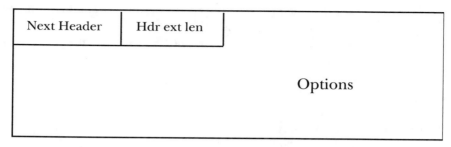

Figure 13.1. Hop-by-Hop Options
Header

increases address space by a billion x a billion x a billion times. A comparison of this increase indicates:

IP Version	Size of Address Space
IPv4	32 bits = 4,294,967,296
IPv6	128 bits = 340,282,366,920,938,463,463,374,607,431,768,211,456

Figure 13.2. Comparative
Address Space

Tunnels for IPv4 over IPv6 or IPv6 over IPv4 can be manually configured. When dealing with the primary aspects of transition this may be employed to permit two IPv6 domains to interact via an IPv4 infrastructure. The manually configured static tunnels are then considered as if they were a normal data link.

Automatic encapsulation (where the IPv4 tunnel endpoint address is set from the IPv4 address embedded in the IPv4 compatible destination address of IPv6 packet) requires a pathway between IPv4 routes and IPv6 routes for destinations using IPv4-compatible addresses. If you look at a packet which begins as an IPv6 packet and is then encapsulated in an IPv4 packet in the middle of its path from source to destination, then this packet must find an encapsulator at a specified part of its path. In addition, this packet needs to adhere to a standard route for the while path from source to destination.

Dual-IP-Layer Procedures

In the standard dual-IP-layer transition method, routers may individually support IPv4 and IPv6 routing. In terms of other sections of the transition including DNS support, it is important to choose the source host regarding whether to transmit IPv4 or IPv6 packet format (depicted in Figure 13.3). The action of forwarding IPv4 packets has a foundation in the routes acquired through operating IPv4-specific routing protocols. In addition, IPv6 packets incorporates IPv6 packets with IPv4 compatible addresses which is founded on routes obtained through operating IPv6 specific routing protocols (illustrated by the IPv6 Routing Header in Figure 13.4). This indicates that individual occurrences of routing protocols are employed for both IPv4 and IPv6.

This could be somewhat altered so it could employ an individual occurrence of an integrated routing protocol to handle routing for both IPv4 and IPv6. Furthermore, this change does not alter the basic dual-IP-layer character of the transition.

Primary testing of IPv6 with IPv4 compatible addressed can help in forwarding of IPv6 packets without operating any IPv6 compatible routing protocol. In this event, a dual IPv4 and IPv6 router can operate routing protocols for just IPv4. It then forwards IPv4 packets rooted on routes acquired from IPv4 routing protocols. In addition, it forwards IPv6 packets with an IPv4 compatible destination address rooted on the route for the linked IPv4 address.

Some of the disadvantages with this method includes the fact that it does not precisely permit routing of IPv6 packets through IPv6 capable routers at a time when it needs to route around IPv4 only routers. In addition, it does not create routes for non-compatible IPv6 addresses. When using the particular mechanism, the routing protocol does not inform the router if the neighboring routers are IPv6 compatible. Instead, neighbor discovery can be employed to calculate this. When an IPv6 packet must be forwarded to an IPv4 only router it can be encapsulated to the destination host.

Inside the IPv6 Packet

IPv6 PACKET FORMAT	Octets
IPv6 header	40
Hop-by-hop options header	Variable
Routing header	Variable
Fragment header	8
Authentication header	Variable
Encapsulating security payload header	Variable
Destination options header	Variable
TCP header	20
Application header	Variable

Figure 13.3. IPv6 Packet Format

IPv6 Header	Routing Header	TCP Header
		+
Next Header: Routing	Next Header: TCP	Data

Figure 13.4. Routing Header

13.7. STATIC TUNNELS

Tunneling methodologies are used to a large extent and are deployed for bridging non-IP network layer protocols such as Appletalk, CLNP, and IPX via IPv4 routed foundations. IPv4 tunneling is basically an encapsulation of packets within IPv4 datagrams that are forwarded over IPv4 foundations between tunnel endpoints. When dealing with a tunneled protocol, a tunnel emerges as a single hop link, where these links between the host and subnet are depicted in Figure 13.5. This can best be illustrated by routers which

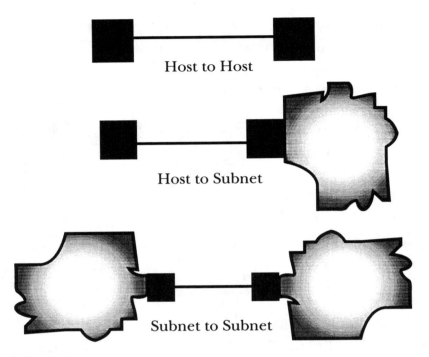

Figure 13.5. Links between the Host and Subnet

create a tunnel over a network layer foundation and can interoperate over the tunnel as though it were a one-hop point-to-point link. When a tunnel is created, routers at the tunnel endpoints can create routing adjacencies and substitute routing information.

13.8. AUTOMATIC TUNNELING

Automatic tunneling can be utilized when IPv4 routing links both the transmission and reception nodes. The way in which automatic tunneling can function involves both nodes to be designated IPv4 compatible IPv6 addresses. Automatic tunneling can be pertinent when either or both the source or destination hosts do not possess any adjacent IPv6-capable router. An adjacent router includes routers which are logically adjacent by a manually configured point-to-point tunnel that is considered as though it were a simple point-to-point link.

When using automatic tunneling, the consequent IPv4 packet is forwarded by IPv4 routers as a standard IPv4 packet, using IPv4 routes acquired from routing protocols. There are no special issues pertinent to IPv4 routing in this case. There are routing issues that relate to how IPv6 routing operates in a method that is compatible with automatic tunneling as well as a way in which tunnel endpoint addresses are chosen during the encapsulation process. Automatic tunneling is excellent from a source host to the destination host, from a source host to a router, as well as from a router to the destination host.

13.9. HOST TO HOST AUTOMATIC TUNNELING

When both the source and destination hosts utilize the IPv4 compatible IPv6 addresses, it is then possible for automatic tunneling to be employed for the complete path from the source host to the destination host. In this event, the IPv6 packet is encapsulated in an IPv4 packet by the source host, after which it is forwarded by routers as an IPv4 packet to the destination host. This permits initial deployment of IPv6 capable hosts to be completed prior to the update of any routers.

A source host utilizes Host to Host automatic tunneling, given that the source address is an IPv4 compatible IPv6 address, the destination address is an IPv4 compatible IPv6 address. The source host has no knowledge of one or more neighboring IPv4 capable routers, or the source and destination exist on the same subnet.

When these conditions have been met, the source host may encapsulate the IPv6 packet in an IPv4 packet using a source IPv4 address that is taken from the associated source IPv6 address. It also employs the destination IPv4 address which is taken from the analogous destination IPv6 address.

When host to host automatic tunneling is employed, the packet is forwarded as a standard IPv4 packet throughout its complete path, and is decapsulated. For example, the IPv4 header is removed, but only by the destination host.

When the source host has a neighboring IPv6 router, or if the source and destination exist on the same subnet, then automatic tunneling does not need to be employed. The packet can be transmitted in raw IPv6 form and forwarded through IPv6 routing as shown by both the transport and tunnel modes illustrated in Figure 13.6.

13.10. HOST TO ROUTER DEFAULT TUNNELING

There are some events where a configured default tunnel can be employed to encapsulate the IPv6 packet for transmission from the source host to an IPv6 backbone. This needs the source host to be configured with an IPv4 address to use for tunneling to the backbone.

Configured default tunneling is especially important if the source host is not aware of any local IPv6 capable router. This indicates that the packet is not able to be forwarded as a standard IPv6 packet directly over the link-layer, or when the destination host doesn't possess an IPv4-compatible IPv6 address. This indicates that the host to host tunneling cannot be used.

Host to router configured default tunneling may alternatively be employed when the host is not aware of a local IPv6 router. In this event, it is up to the host whether it prefers to transmit a native IPv6 packet to the IPv6 capable router or wishes to transmit an encapsulated packet to the configured tunnel endpoint.

In the same way a host to router default configured tunneling can be employed when the destination address is an IPv4 compatible IPv6 address. A source host can utilize the host to router configured default tunnel given that the source address is an IPv4 compatible IPv6 address. The source host is not aware of one or more neighboring IPv4 capable routers, and the source host has been configured with an IPv4 address of an dual router which can perform as the tunnel endpoint.

When all of these condition have been met, then the source host may encapsulate the IPv6 packet in an IPv4 packet, utilizing a source IPv4 address that is extracted from the linked source IPv6 address. It can then employ a destination IPv4 address that is analogous to the configured address of the dual router that serves as the tunnel endpoint.

When host to router configured default tunneling is employed, the packet is forwarded as a standard IPv4 packet from the source host to the dual

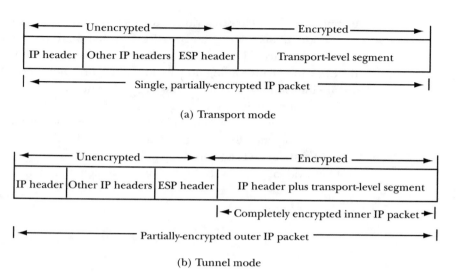

(a) Transport mode

(b) Tunnel mode

Figure 13.6. Transport and
Tunnel Mode

router serving as tunnel endpoint. It is then decapsulated by the dual router, and then forwarded as a standard IPv6 packet by the tunnel endpoint.

13.11. CONCLUSION

When route leaking is employed, IPv4 routes that are obtained by an inter-region dual router may need to be injected into an IPv6 routing region. This type of an inter-region dual router may employ BGP-4 for IPv4 inter-domain routing. Due to the fact that the Inter-Domain Routing Protocol (IDRP) has been taken for IPv6 inter-domain routing, IDRP may wish to be used to generate the IPv4 route into IPv6 routing domains.

When routes acquired with BGP are injected into IDRP, it would be preferable to preserve routing attributes linked with the routes so as to lessen the effect of the inter-region route leaking onto the routing integrity. Due to the fact that nearly all routing attributes are carried in BGP-4 and are also present in IDRP — the mapping of the BGP-4 attributes to the IDRP attributes is direct. However, due to the fact that both addresses and routing domain identifiers are carried by IDRP and BGP-4 are reserved from different number spaces. There is a requirement to make certain that 32-bit IPv4 addresses and 16-bit routing domain identifiers or Autonomous System numbers are individually depicted in the larger IPv6 number space.

IPv6 domain identifiers are assigned from the 128-bit IPv6 address space and IPv6 addresses with 96 leading zero bits, they are taken to depict addresses designated from the IPv4 address space. It will be normal to reserve IPv6 addresses to be used as routing domain identifiers with 112 leading zero bits to individually depict IPv4 Autonomous System numbers.

Security Management

14

14.1. INTRODUCTION

This chapter deals with several aspects regarding the security architecture. That security is then translated in to dealing with the IP Encapsulation Security Payload (ESP).

First, let us begin by discussing the Authentication Header. It is a method that can yield a powerful authentication mechanism for IP datagrams. In addition, it also yields non-repudiation. However, this is dependent on the type of cryptographic algorithm that is employed, as well as how keying is executed. This is best illustrated by using an asymmetric digital signature algorithm (e.g., RSA) which can supply non-repudiation. The authentication and security parameters index format is shown in Figure 14.1.

The ability to keep items secure and safeguard your traffic analysis (illustrated by Figure 14.2) is not given by the Authentication Header. Users who wish their information kept secure need to look at the IP Encapsulating Security Protocol (ESP) that may be used together with the Authentication Header.

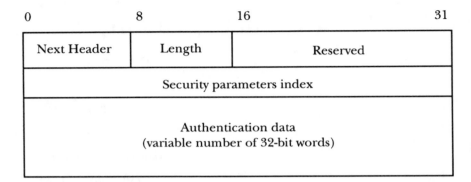

Figure 14.1. Authentication Data
Format

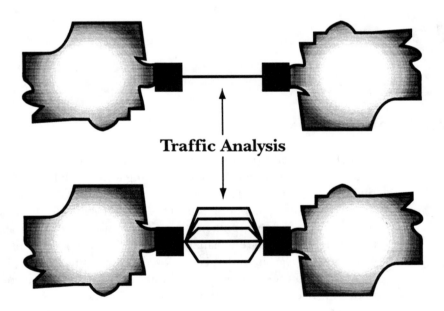

Figure 14.2. Traffic Analysis

14.2. NUTS AND BOLTS

The IP Authentication Header tries to yield security by calculating authentication information on an IP datagram. This authentication information is determined using all of the fields in the IP datagram that do not change during transport. The fields or options which are required to be changed in transit such as the hop count, time to live, ident, fragment offset, or routing pointer are believed to be 0 for the computation of the authentication data. This yields more security than exists in IPv4 and may be adequate for the needs of many users.

The utilization of this technical description will expand the IP protocol operating costs in end systems that also share the load as well as increasing the communications latency. The increased latency is mainly due to the computation of the authentication data by the transmitter and the computation and comparison of the authentication data by the receiver for each IP datagram which has an Authentication Header. The overall impact will be different depending on which authentication algorithm is used as well as other factors.

The Authentication Header can work correctly without altering the complete Internet foundation. The authentication data is conveyed in its own payload. Systems that do not share in the authentication can ignore the Authentication Data. When the Authentication Header is used with IPv6, it is usually placed after the Fragmentation and End-to-End headers, but prior to the ESP and transport-layer headers. The information in the other IP headers is employed to route the datagram from origin to destination. When employed with IPv4, the Authentication Header instantly succeeds the IPv4 header.

When a symmetric authentication algorithm is employed and intermediate authentication is preferred, then the nodes operating this type of intermediate authentication would be given the appropriate keys. Possession of those keys would allow any one of those systems to forge traffic while pretending to be from the actual sender to the legitimate receiver, or optionally to alter the contents of what would normally be considered legitimate traffic. In some mediums, intermediate authentication might be preferred.

Should an asymmetric authentication algorithm be employed while the routers are aware of the proper public keys and authentication algorithm, then the routers which have the authentication public key would be able to authenticate the traffic being handled without having the ability to forge or modify what would normally be considered legitimate traffic. In addition, Path MTU Discovery must be used when intermediate authentication of the Authentication Header is preferred and IPv4 is being used. This is due to the fact that when using this method it is not possible to authenticate a fragment of a packet.

Key Management

Key management is an integral part of the IP security architecture. The IP Authentication Header attempts to decouple the key administration or management methods from the security protocol method. In fact, the only coupling between the key management protocol and the security protocol is through the Security Parameters Index (SPI). This form of decoupling allows numerous different key management methods to be employed. In addition, it also allows the key management protocol to be fixed without degrading the security protocol implementations.

The key management method is employed for the purpose of stipulating several parameters for each Security Association. This includes both the keys as well as other information, such as the authentication algorithm and mode employed by the communicating participants. The key management method both establishes and sustains a logical table that is composed of several parameters for each current security association. An implementation of the IP Authentication Header will be required to read that logical table of security parameters to figure out the best way in which to process each datagram which has an Authentication Header. This is also used to illustrate the method that determines which algorithm/mode and key to employ in authentication.

Authentication Headers

The Authentication Header (AH) may emerge after any other headers which are inspected at each hop, and prior to any other headers which are not inspected at an intermediate hop. The authentication data is the output of the authentication algorithm computer over the complete IP datagram. The authentication computation has to consider the Authentication Data field as well as all fields that are usually modified in transit such as TTL or Hop Limit as though those fields were composed of zeros.

Sensitivity

IPv6 will usually use implicit Security Labels as opposed to explicit labels that are now used with IPv4. There are some events, where users elect to convey explicit labels besides using the implicit labels given by the Authentication Header. Explicit label options need to be defined for use with IPv6. Furthermore, implementations can also support explicit labels besides that of implicit labels. However, implementations are not necessary to support explicit labels. When explicit labels are being used then the explicit label needs be incorporated in the authentication calculation.

14.3. AUTHENTICATION DATA

The authentication data conveyed by the IP Authentication Header is normally computed by employing a message digest algorithm such as MD5 which can either encrypt the message digest or keying the message digest directly. Just the algorithms that are believed to be cryptographically strong one-way functions need to be used with the IP Authentication Header.

When operating on an outgoing IP packet for Authentication, the initial step is for the sending system is to find the proper Security Association. All Security Associations are unidirectional. The choice of the appropriate Security Association for an outgoing IP packet is founded primarily upon the sending user id as well as the Destination Address. When host-oriented keying is employed, all sending user ids will have the same Security Association in a specified destination. When user-oriented keying is used, then different users or different applications of the same user can use different Security Associations. The specific Security Association chosen will indicate which algorithm, algorithm mode, key, and other security properties are pertinent to the outgoing packet.

Fields which must be modified during transit from the sender to the receiver such as the TTL and HEADER CHECKSUM for IPv4 or Hop Limit for IPv6 besides that of the value at the receiver is not known with certainty by the sender. These items are all incorporated in the authentication data computation. When dealing with fields modified in transit, the value conveyed in the IP packet is substituted by the value zero for the purpose of the authentication calculation. When the field's value is replaced with zero as opposed to eliminating these fields, alignment is preserved for the authentication computation.

The sender needs to calculate the authentication over the packet as that packet will appear at the receiver. This requirement is in a sequential order to permit for future IP optional headers in which the receiver may not know about yet the sender certainly knows about if it is incorporating such options in the packet. This also allows the authentication of data which will change in transport, however its value at the final receiver is known with certainty by the sender beforehand.

In IPv4, the time to live and the header checksum fields are the only fields within the IPv4 base header, which are handled specifically for the Authentication Data calculation. Reassembling the fragmented packets happens before the processing of the local IP Authentication Header implementation.

There are no other fields within the IPv4 header that will vary in transport from the standpoint of the IP Authentication Header implementation. The time to live and header checksum fields of the IPv4 base header need to be set to all 0s for the Authentication Data computation. All other IPv4 base header fields are operated on normally with its actual contents. Due to the fact that IPv4 packets are subjected to intermediate fragmentation in routers. IPv4 Implementations need to use Path MTU Discovery when the IP Authentication Header is being used.

The IPv6 hop limit field is the only field in the IPv6 base header which is handled specifically for Authentication Data calculation. The value of the hop limit field is 0 for the intent of Authentication Data calculation. All of the other fields in the base IPv6 header need to be included in the Authentication Data calculation through standard procedures for computing the Authentication Data.

When a packet has received an IP Authentication Header, the receiver primarily uses the Destination Address and SPI value to find the correct Security Association. The receiver then individually verifies that the Authentication Data fields as well as the received data packet are similar. The Authentication Data field is believed to be 0 for the intention of making the authentication calculation. The method by which this is achieved is algorithm dependent. If the processing of the authentication algorithm designates that the datagram is valid, then it is accepted. When the algorithm designates that the data and the Authentication Header do not match, then the receiver needs to eliminate the received IP datagram as invalid. It must then record the authentication failure in the system or audit log. When this type of failure occurs, the recorded log data needs to include the SPI value, date/time received, clear-text Sending Address, clear-text Destination Address, and clear-text Flow ID.

Authentication Security

In this section we have carefully looked at the authentication mechanism for IP. This method is not a remedy for numerous security issues, which commonly exists in any Internetwork, however it yields the means by which to create a secure foundation.

Users must realize the quality of what they achieve is completely dependent upon the strength of whichever cryptographic algorithm has been instituted. The strength of the key which is used and the accuracy of that algorithm's implementation are both dependent upon the security of the key management implementation as well as its implementation and accuracy of the IP Authentication Header and IP implementations in all of the associated systems. Should any of these rules fail, then the user doesn't receive any meaningful security implementation.

Users who must have security, need to take into account the IP Encapsulating Security Payload (ESP). Users who need to be defended from traffic analysis may decide to employ an appropriate link encryption.

One aspect involves carefully watching out for active attacks. They are very common on the Internet today, but the presence of active attacks indicates that unauthenticated source routing can be unidirectional — receive only, or with responses succeeding the initial received source route which designate an important security risk. This is true except that all received source routed packets are authenticated via the IP Authentication Header or through some other cryptologic mechanism.

14.4. SECURITY ARCHITECTURE FOR THE INTERNET PROTOCOL

There are two distinct headers that are used to yield security services in both IPv4 and IPv6. These headers include:

- IP Authentication Header (AH)
- IP Encapsulating Security Payload (ESP) header

There are a several methods in which these IP security mechanisms can be used. The IP Authentication Header is created to yield both integrity and authentication without confidentiality to IP datagrams. The absence of confidentiality makes certain that implementations of the Authentication Header will be commonly available on the Internet. This is true even in locations where the export, import, or where encryption use is designed to yield confidentiality. The Authentication Header sustains security between:

- At least two hosts implementing AH
- Between two or more gateways implementing AH
- Between a host or gateway implementing AH and a set of hosts or gateways.

A security gateway is a system that performs as the communications gateway between external untrusted systems and trusted hosts on their own subnetwork. It also yields security services for the trusted hosts when they communicate with the external untrusted systems. A trusted subnetwork comprises hosts and routers that trust each other not to operate in active or passive attacks. In addition, they trust that the foundation of the communications channel won't be attacked.

In a situation where a security gateway is yielding services for at least one host on a trusted subnet, the security gateway becomes liable for establishing the security association on behalf of its trusted host in addition to yielding security services between the security gateway and the external systems. At this point, only the gateway has to implement AH, however all of the systems behind the gateway on the trusted subnet may benefit from the AH services between the gateway and external systems.

14.5. IP ENCAPSULATING SECURITY PAYLOAD

The IP Encapsulating Security Payload (ESP) provides integrity, authentication, and confidentiality to IP datagrams. The ESP supports security between at least two hosts that implement ESP, between two or more gateways implementing ESP, and between a host or gateway implementing ESP and a set of hosts and/or gateways. The security gateway is a system that acts as the communications gateway between external untrusted systems and trusted hosts on their own subnetwork. It also provides security services for the trusted hosts when they communicate with external untrusted systems. A trusted subnetwork maintains hosts and routers which trust each other not to involve themselves in active or passive attacks. ESP does not give non-repudiation and protection from traffic analysis. The IP Authentication Header (AH) may yield non-repudiation if employed with specific authentication. The IP Authentication Header may be used together with ESP to give authentication. Users who wish the integrity and authentication without confidentiality can use the IP Authentication Header (AH) in lieu of ESP.

Gateway-to-gateway encryption is advantageous for creating private virtual networks throughout an untrusted backbone such as the Internet. When there is a security gateway that is yielding services for one or more hosts on a trusted subnet, the security gateway is liable for creating the security relationship for its trusted host as well as providing security services between the security gateway and the external systems. Essentially, only the gateway can implement ESP, while all of the systems behind the gateway on the trusted subnet can take advantage of ESP services between the gateway and external systems.

The IP Encapsulating Security Payload (ESP) tries to allow for both confidentiality and integrity by encrypting data to be protected and sending the encrypted data in the data portion of the IP Encapsulating Security Payload. With respect to the user's security requirements, this method may be employed to encrypt either a transport-layer segment such as TCP, UDP, ICMP, IGMP, or a whole IP datagram. Encapsulating the protected data is important as it arranges confidentiality for the whole original datagram.

When dealing with Tunnel-mode ESP, the initial IP datagram is sent in the encrypted portion of the Encapsulating Security Payload. Then the whole ESP frame is set within a datagram having unencrypted IP headers. The data in the unencrypted IP headers is utilized to route the secure datagram from the origin to destination. An unencrypted IP Routing Header can be incorporated between the IP Header and the Encapsulating Security Payload.

When dealing with transport-mode ESP, the ESP header is encased into the IP datagram just before to the transport-layer protocol header. Bandwidth is conserved in this mode due to the fact that there are no encrypted IP headers or IP options.

In the case of IP, an IP Authentication Header can be available as a header of an unencrypted IP packet, as a header succeeding the IP header, and prior to the ESP header in a Transport-mode ESP packet. It may also act as a header within the encrypted section of a Tunnel-mode ESP packet.

The Encapsulating Security Payload is constructed a bit differently than other IP payloads. The first aspect of the ESP payload is composed of the unencrypted fields of the payload. The next component is composed of encrypted data. The fields of the unencrypted ESP header communicate with the intended receiver with regards to how to correctly decrypt and operate the encrypted data. The encrypted data component incorporates protected fields for the security protocol as well as the encrypted encapsulated IP datagram. The idea behind a Security Association is essential to ESP.

ESP Syntax

The Encapsulating Security Payload (ESP) emerges at any point subsequent to the IP header, but prior to the final transport-layer protocol. The Internet Assigned Numbers Authority has designated Protocol Number 50 to ESP. The header immediately prior to ESP header will always possess the value 50 in its Next Header in either the (next header) IPv6 or IPv4 (protocol field.) ESP is composed of an unencrypted header succeeded by encrypted data. The encrypted data incorporates both the protected ESP header fields as well as the protected user data. This is either the entire IP datagram or an upper-layer protocol.

The Goals

The goal of the overall security architecture as well as its component mechanisms make certain that IPv4 and IPv6 will have solid cryptographic security mechanisms accessible to users who wish for security. These mechanisms are established to prevent unfavorable problems on Internet users who utilize security mechanisms for their traffic. These mechanisms are meant to be algorithm-independent, therefore cryptographic algorithms can be changed without impacting the other sections of the implementation. These security mechanisms are important for making certain that security policies are followed.

14.6. IP LAYER SECURITY

There are two cryptographic security methods for IP:

- Authentication Header: this yields both integrity and authentication without confidentiality
- Encapsulating Security Payload: this always yields confidentiality, and perhaps integrity and authentication depending on the algorithm and mode. The two IP security methods may be used individually or can be combined.

14.7. AUTHENTICATION HEADER

The IP Authentication Header possesses authentication information for its IP datagram. It accomplished this by calculating a cryptographic authentication function over the IP datagram and employing a secret authentication key in the computation. The sender calculates the authentication data before transmitting the authenticated IP packet. Fragmentation occurs after the Authentication Header operation for outbound packets, but before the Authentication Header operates on inbound packets.

The Authentication Header yields a much stronger security that exists in the majority of the Internet and neither needs to affect the ability to export or significantly increase the dollar cost of implementation. While the Authentication Header may be implemented by a security gateway for hosts on a trusted network behind that security gateway, this mode of operation is not suggested. Instead, the Authentication Header needs to be used from the initial to the final destination.

Both IPv4 and IPv6 need to support the Authentication Header with MD5 as a minimum of the MD5 algorithm employing a 128-bit key. An implementation can support alternate authentication algorithms besides that of the keyed MD5.

14.8. ESP MODES

There are two modes within ESP.

- Tunnel mode: which encapsulates the whole IP datagram within the ESP header.
- Transport mode: which encapsulates an upper-layer protocol such as UDP or TCP) within ESP.

ESP operates between hosts, between a host and a security gateway, or between security gateways. There is support for a security gateway that allows trustworthy networks inside a security gateway to eliminate encryption and effectively curtail the performance and costs caused by encryption. However, it still yields confidentiality for traffic transiting untrustworthy network segments. When both hosts directly implement ESP (and there is not any intervening security gateway) then they may employ the Transport-mode in which only the upper layer protocol data is encrypted while there is no encrypted IP header.

The encapsulating security method employed by ESP can significantly impact network performance in cooperating systems (the common operating environment hierarchy is illustrated in Figure 14.3). However, ESP usage need not negatively impact routers or other intermediate systems that are not sharing in the specific ESP association. Protocol processing in shared systems will be more complex when encapsulating security is employed as they need more time and more processing power. Encryption usage will also expand the communications latency. This increased latency is mostly due to the encryption and decryption needed for each IP datagram that has an Encapsulating Security Payload.

Security Methods

In the majority of cases, the IP Authentication Header can be combined with the IP Encapsulating Security Protocol to achieve the needed security properties. The Authentication Header always yields integrity and authentication and can give non-repudiation if employed with certain authentication algorithms. The Encapsulating Security Payload always yields integrity and confidentiality besides providing authentication when used with specific authenticating encryption algorithms. Joining the Authentication Header to an IP datagram before encapsulating that datagram via the Encapsulating Security Protocol is preferable for users who want to have strong integrity, authentication, and confidentiality.

Firewalls

Firewalls are very common on the Internet. Even though they do impose restrictions on some people, they will endure. Both IP mechanisms can be used to expand the security provided by firewalls.

Firewalls employed with IP usually require the ability to parse the headers and options to decide the transport protocol that is in use as well as the port number for that protocol. Essentially, authentication can be performed both within an organization but also end to end with remote systems across the Internet.

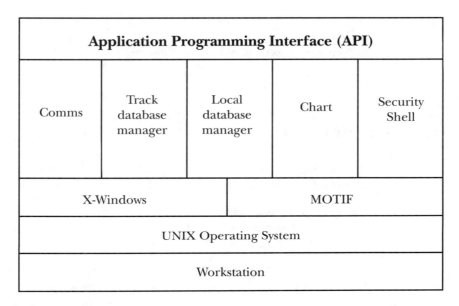

Application Programming Interface (API)				
Comms	Track database manager	Local database manager	Chart	Security Shell
X-Windows		MOTIF		
UNIX Operating System				
Workstation				

Figure 14.3. Common Operating Environment

IP Authentication via Keyed MD5

The confidential authentication key shared between the communicating party's needs to be a cryptographically strong random number instead of a common string that someone can guess after repeated tries. The shared key is not limited by this transform to any specific size. Lengths as long as 128 bits need to be supported by the implementation, even though any specific key may be shorter. Longer keys are suggested.

With respect to data size, MD5 has a 128-bit output that is 64-bit aligned. In terms of performance, MD5 software speeds are sufficient for commonly deployed LAN and WAN links. However, new link technologies may find this method too slow for practical applications.

MD5 Security

It is important to note that the quality of security given to users is very much dependent upon the strength of the MD5 hash function, the accuracy of that algorithm's implementation, the security of the key management method and implementation, the strength of the key, and upon the accuracy of the implementations in all of the associated nodes.

14.9. ESP PROCESSING

It is important to look at the procedure involved when ESP is in use between two communicating parties. There are two modes of use for ESP.

- Tunnel mode: which encapsulates an entire IP datagram inside ESP
- Transport Mode: which encapsulates a transport-layer such as a UDP, or TCP frame inside ESP.

Transport-mode is the same as restricting its use to TCP and UDP. An ICMP message can be transmitted using the Transport mode or the Tunnel-mode with respect to the particular situation. ESP processing happens just before the IP fragmentation on output and after IP reassembly on input. When dealing with Tunnel-mode ESP, the ESP header succeeds all of the end-to-end headers such as the Authentication Header and instantly emerges just prior to a tunnelled IP datagram.

The sender acquires the initial IP datagram, encapsulates it into the ESP, utilizes the sending user id and Destination Address as data to find the correct Security Association, and then uses it for the appropriate encryption transform. When there is no valid Security Association in place for this session or in a situation where the receiver has no key, the receiver needs to eliminate the encrypted ESP and the failure needs to be recorded in the system or audit log. In fact, the receiver may not want to react by immediately informing the sender of this failure due to the strong possibility that he may be easily exploited through denial of service attacks.

When decryption succeeds, the initial IP datagram is then removed from the decrypted ESP. This initial IP datagram is then operated on per the normal IP protocol specifications. In the case of a system alleging to provide multilevel security, there are additional appropriate mandatory access controls which need be applied based on the security level of the receiving operation as well as the security level linked with this Security Association. When those mandatory access controls don't work, then the packet needs to be eliminated and the failure needs to be logged using implementation specific procedures.

When dealing with transport-mode ESP, the ESP header succeeds the end-to-end headers and instantly goes before a transport-layer. The sender takes the initial transport layer frame, encapsulates it into the ESP, and utilizes at least the sending user id and Destination Address to find the appropriate Security Association. It is then used specifically for the proper encryption transform. If host-oriented keying is being used, then all sending user ids on a system will have the same Security Association for a specific Destination Address. When no key has been established, then the key management mechanism is employed to establish a encryption key for this communications session before encryption. The encrypted ESP is then encapsulated as the last payload of a cleartext IP datagram.

The receiver operates on the cleartext IP header and cleartext optional IP headers and temporarily stores pertinent information such as the source and destination addresses, Flow ID, Routing Header. It then decrypts the ESP using the session key that has been established for this traffic, which possesses the combination of the destination address and the packet's Security Association Identifier (SAI) to find the correct key.

When a key doesn't exist for this session or the attempt to decrypt fails, the encrypted ESP must be eliminated and the failure needs to be recorded in the system log or audit log. When such a failure occurs, the recorded log data needs to include the SPI value, date/time received clear-text Sending Address, clear-text Destination Address, and the Flow ID. The log data can also incorporate other information about the failed packet. If decryption does not work properly for some reason, then the resulting data will not be parsable by the implementation's protocol engine. Therefore, it is possible to detect failed decryption.

When decryption succeeds, the initial transport-layer frame (i.e., ICMP, UDP, or TCP) is eliminated from the decrypted ESP. The data from the cleartext IP header and the decrypted transport-layer header is a combination that is used to determine which application the data needs to be sent to. The data is then transmitted through the appropriate application as normal per the IP protocol specification. In the event where a system asserts that it can provide multilevel security more Mandatory Access Controls need to be applied rooted on the security level of the receiving process and the security level of the received packet's Security Association.

Authentication

There are transforms that provide authentication in addition to confidentiality and integrity. When this type of a transform is not used, then the Authentication Header can be used together with the Encapsulating Security Payload. There are two different methods involved when using the Authentication Header with ESP. Choosing one depends on which data is to be authenticated. The location of the Authentication Header then determines which set of data is being authenticated.

In the first use, the entire received datagram is authenticated. This incorporates both the encrypted and unencrypted portions. Even though only the data transmitted after the ESP Header is confidential, in this event the sender primarily applies ESP to the data which is protected.

The final step involves the IP Authentication Header being calculated over the resulting datagram with respect to the normal method. When the receiver obtains the data, he or she first verifies the authenticity of the entire datagram by employing the normal IP Authentication Header process. Then, if authentication is successful, decryption using the normal IP ESP process happens. If decryption is successful, then the resulting data is sent up to the upper layer.

When authentication process is applied only to the data protected by Tunnel-mode ESP, then the IP Authentication Header would be sent normally within that protected datagram. However, if the Transport-mode ESP were being used, then the IP Authentication Header would be sent before the ESP header and would be computed across the entire IP datagram.

When the Authentication Header is encapsulated within a Tunnel-mode ESP header, both headers will have specific security classification levels linked to them. In addition, if the two security classification levels are not the same, then an error has occurred. That error must be recorded in the system log or audit log employing the procedures as previously outlined in this chapter. It is not necessarily an error for an Authentication Header located outside of the ESP header to have a dissimilar security classification level to the ESP header's classification level. This could be valid because the cleartext IP headers might have a different classification level after the data has been encrypted employing ESP.

14.10. CONCLUSION

This chapter deals with the security architecture for IPv6 with some illustrations into IPv4. This security implementation is further exemplified through the demonstration of the IP Encapsulating Security Payload. Security is illustrated and is defined in terms of strength afforded for each user.

Utilization of the Authentication Header will expand the IP protocol processing costs in participating systems. It will also expand the communications latency. The extended latency is mostly due to the computation of the authentication data by the sender and the computation and comparison of the authentication data by each receiver for each IP datagram which has an Authentication Header.

That strength, however, is dependent on the remaining sections of this chapter and deals with Keyed MD5 with regards to the IP Authentication and its associated header.

IPv6 Architectural Specifics

15

15.1. INTRODUCTION

This chapter looks at the DES-CBC security transform for the IP Encapsulating Security Payload (ESP) described in Chapter 14. As discussed earlier, the Encapsulating Security Payload (ESP) yields confidentiality for IP datagrams as it encrypts the payload data to be protected. In this section we will look at how ESP uses the Cipher Block Chaining (CBC) mode. However, it is important to point out that security relies completely upon the power of the US Data Encryption Standard (DES) algorithm. The accuracy of that algorithm's implementation, the security of the key management mechanism, and the power of the key all depend on the accuracy of the implementations that are present in the cooperating nodes.

Any implementation that states it has conformance or compliance with the Encapsulating Security Payload specification is required to implement this DES-CBC transform. This section builds upon the Security Architecture for the Internet Protocol outlined in the last chapter which designates the overall security plan for IP, and yields an important foundation for this specification.

15.2. SECRET KEYS

The secret DES key is used jointly between the communicating parties measures eight octets in length. This key is composed of a 56-bit quantity employed by the DES algorithm. The 56-bit key is recorded as a 64-bit eight octet quantity, which has the least significant bit of each octet employed as a parity bit. Both encryption and authentication in transport and tunnel modes are shown in Figure 15.1.

The specific mode of DES needs an Initialization Vector (IV) which measures eight octets in length. Each datagram has its own IV. This incorporates the IV in each datagram to make certain that decryption of each received datagram can be executed, even when other datagrams are eliminated or when datagrams are resequenced in transport.

The selection mechanism of IV values relies upon implementation. A common method is a counter, which starts with a randomly chosen value. This yields an easy method for preventing repetition, and is adequately powerful for practical use. Furthermore, crypto-analysis may employ the rare coincidental development when an associated bit position in the first DES block increments in an analogous fashion.

There are implementations that illustrate variable values that usually occur through a false number generator. It is important to be careful regarding the succession — that the number generator is long enough to avert repetition during the lifetime of the session key.

The DES algorithm works on blocks of eight octets. This often necessitates padding succeeding the end of the unencrypted payload data. Both the input and output conclude in the amount number of octets, which allow in place encryption and decryption.When the length of the data to be decrypted is not an integral multiple of eight octets when received, then an error is implied.

15.3. THE INITIALIZATION VECTOR

The size of this field is variable, even though it has a constant for all DES-CBC datagrams of the same SPI and IP Destination. Octets are transmitted in network order in which the most significant octet goes first.

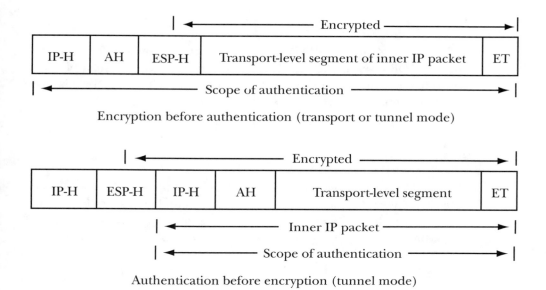

Figure 15.1. Encryption and
Authentication

IP-H = IP based header plus extensions headers
ESP-H = Encapsulating security payload header
ET = Encapsulating security payload trailing fields
AH = Authentication header

Figure 15.1. Encryption and
Authentication

The size needs to be a multiple of 32-bits. The size is most likely determined by the key management mechanism. Once the size is 32-bits, a 64-bit Initialization Vector is formed from the 32-bit value concatenated with the bit-wise complement of the 32-bit value. This is a common field size as it aligns the Payload Data for both 32-bit and 64-bit processing.

All conformant implementations need to also correctly process a 64-bit field size. This yields precise compatibility with existing hardware implementations. It is intended that the values not repeat during the lifetime of the encryption session key.

The Algorithm

When dealing with DES-CBC, the base DES encryption function operates on the XOR of each plaintext block with the previous ciphertext block to provide the ciphertext for the current block. This yields re-synchronization when datagrams are lost.

Used Ciphers

IPv6 and SSLv3 are cipher independent. This is advantageous because ciphers are changing and cipher attacks are more successful for small keylength, the protocol can be established to use another, more sophisticated encryption algorithm. However, both protocols have defined algorithms, including:

IPv6			SSL	
Authentication	**Hash size byte**			**Hash size byte**
Keyed MD5	16		MD 5	16
			SHA	20
Encryption	**Key Bits**		**Encryption**	**Key Bits**
DES CBC	56		Fortezza	96
			IDEA CBC	128
			RC2 CBC 40	40
			RC4 40	40
			RC4 128	128
			DES40 CBC	40
			DES CBC	56
			3DES EDE CBD	168

Figure 15.2. Encryption Standards

Decryption

The SPI field is first removed and inspected. This is utilized as an index into the local Security Parameter table to locate the negotiated parameters and decryption key. The negotiated model of the IV decides the size of the IV field. These octets are removed, and an appropriate 64-bit IV value is established.

The encrypted section of the payload is decrypted using DES in the CBC mode. The Payload Type is then removed and inspected. If it so happens that it is unrecognized, the payload is eliminated with a proper ICMP message.

The Pad Length is then removed and inspected. The designated numbers of pad octets are removed from the end of the decrypted payload, and the IP Total/Payload Length is adjusted correspondingly. The IP Headers as well as the remaining section of the decrypted payload are both sent to the protocol receive routine determined by the Payload Type field.

15.4. SECURITY

It is important for users to realize that the overall quality of the security described here totally relies on the strength of the DES algorithm, the accuracy of that algorithm's implementation. The security of the key management method, implementation, and strength of the key depend on the accuracy of the implementations throughout all of the participating nodes.

In addition, applications may choose to be cautious so that they do not select weak keys, even though the odds of choosing one at random are not significant. Both the cut and paste attack carries out the foundation behind the Cipher Block Chaining algorithms. Once a block is destroyed in transmission on decryption both it as well as the following block will be unintelligible by the decryption process. However, all subsequent blocks will be decrypted correctly. Once a hacker has legitimate access to the same key, this functionality can be utilized to insert or replay formerly encrypted data of other users of the same engine. This effectively divulges the plaintext. The standard ICMP, TCP, UDP transport checksum can observe this attack, however by itself it is not considered cryptographically strong. In this situation, user or connection oriented integrity checking is required.

At least one block of known plaintext is enough to recover a DES key. Due to the fact that IP datagrams usually begin with a block of known and/or guessable header text, frequent key changes will not guard against a hacker attack. Furthermore, DES is not recommended as a good encryption algorithm for the protection of even moderate value information. Triple DES is, however, a better choice for this type of purpose. Notwithstanding these potential risks, the level of privacy yielded by use of ESP DES-CBC in the Internet environment is far better than transmitting the datagram as cleartext.

Neighbor Discovery

Neighbor Discovery (ND) protocol for IPv6 is outlined in this section. Nodes that include both hosts and routers employ Neighbor Discovery to decide the link-layer addresses for neighbors that are known to exist on attached links. They can then instantly purge cached values which are invalid. Hosts also employ Neighbor Discovery to locate neighboring routers that wish to forward packets on their behalf. In addition, nodes employ the protocol to actively record which neighbors are reachable and which are not. Finally, they are used to detect changed link-layer addresses. Once a router or the path to a router fails, a host actively looks for functional options.

15.5. THE PROTOCOL

This protocol can assist in providing a solution for a set of problems associated with the interaction between nodes attached to the same link. It designates a method for solving Router Discovery that illustrated the method in which hosts find routers that live on an attached link.

The methods also include prefix discovery:

- Tells how hosts discover the set of address prefixes that designate which destinations are on-link for an attached link.
- Points out that nodes use prefixes to make a distinction as to destinations which exist on-link from those only reachable through a router.

Parameter Discovery:

- Determines how nodes acquire information about link parameters:
- The link MTU or particular Internet parameters (e.g., the hop limit value to place in outgoing packets).
- Address Autoconfiguration: how nodes automatically configure an address for an interface.
- Address resolution: explains how nodes distinguish the link-layer address of an on-link destination (e.g., neighbor given only the destination's IP address).
- Next-hop determination: this is the algorithm for mapping an IP destination address to the IP address of the neighbor where traffic is sent to its destination. The next-hop may be a router or the destination itself.
- Neighbor Unreachability Detection: explains the way in which nodes find out that a neighbor is no longer reachable. Neighbors used as routers: is where alternate default routers can be tried. Routers and hosts find that address resolution can be executed again.
- Duplicate Address Detection: explains how a node determines that an address it wants to use is not already in use by another node. Redirect: is the method in which a router informs a host of a better first-hop node that will arrive at a specific destination.

Neighbor Discovery designates five unique ICMP packet types:

- A pair of Router Solicitation
- Router Advertisement messages
- A pair of Neighbor Solicitation
- Neighbor Advertisements messages
- A Redirect message.

The messages are useful with regards to Router Solicitation. At the time when an interface is active, hosts can transmit Router Solicitations that request routers to create Router Advertisements instantly as opposed to their next scheduled time. A Router Advertisement occurs when Routers advertise their existence along with several link and Internet parameters. This can occur every so often or in response to a Router Solicitation message. Router Advertisements are composed of prefixes that are employed for on-link determination, address configuration, as well as values which include a recommended hop limit value.

Neighbor Solicitation is transmitted by a node to either decide the link-layer address of a neighbor or to verify that a neighbor is still reachable through a cached link-layer address. Neighbor Solicitations are also utilized for Duplicate Address Detection. However, while a Neighbor Advertisement is a reply to a Neighbor Solicitation message, a node can transmit unsolicited Neighbor Advertisements to declare a link-layer address change. A Redirect is then utilized by routers to notify hosts of a better first hop for a destination.

When dealing with multicast capable links, each router regularly multicasts a Router Advertisement packet communicating its availability. A host receives Router Advertisements from all routers, it then creates a list of default routers. Routers create Router Advertisements frequently enough so that hosts will be aware of their presence within a few minutes. However, this time interval is not frequently enough to depend upon an absence of advertisements to detect router failure. Yet, another Neighbor Unreachability Detection algorithm yields failure detection.

Router Advertisements are composed a list of prefixes used for on-link determination as well as autonomous address configuration. Flags are associated with the prefixes to determine the intended uses of a specific prefix. Hosts use the advertised on-link prefixes to create and sustain a list that is used in determining when a packet's destination is on-link or beyond a router. Remember that a destination can be on-link although it is not covered by any advertised on-link prefix. In this event, a router can transmit a Redirect informing the sender that the destination is a neighbor.

Router Advertisements permit routers to notify hosts how to perform Address Autoconfiguration. In addition, routers can designate whether hosts should use stateful (DHCPv6) as well as stateless (autonomous) address configuration.

Router Advertisement messages are composed of Internet parameters including the hop limit which hosts can employ in outgoing packets as well as link parameters including the link MTU. This promotes centralized administration of critical parameters which can be set on routers and automatically reproduce to all attached hosts.

Nodes are able to achieve address resolution by multicasting a Neighbor Solicitation that requests that the target node return its link-layer address. Neighbor Solicitation messages now are multicast to the solicited-node multicast address of the target address. The target sends back its link-layer address as a unicast Neighbor Advertisement message. An individual request-response pair of packets is enough for both the initiator and the target to determine each other's link-layer addresses. The initiator incorporatess its link-layer addresses in the Neighbor Solicitation.

Neighbor Solicitation messages can also be employed to find out if more than one node has been designated to the same unicast address. Neighbor Unreachability Detection find the failure of a neighbor, or the failure of the forward path to the neighbor. This action necessitates positive confirmation that packets transmitted to a neighbor are actually getting to that neighbor and being processed correctly by its IP layer. Neighbor Unreachability Detection employs confirmation from two sources. The upper-layer protocols yields a positive confirmation that a connection is producing forward progress which involves previously sent data that is known to have been delivered correctly. When positive confirmation is not expected through these actions, a node transmits unicast Neighbor Solicitation messages that solicit Neighbor Advertisements as reachability confirmation from the next hop. To decrease unnecessary network traffic, probe messages are only transmitted to neighbors to which the node is actively sending packets.

Neighbor Discovery is able to work with link-layer address change. This involves a node that understands its link-layer address has changed. It can then multicast a few unsolicited Neighbor Advertisement packets to all nodes to instantly update cached link-layer addresses which have become invalid.

Remember, that transmitting unsolicited advertisements is just a performance enhancement. The Neighbor Unreachability Detection algorithm makes certain that all nodes will reliably discover the new address, though the delay may be somewhat longer.

Inbound load balancing involves nodes which are replicated interfaces, and may want to load balance the reception of incoming packets via multiple network interfaces on the same link. These types of nodes have several link-layer addresses assigned to the same interface. One single network driver may represent multiple network interface cards as a single logical interface having multiple link-layer addresses. Load balancing is achieved by permitting routers to eliminate the source link-layer address from Router Advertisement packets. This effectively forces neighbors to utilize Neighbor Solicitation messages to obtain information on link-layer addresses of routers. Returned Neighbor Advertisement messages may have link-layer addresses that differ with regards to who issued the solicitation.

Anycast addresses designate one of a set of nodes which yield an equivalent service, and several nodes on the same link may be configured to distinguish the same Anycast address. Neighbor Discovery handles anycasts by having nodes expect to receive several Neighbor Advertisements for the same target. All advertisements for anycast addresses are tagged as being non-override advertisements. This invokes particular rules to conclude which of probably several advertisements needs to be used.

Proxy advertisements originate from a router that wants to accept packets for a target address that is incapable of answering Neighbor Solicitations. At this point, a router can send a non-Override Neighbor Advertisement. At the present time there aren't any uses of proxy. However proxy advertising may possible be employed to take care of cases such as mobile nodes which have moved off-link. It is not meant as a general method to handle nodes that don't implement this protocol.

15.6. IPV4 CONTRAST

The IPv6 Neighbor Discovery protocol is analogous to a group of IPv4 protocols ARP, ICMP Router Discovery, and ICMP Redirect in ICMPv4. In IPv4 there is no standard protocol or mechanism for Neighbor Unreachability Detection. Even though Hosts Requirements do not designate some possible algorithms for Dead Gateway Detection, as it is a subset of the problems Neighbor Unreachability Detection tackles.

The Neighbor Discovery protocol yields several improvements over the IPv4 set of protocols such as the fact that Router Discovery is a section of the base protocol set and it isn't necessary to snoop the routing protocols. There are also Router advertisements which convey link-layer addresses so that there is no additional packet exchange required to resolve the router's link-layer address.

Router advertisements convey prefixes for a link, but there is no requirement to have a separate method to configure the netmask. Router advertisements allow for Address Autoconfiguration, while Routers can advertise an MTU for hosts to employ on the link. This makes certain that all nodes employ the same MTU value on links lacking a well-defined MTU.

Address resolution multicasts cover over 4 billion multicast addresses. This effectively decreases address resolution affiliated interrupts on nodes besides that of the target. In addition, non-IPv6 machines need not be interrupted at all. Redirects possess the link-layer address of the new first hop, while individual address resolution is not required upon reception of a redirect.

Several prefixes may be affiliated with the same link. The default is that hosts learn all on-link prefixes from Router Advertisements. Yet, routers can be configured to eliminate some or all prefixes from Router Advertisements. In this event hosts assume that destinations are off-link and send traffic to routers. A router can then send redirects as needed.

As opposed to IPv4, the recipient of an IPv6 redirect believes that the new next-hop is on-link. In IPv4, a host ignores redirects designating a next-hop which is not on-link with regards to the link's network mask. The IPv6 redirect method is the same as the XRedirect (extended ICMP Redirect message) facility. It is believed to be advantageous on non-broadcast and shared media links in which it is unattractive or impossible for nodes to know all prefixes for on-link destinations.

Neighbor Unreachability Detection is a component of the base that considerably improves the strength of packet delivery in the presence of:

- Failing routers
- Partially failing or partitioned links and nodes
- Partitioned links and nodes that change its link-layer addresses.

All of these change their link-layer addresses. Mobile nodes can move off-link without sacrificing any connectivity due to stale ARP caches. However, as opposed to ARP, Neighbor Discovery observes half-link failures that employ Neighbor Unreachability Detection and avoids transmitting traffic to neighbors where two-way connectivity is not present.

As opposed to IPv4 Router Discovery, the Router Advertisement messages are not composed of a preference field. The preference field is not required to handle routers of different stability as the Neighbor Unreachability Detection will detect dead routers and switch to a working one.

Employing link-local addresses to solely identify routers for Router Advertisement and Redirect messages makes it possible for hosts to sustain the router associations in the event of the site renumbering to utilize new global prefixes. Employing the Hop Limit equal to 255 trick Neighbor Discovery is not susceptible to off-link senders that transmit ND (Neighbor Discovery) messages. When dealing with IPv4 off-link senders can send both ICMP Redirects and Router Advertisement messages.

Links

Neighbor Discovery helps links with various properties. These links include:

- Point-to-Point: This involves Neighbor Discovery handles including links that are similar to multicast links.
- Variable MTU: This is where Neighbor Discovery permits routers to designate a MTU for the link, this is what all nodes utilize. All nodes on a link need to use the same MTU (Maximum Receive Unit) to allow multicast to work correctly. If this does not happen when multicasting a sender (unaware which nodes will receive the packet) it will not determine a minimum packet size that all receivers can process.
- Asymmetric reachability: This is where Neighbor Discovery realizes the absence of symmetric reachability (where a node avoids paths to a neighbor that it does not have symmetric connectivity).
- Neighbor Unreachability Detection: This will usually classify half-links and the node will stop using them.

The Host Model

It is as this point that we look at a theoretical model of one possible data structure organization that hosts and some extent routers will sustain in interacting with neighboring nodes. This model primarily deals with the manner of host behavior directly related to Neighbor Discovery. Specifically, it does not concern itself with such issues as source address selection or choosing an outgoing interface on a multihomed host.

15.7. DATA STRUCTURES

Hosts need to have the ability to sustain sections of information for each interface involving the Neighbor Cache. It is a listing of entries regarding individual neighbors where traffic has been sent recently. Entries are entered on the neighbor's on-link unicast IP address and are composed of such information including its link-layer address, a flag which indicates if the neighbor is a router or a host, and a pointer to any queued packets waiting for address resolution to complete.

A Neighbor Cache entry is composed of information utilized by the Neighbor Unreachability Detection algorithm. This includes the reachability state, the number of unanswered probes, as well as the time the next Neighbor Unreachability Detection event is scheduled to occur.

The Destination Cache is a group of entries regarding destinations to which traffic has been sent recently. The Destination Cache incorporates both on-link and off-link destinations and yields a level of indirection into the Neighbor Cache. The Destination Cache maps a destination IP address to the IP address of the next-hop neighbor. This cache is updated with data acquired from Redirect messages. Implementations may find it advantageous to record additional information that is not directly related to Neighbor Discovery in Destination Cache entries including the Path MTU (PMTU) and round trip timers sustained by transport protocols.

The Prefix List is a list of the prefixes that designate a set of addresses that are on-link. Prefix List entries are established from information received in Router Advertisements. Each entry has an equivalent invalidation timer value that is extracted from the advertisement and used to expire prefixes when they become invalid. There is also a special infinity timer value which designates that a prefix remains valid forever, unless another finite value is received in a future advertisement.

The link-local prefix is thought to be on the prefix list with an infinite invalidation timer despite routers that are advertising a prefix for it. Received Router Advertisements SHOULD NOT modify the invalidation timer for the link-local prefix.

The Default Router List is a list of routers to where packets may be transmitted. Router list entries indicate entries in the Neighbor Cache, while the algorithm for choosing a default router accommodate routers which are known to be reachable over those whose reachability is questionable. In addition, each entry also has an affiliated invalidation timer value that is extracted from Router Advertisements employed to delete entries that are no longer advertised.

These types of data structures may be implemented through several methods. One implementation uses an individual longest match routing table for all of the above data structures. Despite the specific implementation, it is crucial that the Neighbor Cache entry for a router is shared by all Destination Cache entries using that router so as to avert redundant Neighbor Unreachability Detection probes.

Also, other protocols such as IPv6 Mobility can possibly increase additional data structures. An implementation is free to implement such data structures in any way it wants. An implementation may merge all conceptual data structures into one routing table.

The Neighbor Cache is composed of information sustained by the Neighbor Unreachability Detection algorithm. An integral component of information is a neighbor's reachability state.

15.8. SENDING ALGORITHMS

When a packet is sent to a destination, a node employs a combination of the Destination Cache, the Prefix List, as well as the Default Router List to decide the IP address of the proper next hop. This procedure is known as a next-hop determination. Once of the IP address of the next hop is known, the Neighbor Cache is queried for link-layer data regarding that neighbor.

Next-hop determination for a specified unicast destination works such that the sender executes a longest prefix match against the Prefix List to decide whether the packet's destination is on-link or off-link. When the destination is on-link, the next-hop address is the same as the packet's destination address. In any other event, the sender chooses a router from the Default Router List. When the Default Router List is empty, the sender believes that the destination is on-link.

In terms of efficiency, next-hop determination is not executed on every packet that is transmitted. However, the results of next-hop determination computations are recorded in the Destination Cache that also has updates obtained from Redirect messages. Once the sending node has a packet to send, it inspects the Destination Cache. When no entries are present for the destination, next-hop determination is summoned to establish a Destination Cache entry.

When the IP address of the next-hop node is known, the sender inspects the Neighbor Cache for link-layer information regarding that neighbor. When no entry is present, the sender establishes one, sets its state to incomplete, starts Address Resolution, and finally queues the data packet waiting for address resolution to be completed.

In terms of multicast capable interfaces Address Resolution, it is composed of sending a Neighbor Solicitation message and waiting for a Neighbor Advertisement. Once a Neighbor Advertisement reply is received, the link-layer addresses is entered in the Neighbor Cache entry and the queued packet is sent. When dealing with multicast packets, the next-hop is always the multicast destination address and is believed to be on-link.

When a Neighbor Cache entry is accessed while sending a unicast packet, the sender checks Neighbor Unreachability Detection related information with respect to the Neighbor Unreachability Detection algorithm. This unreachability check may result in the sender transmitting a unicast Neighbor Solicitation to determine that the neighbor is currently reachable.

The Next-hop determination is completed the first time traffic is transmitted to a destination. When subsequent communication to that destination executes correctly, the Destination Cache entry is still used. Should the communication not work as designated by the Neighbor Unreachability Detection algorithm, the next-hop determination must be performed again.

When a node starts over next-hop determination there aren't any requirements to eliminate the complete Destination Cache entry. It is sometimes advantageous to retain such cached information including the PMTU and round trip timer values that may also be kept in the Destination Cache entry. Routers and multi-homed hosts have several interfaces, as these will then handle multiple entries.

Stale and Unused Information

The data structures employ different means for eliminating possible stale or unused information. There is no requirement to regularly purge Destination and Neighbor Cache entries. Even though stale information can possibly remain in the cache indefinitely, the Neighbor Unreachability Detection algorithm makes certain that stale information is purged instantly if it isn't actually being used.

To restrict the storage required for the Destination and Neighbor Caches, a node may be required to *garbage-collect* old entries. It is important to remember that care must be taken to make certain that enough space is available to hold the working set of active entries. A small cache may result in there being a large number of Neighbor Discovery messages if entries are thrown away and created in quick succession. Any LRU-based policy that only reclaims entries that have not been used in some time is sufficient for garbage collecting unused entries.

A node needs to be able to keep entries in the Default Router List and the Prefix List until their lifetimes expire. However, a node may collect entries too soon if it is low on memory. While some routers may be omitted from the Default Router list, a node needs to retain at least two entries in this list so you can sustain robust connectivity for off-link destinations.

When removing an entry from the Prefix List there is no requirement to purge any entries from the Destination or Neighbor Caches. Neighbor Unreachability Detection will effectively purge any entries in these caches that have become invalid. When taking out an entry from the Default Router List, however, any entries in the Destination Cache that go through that router must perform next-hop determination again to choose a new default router.

15.9. CONCLUSION

In this chapter we have covered two very important issues relating to IPV6. The first involved ESP DES-CBC Transform, while the second involved Neighbor Discovery for IPv6.

The former dealt with secret keys, initialization vectors, algorithms, decryption, and security. While the latter dealt with router advertisements, the contrast between IPv6 and IPv4, unreachability detection, employing link-local addresses, the host, data structures, and the router and the prefix. All in all, we get a better idea of the behavior in which transmission occurs within the IPv6 model.

Internet Protocol Configuration

16

16.1. INTRODUCTION

This chapter deals with the method taken by a host takes in determining how to autoconfigure its interfaces in IPv6. The autoconfiguration operation incorporates creating a link-local address and verifying its individuality on a link, and determining what data needs to be autoconfigured such as the addresses and other information. It is important to note the process involved in creating a link-local address, the procedure for creating site-local and global addresses through stateless address autoconfiguration, and the Duplicate Address Detection operation.

16.2. IPV6 STATELESS ADDRESS AUTOCONFIGURATION

When dealing with addresses, it is also important to determine whether they need to be acquired through the stateless mechanism and/or the stateful mechanism. IPv6 looks at both stateless and stateful address autoconfiguration methods. Stateless autoconfiguration needs no manual configuration of hosts, has minimal configuration of routers, and has no additional servers. The stateless mechanism permits a host to create its own addresses through a combination of locally available information and information advertised by routers. Routers advertise prefixes which determine the subnets affiliated with a link. This occurs while hosts create an interface token that individually identifies an interface on a subnet. Linking them both creates an address. When there aren't any routers, a host can only create link-local addresses. Nonetheless, link-local addresses are adequate for permitting communication among nodes attached to the same link.

When dealing with a stateful autoconfiguration model, hosts acquire interface addresses as well as configuration information and parameters from a server. Servers keep a database which records which addresses have been designated to which hosts. The stateful autoconfiguration protocol permits hosts to acquire addresses, other configuration data, or both of them from a server. Stateless and stateful autoconfiguration can work together. For example, a host may employ stateless autoconfiguration to configure its own addresses, and then use stateful autoconfiguration to acquire other information.

The stateless approach is employed when a site is not especially concerned with the specific addresses hosts use. It only matters that they are unique and correctly routable. The stateful method is employed when a site needs better control over exact address assignments. The site administrator determines the specific type of autoconfiguration that needs to be used through establishing specified fields in Router Advertisement messages.

IPv6 addresses are utilized in an interface for a fixed amount of time. Each address has an affiliated lifetime which indicates how long an address is constrained to an interface. Once a lifetime expires, the binding and address become invalid and the address may be reassigned to another interface somewhere else in the Internet. To effectively deal with the expiration of address bindings easily, an address goes through two specific operations while assigned to an interface.

At first, an address is preferred, this indicates that its use in arbitrary communication is not restricted. At a future time, an address is deprecated in expectation that its current interface binding will become invalid. When it is in a deprecated state, the utilization of an address is depressed, however it is not totally prohibited. When dealing with a new communication such as a new TCP connection it is important to use a preferred address whenever possible. A deprecated address can only be used by applications that have been using it and would have problems switching to another address without a service disruption.

To make certain that all configured addresses are inclined to be unique on a specified link, nodes run a duplicate address detection algorithm on addresses prior to assigning them to an interface. The Duplicate Address Detection algorithm is executed on all addresses, regardless of whether they are acquired through stateless or stateful autoconfiguration.

The autoconfiguration process designated here is pertinent only to hosts and not routers. Due to the fact that host autoconfiguration employs information advertised by routers, routers must be configured by another method. Furthermore, routers are anticipated to successfully pass the Duplicate Address Detection operation on all addresses before assigning them to an interface.

The Router and the Prefix

We now look at the router and host behavior related to the Router Discovery portion of Neighbor Discovery. Router Discovery is used to locate neighboring routers as well as acquire prefixes and configuration parameters related to address autoconfiguration.

Prefix Discovery is the procedure through which hosts acquire the ranges of IP addresses that exist on-link and can be reached directly without the need of a router. Routers send Router Advertisements to determine whether the sender wishes to be a default router. Router Advertisements also are composed of Prefix Information options that list the set of prefixes that identify on-link IP addresses.

Stateless Address Autoconfiguration also needs to acquire subnet prefixes as part of configuring addresses. Even though the prefixes used for address autoconfiguration are logically different from those used for on-link determination, autoconfiguration information is piggybacked on Router Discovery messages to decrease network traffic. The same pre-fixes can be advertised for on-link determination and address autoconfiguration by designating the appropriate flags in the Prefix Information options.

16.3. PROTOCOL BASICS

It is important to look at the representative steps which occur when an interface autoconfigures itself. Autoconfiguration is executed only on multicast capable links and starts when a multicast capable interface is allowed, such as during system startup. Nodes in hosts and routers start the autoconfiguration operation by creating a link-local address for the interface. Appending the interface's token to the well- known link-local prefix creates a link-local address. An interface token solely designates an interface on a subnet.

A node must try to verify that its tentative address is not already in use by another node on the link, before the link-local address can be assigned to an interface and used. Specifically, it transmits a Neighbor Solicitation message that has the tentative address as the target. When another node is currently using that address, it returns a Neighbor Advertisement indicating this. When another node is also trying to use the same address, it transmits a Neighbor Solicitation for the target too. The specific amount of times the Neighbor Solicitation is retransmitted as well as the delay time between consecutive solicitations is link-specific and may be set by system management.

When a node concludes that its tentative link-local address is not unique, autoconfiguration ceases and manual configuration of the interface is needed. To make this recovery easier, it may be possible for an administrator to furnish an alternate interface token which overrides the default token so that the autoconfiguration mechanism is applied through the unique interface token. Optionally, link-local as well as other addresses must be configured manually.

The next step of autoconfiguration involves acquiring a Router Advertisement or deciding that no routers are available. When routers are present, they transmit Router Advertisements that determine what kind of autoconfiguration a host needs to perform. If no routers are available, stateful autoconfiguration must be enabled.

When a node determines that its tentative link-local address is unique, it assigns it to the interface. Now, the node has IP-level connectivity with neighboring nodes. The left-over autoconfiguration steps are executed only by hosts.

Routers transmit Router Advertisements every so often, however the delay between consecutive advertisements will most likely be longer than a host is able to wait for executing autoconfiguration. To acquire an advertisement rapidly, a host transmits at least one router solicitation to the all-routers multicast group. Router Advertisements possess two flags that determine what type of stateful autoconfiguration needs to be executed. A managed address configuration flag indicates whether hosts should use stateful autoconfiguration to acquire addresses. Another stateful configuration flag determines whether hosts can employ stateful autoconfiguration to acquire additional information.

To be safe, all addresses need to be tested as being unique before they can be assigned to an interface. In the event that addresses are created through stateless autoconfig, the unique ability of an address is decided mostly by the section of the address created from an interface token. Therefore, if a node has already verified the link-local address as being unique, then additional addresses set from the same interface token are not required to be tested separately. However, all addresses obtained manually or through stateful address autoconfiguration need to be tested for uniqueness separately. To serve sites which expect the overhead of executing Duplicate Address Detection to be determined, then the utilization of Duplicate Address Detection can be disabled via the administrative setting of a per-interface configuration flag.

To speed the autoconfiguration process, a host may create its link-local address in addition to verifying its uniqueness as it waits for a Router Advertisement. Due to the fact that a router may delay replying to a Router Solicitation for a brief time, the total time required to complete autoconfiguration can be considerably longer if the two steps are done consecutively.

Link-Local Addresses

Autoconfiguration is executed on a per-interface basis on multicast-capable interfaces. When dealing with multi-homed hosts, autoconfiguration is executed individually on each interface. Autoconfiguration operates to a large degree on hosts. However, the exception to this rule is that routers are believed to create a link-local address employing the procedure. Besides that, routers execute Duplicate Address Detection on all addresses before assigning them to an interface.

When creating a link-local address it is important to note that a node creates a link-local address whenever an interface is enabled. An interface may be enabled subsequent to it being initialized at system startup time. For example, the interface may be reinitialized succeeding a temporary interface failure or after it is temporarily disabled by system management. Alternatively the interface may attach itself to a link for the first time, or the interface may be enabled by system management after having been administratively disabled.

Neighbor Solicitation Messages

Upon receipt of a valid Neighbor Solicitation message on an interface, the node action depends on whether the target address is tentative. The target address is not tentative in a case where it is assigned to the receiving interface. When the target address is tentative (while the source address is a unicast address) the solicitation's sender is executing address resolution on the target and will be silently ignored. In all cases, a node can not reply to a Neighbor Solicitation for a tentative address.

When dealing with an unspecified source address of the Neighbor Solicitation, the solicitation is from a node executing Duplicate Address Detection. When the solicitation is from another node, the tentative address is a duplicate and can not be used by either node. When the solicitation is from the node itself, this is because the node loops back multicast packets. The solicitation is not able to determine the presence of a duplicate address.

Testing

It is important to schedule testing so that you can designate conditions under which a tentative address is not unique:

- Should a Neighbor Solicitation (for a tentative address) be received before having sent one, the tentative address is a duplicate. This condition happens when two nodes run Duplicate Address Detection at the same time, but send initial solicitations at different times. This is best illustrated by choosing different random delay values prior to sending an initial solicitation.
- When the actual number of Neighbor Solicitations received is greater than the number predicted based on the loopback semantics (such as when the interface does not loopback packet) but where at

least one solicitation was received, the tentative address is a duplicate. This condition happens when two nodes run Duplicate Address Detection at the same time and send solicitations at approximately the same time.

Global and Site-Local Addresses

Global and site-local addresses are created by adding an interface token to a prefix of proper length. Prefixes are acquired from Prefix Information options that are held in Router Advertisements. The establishment of global and site-local addresses as well as configuration of other parameters indicated here needs to be locally configurable.

Router Advertisements

Router Advertisements are transmitted every so often to the all-nodes multicast address. In order to acquire an advertisement quickly, a host transmits Router Solicitations.

When a link has no routers, a host needs to try to use stateful autoconfiguration to acquire addresses as well as other configuration information. An implementation can yield a method of crippling the request of stateful autoconfiguration. However, the default needs to be enabled. When dealing with autoconfiguration, a link has no routers if no Router Advertisements are received after transmitting a small amount of Router Solicitations.

Configuration Uniformity

Hosts can acquire address information employing both stateless and stateful protocols due to the fact that both may be enabled simultaneously. In addition, values of other configuration parameters (e.g., MTU size and hop limit) will be obtained from both Router Advertisements as well as the stateful autoconfiguration protocol. When the same configuration information is given by several sources, the value of this information needs to be uniform, yet it is not believed to be a fatal error when data is received from several sources that are different. Hosts accept the union of all information received through the stateless and stateful protocols. When inconsistent information is obtained from different sources, the most recently obtained values always have priority over information acquired before.

Security

Stateless address autoconfiguration permits a host to connect to a network, configure an address, and start talking with other nodes without ever registering or authenticating itself with the local site. Even though this permits unauthorized users to connect to and use a network, the threat is within the Internet. Any node with a physical attachment to a network can create an address through various methods that yield connectivity.

The utilization of Duplicate Address Detection leads to the possibility of denial of service attacks. Any node can reply to Neighbor Solicitations for a tentative address, this makes the other node reject the address as a duplicate. This attack is analogous to other attacks that deal with spoofing of Neighbor Discovery messages as they can be addressed by forcing Neighbor Discovery packets be authenticated.

Looping Back to the Sender

Trying to find out if a received multicast solicitation was looped back to the sender or came from another node is dependent upon the implementation. One difficult case arises when two interfaces connected to the same link have the same token and link-layer address. In addition, they both send out packets with the same contents at approximately the same time. This is best illustrated by Neighbor Solicitations for a tentative address as a component of Duplicate Address Detection messages. Even though a receiver will accept both packets, it is not able to determine which packet was looped back and which packet came from the other node just by comparing packet contents where both contents are the same. In this specific case, it is not required to know exactly which packet was looped back and which was sent by another node. When one receives more solicitations than were sent, the tentative address is a duplicate, yet the circumstances may not always be this direct.

16.4. DYNAMIC HOST CONFIGURATION PROTOCOL FOR IPV6

The Dynamic Host Configuration Protocol (DHCPv6) gives configuration parameters to Internet nodes. DHCPv6 is composed of a protocol for delivering node specific configuration parameters from a DHCPv6 server to a client as well as a means for designating network addresses as well as other related parameters to IPv6 nodes. DHCPv6 is created on a client-server model, where specified DHCPv6 servers designate network addresses and automatically deliver configuration parameters to dynamically configurable clients.

DHCPv6 uses both Request and Reply messages to handle a client/server processing model in which both the client and server make certain that the requested configuration parameters have been received and accepted by the client. DHCPv6 also handles optional configuration parameters and processing for nodes via extensions. The IPv6 Addressing Architecture as well as the IPv6 Stateless Address Autoconfiguration yield new features which are not available in IPv4, but are used to clarify the DHCPv6 client procedures.

DHCPv6 Design

Whenever you are responsible for the implementation of the DHCPv6 protocol, it is important to look at the design model from a structural viewpoint. The first step is to look at the DHCPv6 Message Formats and Field Definitions where all fields in DHCPv6 messages need to be initialized to binary zeros by both the client and server unless otherwise specified.

A DHCPv6 Server on the same link as a client sends the DHCPv6 Advertise as a reply to a DHCPv6 Solicit message transmitted to the all DHCPv6 Agents multicast address, then the agent address will be the IP address of one of the server's interfaces. The "S" bit will be set, the agent address will be an address of the server, and there may be zero server addresses transmitted in the DHCPv6 Advertise message. It is an error for the server-count to be zero if the "S" bit has not been set.

When the DHCPv6 Server is transmitting the advertisement in response to a solicitation with the client's link-local address present, the server needs to copy the link-local address into the advertisement. The source IP address of the IP header of any DHCPv6 Advertise message needs to have enough range to be reachable by the DHCPv6 Client. Specifically, the source address of any DHCPv6 Advertise message is transmitted by a DHCPv6 relay which can not be a link-local address. In the event where there are no routers transmitting Router Advertisements, then a DHCPv6 Server needs to be configured on the same link as the prospective clients.

DHCPv6 Message Format

The method involved when a client transmits a DHCPv6 Request message can append extensions when requesting parameters from a DHCPv6 Server. When the client is not aware of a DHCPv6 server address, it needs to first acquire a server address by multicasting a DHCPv6 Solicit message. When the client does not have a valid IP address of sufficient range for the DHCPv6 server to communicate with the client, the client needs to use the unicast IP address of a local DHCPv6 relay as the destination IP address. In any other case, the client can eliminate the server address in the DHCPv6 Request message.

The DHCPv6 reply message format is when the server sends at least one DHCPv6 Reply message as a reply to every DHCPv6 Request received. When the request arrives with the "S" bit set, the client may not send the Request to the server at once, and may employ a neighboring relay agent. In this event, the server sends back the DHCPv6 Reply with the "L" bit set, and the DHCPv6 Reply is addressed to the agent address located in the DHCPv6 Request message. When the "L" bit is set, then the client's link-local address will also be available.

The release message format is when the DHCPv6 Release message is transmitted without the assistance of any DHCPv6 relay. When a client transmits a Release message, it is believed to have a valid IP address with enough range to permit access to the target server. Only the parameters that are designated in the extensions are released. The DHCPv6 server admits the Release message by transmitting a DHCPv6 Reply.

A DHCPv6 client needs to quietly eliminate any DHCPv6 Solicit, DHCPv6 Request, or DHCPv6 Release messages it receives. The DHCPv6 client can hold its configured parameters and resources across client system reboots as well as DHCPv6 client program restarts. Yet, in these situations a

DHCPv6 client needs to transmit a DHCPv6 Request message to verify that its configured parameters and resources are still valid. This Request message needs to have the "C" bit set in order to purify stale client binding information at the server that may no longer be in use by the client. In fact, stale information is that which the client does not incorporate in extensions to such request messages.

DHCPv6 Advertising Messages

When a DHCPv6 client receives a DHCPv6 Advertise message, it may send a DHCPv6 Request message to receive configuration information as well as resources from the DHCPv6 servers recorded in the advertisement. When the Advertising message has 0 server addresses and also doesn't have the "S" bit set, the client needs to quietly eliminate the message. When the server's address is illustrated as a multicast address, the advertisement also needs to be quietly eliminated.

When the "S" bit is set, a DHCPv6 server on the same link as the client sends the DHCPv6 Advertising message. In this event, the client is required use the agent address as the destination address for any subsequent DHCPv6 message transactions transmitted to that server. Advertisements may have extensions, this can permit the DHCPv6 client to choose the configuration which best meets its needs from several possible servers.

DHCPv6 Reply Messages

When a client receives a DHCPv6 Reply message, it is required to inspect whether the transaction ID in the Reply message is the same as the transaction ID of a pending DHCPv6 Request message. When no match is determined, the Reply message needs to be quietly eliminated. If the transaction ID is the same as that of a pending Request and the "L" bit is set — but the source address in the IP header is not the same as the pending agent address — the client needs to eliminate the message and log the event. In the same way, if the transaction ID is the same as that of a pending Request, the "L" bit is not set — but the source address in the IP header is not the same as the pending server address. Therefore, the client needs to eliminate the message and log the event too.

Should the Reply message be acceptable, the client operates each extension, it then extracts the pertinent configuration information and parameters for its network operation. The Error Code located in the Reply message is appropriate for all extensions located in the Reply. Should all expected extensions not be found in the same Reply message, then they are probably located in another Reply that may have a different Error Code, but has the same transaction ID. The DHCPv6 Client needs to continue processing DHCPv6 Reply messages until all requested extensions are tallied. Should some of the requested extensions not be tallied within DHCPv6 Reply messages transmitted by the server, the client needs to resend the complete DHCPv6 Request again along with all extensions as well as the same transaction ID.

A certain amount of configuration information taken from the extensions to the DHCPv6 Reply message needs to remain affiliated with the DHCPv6 server that sent the message. The specific extensions may need this extra part of association with the server, where these resource-server affiliations are used when transmitting DHCPv6 Release messages.

Transmitting DHCPv6 Release Messages

If a DHCPv6 client concludes that a portion of its network configuration parameters are no longer necessary, it needs to enable the DHCPv6 server to release allocated resources that are no longer being used. It accomplishes this task by transmitting a DHCPv6 Release message to the server. The client confers with its list of resource server affiliations in order to find out which server needs to receive the designated Release message. When a client wants to ask the server to release all information and resources pertinent to the client, the client designates no extensions. This action is more desirable than transmitting a DHCPv6 Request message with the "C" bit set and no extensions.

Server Considerations

A server sustains a group of client records referred to as bindings. Each binding is individually identified by the ordered pair of the link-local address and agent address, due to the fact that the link-local address is assured of being unique on the link designated by the agent address. An implementation needs to handle bindings which are composed of at least a client's link-local address, agent address, desired lifetime, and valid lifetime for each client address, and the transaction ID. A client binding may be used to record any other information, resources, and configuration data that will be affiliated with the client.

The DHCPv6 server needs to retain its client bindings across server reboots, as well as a DHCPv6 client that needs to be assigned with the same configuration parameters regardless of server system reboots and DHCPv6 server program restarts. A DHCPv6 server is also required to support fixed or permanent allocation of configuration parameters to designated clients.

Servers which exist on the same link as the client need to utilize the source address in the IP header from the client as the destination address in DHCPv6 response messages transmitted by the server to the client. In addition, a server needs to ignore any DHCPv6 Advertisements, DHCPv6 Replies, or DHCPv6 Reconfigure message it receives.

16.5. DHCPV6 MESSAGES

When a DHCPv6 Solicit message is received at the All DHCPv6 Servers multicast address, the DHCPv6 Server needs to check to make certain that the source address is not a link-local address. When the source address is a link-local address, the server is required to quietly eliminate the packet. Should any solicitation have the "L" bit set without the "A" bit also being set, then the server needs to eliminate the packet and log the error. When the UDP length is not the same as the length designated by the format of the DHCPv6 Solicit message, the server is required to drop the packet and log the error.

At the time of both receiving and verifying the accuracy of a DHCPv6 Solicit message, a server builds a DHCPv6 Advertisement message and sends it on the same link over which the solicitation was received from. The destination address of the advertisement needs to be the source address of the solicitation. The DHCPv6 server needs to use an IP address of the interface on which it had received the Solicit message as the source address field of the IP header of the message.

The DHCPv6 server can augment extensions to the Advertisement in an effort to yield the soliciting node with the best possible information with respect to the services and resources where the server may be able to make available.

In addition, the DHCPv6 server needs to make certain that the client's link-local address field of the Request message is composed of an address that could be a valid link-local address. When this is not the case, the message needs to be quietly eliminated. In any other case, it looks for the presence of the "S" bit. When this is set, the server needs to inspect that the server address to determine if it matches the destination IP address where the Request message was received by the server. Should the server address not match, the Request message needs to be quietly eliminated. When the received agent address and link-local address do not match any binding recognized by the server, then the server can establish a new binding for the formerly unknown client.

DHCPv6 Message Processing

Should a DHCPv6 server be required to change the configuration affiliated with any of its clients, it creates a DHCPv6 Reconfigure message and transmits it to each client. The reconfiguration can be transmitted to a multicast address selected by the server and transmitted to each of its clients concurrently.

In terms of request message processing, when a relay receives a DHCPv6 Request message, it needs to determine that the message is received from a link-local address. The link-local address must match the link-local address field in the Request message header, and the agent address field of the message must match an IP address affiliated with the interface where the DHCPv6 Request message was received. In the event that any of these checks fail, the relay needs to quietly eliminate the Request message.

The relay is required to determine whether the "S" bit is set in the message header. If it is not, the datagram is eliminated, and the relay is required to return a DHCPv6 Reply message to the source address of the Request message.

Should the received request message be acceptable, the relay then sends the DHCPv6 Request message to the DHCPv6 server located in the Server Address field of the received DHCPv6 Request message. All of the fields of DHCPv6 Request message header sent by the relay are duplicated over without changes from the DHCPv6 Request received from the client. Only the fields in the IP header will be different from the datagram received from the client, instead of the payload.

DHCPv6 Security

DHCPv6 clients and servers usually have to authenticate the messages they exchange. This is best illustrated when a DHCPv6 server verifies that a DHCPv6 Request initiated from the client is determined both by the link-local address and agent address fields within a Request message header. On the contrary, it is usually fundamental for a DHCPv6 client to make certain that the configuration parameters and addresses it has received were transmitted by an authoritative DHCPv6 server. In the same way, a DHCPv6 server needs only accept a DHCPv6 Release message that is most likely from one of its clients.

The IPv6 Authentication Header can yield security for DHCPv6 messages when both endpoints have a proper IP address. However, a client usually has only a link-local address, and this type of an address is not enough for a DHCPv6 server that is off-link. When the DHCPv6 relay is involved, the DHCPv6 message must have the relay's address within the IP destination address field even if the client's objective is to deliver the message to the DHCPv6 server.

16.6. DHCPV4 AND DHCPV6 COMPARISON

The difference between these two protocols is that IPv6 has built-in support for a new model and structure for communications and autoconfiguration of addresses. DHCPv6 has a design that is able to take advantage of the intrinsic benefits of Ipv6. Furthermore, enhanced functionality has been added specifically to support the growth and the presence of mature Internet users in the industry.

In terms of IPv6 structural changes, the link-local address permits a node to have an address immediately when the node boots. This indicates that all clients have a source IP address at all times to find a server or relay agent on the local link. The requirement for bootup compatibility and broadcast flags is eliminated, which allows a great deal of freedom in specifying the new packet formats for the client and server interaction.

Multicast and the scoping methods with IPv6 allow the structure of discovery packets that would intrinsically designate their range by the multicast address for the function needed. Stateful autoconfiguration has to live and blend with stateless autoconfiguration which supports Duplicate Address Detection as well as the two IPv6 lifetimes, to facilitate the dynamic renumbering of addresses and the management of those addresses. Multiple addresses per interface are built-in IPv6. The majority of DHCPv4 options are not needed now due to the fact that the configuration parameters are either acquired through IPv6 Neighbor Discovery or the Service Location protocol.

DHCPv6 Architecture/Model Changes is indicated in the message type is the first byte in the packet. IPv6 Address allocations are now supported in a message extension in contrast to the main header. While Client/Server bindings are now required to take advantage of the client's link-local address to always allow communications either directly from an on-link server, or from a remote server through an on-link relay-agent. Servers are now discovered by a client solicitation and server or relay-agent advertisement model.

The client recognizes if the server is on-link or off-link. The client (after a solicitation) will be returned the addresses of available servers that are from an on-link server or from an on-link relay-agent as agents yielding the advertisements. The on-link relay-agent will acquire the location of remote server addresses from system configuration or by the utilization of a site wide DHCPv6 Multicast packet.

The server believes the client receives its responses unless it receives a retransmission of the same client request. This allows for recovery in the event where the network has faulted. DHCPINFORM is elemental in this new packet structure, therefore a client can request configuration parameters besides that of IPv6 addresses in the optional extension headers (IPv6 Next Headers are shown with variable lengths in Figure 16.1).

Octets

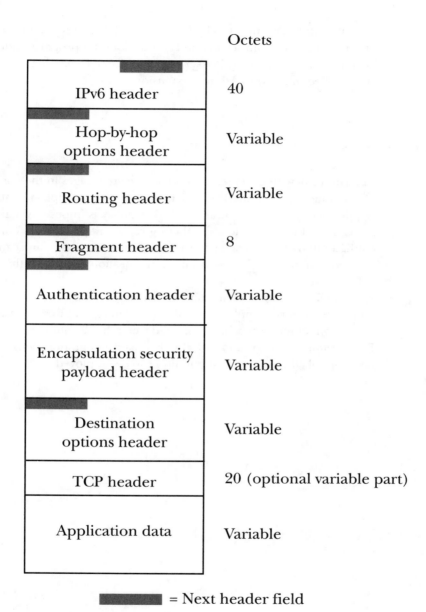

IPv6 header	40
Hop-by-hop options header	Variable
Routing header	Variable
Fragment header	8
Authentication header	Variable
Encapsulation security payload header	Variable
Destination options header	Variable
TCP header	20 (optional variable part)
Application data	Variable

= Next header field

Figure 16.1. IPv6 Next Headers

Clients are required to listen to their UDP port for the new Reconfigure message type from servers, unless they join the proper multicast group as determined by the DHCPv6 server. In addition, Dynamic Updates to DNS are handled in the IPv6 Address extension.

16.7. CONCLUSION

In terms of new Internet features, there are advantages in the configuration of Dynamic Updates to DNS which handle several implementation policy requirements. The configuration of what policy is imposed when addresses are censured for dynamic renumbering can be implemented. Furthermore, configuration of how relay-agents find remote servers for a link can be implemented. There has also been an Authentication extension that has been added.

A client in an implementation can request the configuration of extra addresses for server applications. While reclaiming addresses designate with very long lifetimes can be implemented using the Reconfigure message type. Furthermore, configuration of closely linked integration between stateless and stateful address autoconfiguration can be employed.

Interfaces and Extensions

17

17.1. INTRODUCTION

The goal is to provide specifications to execute changes to the sockets API to support IPv6. These changes are for TCP and UDP based applications. There is a large degree of portability regarding current applications using IPv4 raw sockets. However, this is primarily due to the fact that IPv4 implementations began from a common Berkeley source code that permits programs such as Ping and Traceroute to compile with little effort on many hosts that support the sockets API. In using IPv6, however, there is no common source code base that implementors can use. Therefore, the prospect for divergence at this level between different implementations is extensive. In order to avert a total lack of portability amongst applications that use raw IPv6 sockets, a degree standardization is required.

17.2. OVERALL STRUCTURE

Several advanced applications inspect fields in the IPv6 header and set and look at fields in the various ICMPv6 headers. Common structure definitions for these headers are necessary, together with common constant definitions for the structure participants. At the time when an *include file* is specified, that include file is permitted to incorporate other files that do the actual definition.

IPv6 raw sockets are utilized to bypass the transport layer — TCP or UDP. When using IPv4, raw sockets are employed to access ICMPv4, IGMPv4, as well as to read and write IPv4 datagrams which have a protocol field that the kernel does not process. This is best illustrated through a routing daemon for OSPF, due to the fact that it uses IPv4 protocol field 89. When employing IPv6 raw sockets, they will be used for ICMPv6 and to read and write IPv6 datagrams which have a next header field that the kernel does not process. This is illustrated by a routing daemon for the Inter-Domain Routing Protocol (IDRP).

All data transmitted through raw sockets needs to be in network byte order and all data received through raw sockets will be in network byte order. This is dissimilar from the IPv4 raw sockets, as they did not designate a byte ordering and typically used the host's byte order.

IPv4 raw sockets are different in that complete packets or IPv6 packets with extension headers cannot be transferred through the IPv6 raw sockets API. Instead, additional data objects are employed to transfer the extension headers. All of the fields within the IPv6 header that an application may wish to change can be altered by the application.

Checksums

The kernel will compute and insert the ICMPv6 checksum for ICMPv6 raw sockets. When dealing with other raw IPv6 sockets, the application needs to set the new IPV6_CHECKSUM socket option in to have the kernel calculate and record a checksum. This option stops applications from having to execute source address selection on the packets they transmit. The checksum will integrate the IPv6 fake-header. This new socket option also designates an integer offset into the user data of where the checksum is to be placed.

Type Filtering

ICMPv4 raw sockets acquire the majority of ICMPv4 messages received by the kernel. However, ICMPv6 is a set of ICMPv4, which includes functionality of both IGMPv4 and ARPv4. This indicates that an ICMPv6 raw socket can possibly receive many more messages than would be received with an ICMPv4 raw socket. This would include ICMP messages that are the same as ICMPv4, together with neighbor solicitations, neighbor advertisements, as well as membership messages.

The majority of applications that utilize an ICMPv6 raw socket only deal with a small subset of the ICMPv6 message types. To transfer nonessential ICMPv6 messages from the kernel to the user can involve an increased amount of overhead. Essentially, this API incorporates a method of filtering ICMPv6 messages by the ICMPv6 type field.

TCP and Ancillary Data

Transmission and reception of ancillary data is simple when employing UDP as the application calls sendmsg() and recvmsg() instead of sendto() and recvfrom(). However, there are certain events where a TCP application wishes to transmit or receive this optional information. This can best be illustrated through a TCP client which wishes to designate a source route. It is important to note that this is required to be completed before calling connect(). In the same way, a TCP server may wish to know the received interface after accept() returns together with any destination alternatives.

17.3. IDENTIFYING THE INTERFACE

Some applications must recognize the interface on which a packet was received. In addition, some applications are required to designate the interface on which a packet is to be sent. Thus a method is necessary to designate the interfaces on a system.

When an interface is recognized by the system, the kernel designates a unique positive integer value referred to as the *interface index* to that interface. These items are small positive integers that begin at 1. In addition, there may also be gaps so that there is no current interface for a specific interface index.

The method involved in obtaining that interface index is not a simple task. Due to the fact that the interface index is commonly used throughout this API, a new ioctl() command is designated to retrieve it called SIOCGIFINDEX. This command employs the standard ifreq structure. The ifreq structure is employed by many of the existing interface ioctls to designate or acquire information or attributes of an interface. When it is given an interface name it returns the interface index in the ifr_ifindex member of the ifreq structure. Remember, the ifreq structure is employed by several existing interface ioctls to determine or acquire information or attributes regarding an interface.

The Outgoing Interface

An application may be required to designate either or both of the outgoing interface, and the source address. The source address can also be determined by calling bind() prior to each output operation, but providing the source address together with the data consumes less overhead such as in system calls and needs less state to be recorded and protected in a multi-threaded application.

17.4. THE DESTINATION

There are a variable amount of destination options that can appear in at least one destination option header. A destination option header that emerges prior to a routing header is processed by the first destination in addition to any subsequent destinations designated in the routing header. However, a destination options header emerges after a routing header (shown in Figure 17.1) is processed only by the final destination. Each option in a destination options header is TLV-encoded with a type, length, and value very similarly to the hop-by-hop options.

To receive destination options, the application must turn on the IPV6_ RXDSTOPTS socket option. Every individual option is returned as an ancillary data object designated by a cmsghdr structure. The cmsg_level member will be IPPROTO_DSTOPTS, the cmsg_type member will be the option type, and the first byte of cmsg_data[] is the first byte of the option data.

However, to send at least one destination option, the application designates them as ancillary data in a call to sendmsg(). In addition, no socket option needs to be set.

Each option is designated as an ancillary data object by a cmsghdr structure. The cmsg_level member is fixed to IPPROTO_DSTOPTS, the

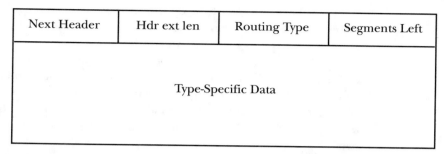

Next Header	Hdr ext len	Routing Type	Segments Left
Type-Specific Data			

Figure 17.1. Routing Header

cmsg_type member is fixed to the option type, while the first byte of cmsg_data[] is the first byte of the option data.

The Source Route

Source routing within IPv6 is achieved by designating a routing header as an extension header. It is possible that there are different types of routing headers. This type handles as many as 24 intermediate destinations, each of which is designated as a loose or a strict hop.

Source routing with the IPv4 sockets API must have the application to create the source route in the format which emerges as the IPv4 header option. This necessitates the possession of intrinsic knowledge regarding the IPv4 options format. This API designates seven functions that the application calls to create and inspect a routing header.

17.5. ANCILLARY DATA AND IPV6 EXTENSION HEADERS

There are three IPv6 extension headers that can be designated by the application and returned to the application via ancillary data. The commands include sendmsg() and recvmsg() with hop-by-hop options, destination options, and the routing header. When there are several ancillary data objects which transferred through the sendmsg() or recvmsg() where these objects are indicative of any of these three extension headers, their placement in the control buffer is directly linked to their location in the associated IPv6 datagram. This API forces some ordering constraints when using several ancillary objects with sendmsg().

When several hop-by-hop options have unique option types that are designated, these options may be resequenced by the kernel to decrease padding in the hop-by-hop options header. Hop-by-hop options may emerge anywhere in the control buffer and will always be collected by the kernel and put into a single hop-by-hop options header which appears just after the IPv6 header.

Analogous rules work on the destination options. This includes those of the same type that will appear in the same order as they are specified, while those with different types may be reordered. However, the kernel will set up two destination options headers. One of them goes before the routing header while one goes after the routing header. If the application designates a routing header, then all destination options that appear in the control buffer prior to the routing header will appear in a destination options header prior to the routing header. Then these options may be resequenced, subject to the two rules that we have just stated. In the same way, all destination options that appear in the control buffer after the routing header will emerge in a destination options header subsequent to the routing header, while these options may be re-sequenced.

Neighbor Reachability

When a standard method is designated for the UDP application to explain the kernel that it is making forward progress with a specified peer. This may effectively save unnecessary neighbor solicitations as well as neighbor advertisements.

17.6. THE FUTURE OF IPV6

The IETF began its attempt to choose an heir to IPv4 at a time when projections suggested that the Internet address space would be increasingly limited in its resources. In addition, there were several actions that began looking into ways resolve these address restrictions yielding increased functionality. The IETF created the IPng Area in late 1993 to look into ways in which to develop IPng technical methods.

Class	First Byte	Network Mask
A	1. — 127.	255.0.0.0
B	128. — 191.	255.255.0.0
C	192. — 223.	255.255.255.0

Figure 17.2. Internet Address Classes and Network Masks

All in all there were several movements which led to IPv6 being born. This protocol had a simplified header with a hierarchical address structure that allowed severe route aggregation that also made it big enough to meet the needs of the Internet in the long term. The protocol also incorporates packet-level authentication as well as encryption along with plug and play autoconfiguration. The structural alterations involved the way in which IP header options are encoded to expand the flexibility to interject new options in the future while increasing performance. It also incorporates the capability to classify traffic flows.

17.7. WHAT MAKES IPV6 A PROTOCOL?

IPv6 has the current address assignment policies that are adequate with no pressing need to recover underutilized designated network numbers. In addition, there is no current requirement to renumber large sections of the Internet. CIDR-style designations of sections of unassigned Class A address space needs to be taken into account. In addition, Simple Internet Protocol Plus (SIPP) specifications involving the 128 bit version is adopted as the foundation for Ipng.

17.8. REASONS TO ADOPT IPV6

Users have numerous reasons to switch to an IPv6 system:

1. Expanded multimedia support. Some users need this functionality.
2. Expanded Addressing. As address space runs out, it will become very important to have an IPv6-compliant system. This permits referencing of old IPv4 addresses as well as new IPv6 addresses.
3. Mandated IPv6 compliancy. Some forward-thinking organizations may require their systems to be IPv6-compliant.

Figure 17.3. Reasons to Adopt IPv6

There are recommendations regarding the use of non-IPv6 addresses in IPv6 environments as well as IPv6 addresses in non-IPv6 environments. It will be important for groups to work to a point where use of specific address environments is more clearly defined.

Looking into IPv4

When looking into the current 32 bit IPv4 address structure, over 4 billion hosts on as many as 16.7 million networks can be named. However, the actual address designation efficiency is much less. In fact, this type of inefficiency is worsened by the granularity of assignments that employ Class A, B and C addresses (shown in Figure 17.4).

The best fix involves the designation of several Class C addresses to substitute for Class B addresses involved its own problem by increasingly expanding the size of the routing tables in the backbone routers which are already growing at a phenomenal rate. There is problem in accepting either restricting the rate of growth and ultimate size of the Internet or disrupting the network by altering to new methods or technologies.

17.9. RUNNING ON EMPTY

It was important to look into creating a proper estimate of the time remaining prior to exhausting the IPv4 address space so as to determine the range of the IPng effort. If the time remaining was analogous to that needed to deploy a replacement, then we would have chosen the IPng which would only fix the address restrictions since we would not have had sufficient time to create any other features. If more time looked as though it were available, we could look into additional improvements.

The IETF created an Address Lifetime Expectations (ALE) Working Group to create an estimate for the remaining lifetime of the IPv4 address space founded on currently known and available technologies. The ALE Working Group looked into the current allocation statistics. They then concluded that the Internet would use up the IPv4 address space between 2005 and 2011. Some members of the IPv4 ALEs and large Internet mailing lists called into question the reliability of this projection.

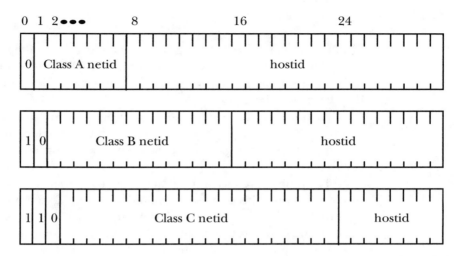

*Figure 17.4. Class A, B, and C
Addresses*

When people believe in this projection, they assume there are no standard shifts in IP usage. If someone were to create a new application, for example the ultimate rise in the demand for IP addresses could over-estimate the time available.

There may also be a difficulty with the data used to make the projection. The InterNIC designate IP addresses in large groups to regional Network Information Centers (NICs) as well as network providers. The NICs and the providers then re-allocate addresses to their customers. The ALE projections employed the InterNIC assignments without considering to the actual rate of assignment of addresses to the end users. They completed the projection this way since the accuracy of the data seemed higher. Using this once removed data may however increase a level of over-estimation since it presumes the rate of large block allocation will continue. These factors decrease the reliability of the ALE estimates but they point to the fact that there is enough time remaining in the IPv4 address space to add features in IPng besides increasing the address size with respect to the time needed for development, testing, and deployment.

17.10. ROUTING TABLES

Another issue in Internet scaling is the expanding size of the routing tables needed in the backbone routers. Adopting the CIDR block address designation and grouping routes decreased the size of the tables for a time, but they are now increasing.

Providers are not required to work harder to advertise their routes only in groups. Providers though, should suggest that their new customers should renumber their networks in the best interest of the complete Internet community.

The problem results in consuming all of the IPv4 address space and may be controversial if this problem is ignored and if routers are not able to keep up with the table size growth. Prior to implementing CIDR the backbone routing table was growing at a rate about 150% as fast as memory technology.

It is important to note that though IPng addresses are created with aggregation with regards to switching to IPng, this will not solve the routing table size problem unless the addresses are designated strictly to maximize the effect of such aggregation. This efficient advertising of routes can be sustained since IPng incorporates address autoconfiguration methods to permit easy renumbering if a customer chooses to switch providers. Customers who receive service from more than one provider may restrict the ultimate efficiency of any route aggregation.

Address Assignment

The IESG looked into proposing more strict assignment policies, regaining some addresses already designated, or making a significant effort to renumber important portions of the Internet. The IPng Area Directors approve the current address designation policies to look at the ALE projections. No one should involve particular efforts to recover underutilized addresses already designated or to renumber actively major portions of the Internet. Network service providers should assist new customers in renumbering their networks to conform to the provider's CIDR assignments.

The ALE Working Group looks into considering designating CIDR-type address blocks out of the unassigned Class A address space. The IPng Area Directors agree with this recommendation.

17.11. IPNG TECHNICAL ASPECTS

The IESG yielded an outline with regards to the type of criteria to designate the appropriateness of an IPng proposal. The IETF then looked into the appropriate methods with the Selection Criteria.

When looking into the specifications of IPv6, it is important to designate the proposed protocol. In terms of structural ease, the IP-layer protocol needs to be as simple as possible with functions which exist elsewhere that are more suitably performed at protocol layers other than the IP layer.

In terms of topological flexibility, the routing structure and protocols of IPng need to permit several different network topologies. They must not infer that the network's physical structure is a tree. In terms of performance, an effective router must be able to process and forward IPng traffic at speeds that are able to completely use high-speed media all the time. In terms of the robust service, the network service as well as its affiliated routing and control protocols need to be powerful.

The overall transition makes certain that the protocol must have a direct transition plan from IPv4. It must also have an independent aspect to media so that the protocol can work across an internetwork of several different LAN and WAN media. Each must have individual link speeds that vary from a ones of bits per second to hundreds of gigabits per second. The datagram service is where the protocol must support an unreliable datagram delivery service.

In terms of ease of configuration, the protocol must allow easy and adequately distributed configuration and operation. Automatic configuration of hosts and routers is needed. But the issue of security is always a focus in that the IPng needs to provide a secure network layer. This is further extended to having unique names; this is where the IPng must designate unique names to all IP-Layer objects within the global Internet. Also, these names may or may not have any location, topology, or routing importance. In addition, the ability to access standards is where the protocols that designate IPng as well as its associated protocols need to be as available and redistributable.

17.12. SERVICE AND SUPPORT

In terms of multicast support, IPv6 needs to support both unicast and multicast packet transmission. Dynamic and automatic routing of multicasts are also needed. With regards to extensibility, the protocol has to be extensible so that it is able to grow to meet the future service needs of the Internet. This growth must be acquired without needing network-wide software upgrades. In terms of the service classes, IPv6 needs to permit network devices to link packets with specific service classes and give them the services designated by those classes.

In terms of mobility, it is important to acquire support for mobile hosts, networks, and internetworks. With regards to the control protocol, there must be a fundamental level of support for testing and debugging networks. This support also extends to tunneling where IPng has to permit users to create private internetworks on top of the basic Internet infrastructure. Both private IP-based internetworks as well as private non-IP based internetworks need to be supported.

Adding a scope field to multicast addresses increases the scalability of multicast routing. However, there is a new kind of address designated as a cluster address. It is meant to designate topological regions as opposed to individual nodes. The utilization of cluster addresses in combination with the IPv6 source route capability permits nodes greater control over the path their traffic uses.

There is also an easier header format in which some IPv4 header fields have been eliminated or made optional to decrease the common case processing cost of packet handling. It also makes certain that the bandwidth overhead of the IPv6 header is as low as it can be despite the increased size of the addresses. Although the IPv6 addresses are four times greater than the IPv4 addresses, the IPv6 header is only double the size of the IPv4 header.

Several IPv6 options are placed in separate optional headers between the IPv6 header and the transport-layer header. Due to the fact that the majority of IPv6 option headers are not inspected or processed by any router along a packet's delivery path until it arrives at its final destination. In fact, an organization will see an advantage in their router performance. There is an increased improvement for IPv6 options of discretionary length (not restricted to 40 bytes). This functionality in addition to the method, in which they are processed, allows IPv6 options to be employed for functions that were not pragmatic in IPv4.

One of the main functions of IPv6 is the power to encode (within an option) the action in which a router or host can execute if the option is not know. This allows the successive deployment of additional features into an operational network with a little danger of disruption.

In addition, support for authentication and privacy is included in IPv6 that integrates the designation of an extension that yields support for authentication and data integrity. This extension is integrated as a fundamental aspect of IPv6 that involves support that is required in all implementations. IPv6 also incorporates the designation of an extension that can handle confidentiality through encryption. The level of support for this extension will be greater once present in all implementations.

Support for autoconfiguration within IPv6 and pertains to plug and play configuration of node addresses on an isolated network as well as the functionality offered by DHCP. In addition, there is support for source routes that includes an extended function source routing header which is meant to support the Source Demand Routing Protocol (SDRP). The goal of SDRP is to handle source-initiated selection of routes to supplement the route choice yielded by existing routing protocols for both inter-domain and intra-domain routes.

There is an easy and flexible transition from IPv4 that involves the IPv6 transition plan whose goal is to meet a select group of requirements such as:

- Incremental upgrade where existing installed IPv4 hosts and routers can be upgraded to IPv6 at any time without relying on any other hosts or routers which are being upgraded.
- Incremental deployment is a relatively new aspect for IPv6 hosts and routers that can be installed at any time without any prerequisites.
- Easy Addressing deals with the existing installed IPv4 hosts or routers as they are upgraded to IPv6, they may continue to utilize their existing address. However, they need not be assigned new addresses.
- Low start-up costs hardly involve any preparation work so as to either upgrade existing IPv4 systems to IPv6 or to deploy new IPv6 systems.

There is also quality of service capabilities, which is a relatively new capability that is designed to activate the labeling of packets which are property of specific traffic flows in which the transmitting host has asked for special handling. This may include non-default quality of service or real-time service.

Autoconfiguration of Addresses

As data networks grow to be more and more complex, the requirement allowing the bypass of some degree of complexity facilitates a movement towards plug and play. The user is no longer expected to be able to comprehend the mechanics of the network structure or to know how to configure the network software in their host. In fact, a user should be able to unpack a new computer, plug it into the local network and have it work without the requirement of entering any unique information.

Plug and play functionality is one requirement where the host needs to have the ability to obtain an address dynamically. This can accomplished either when attaching to a network for the first time or when the host must be readdressed due to the fact that the host moved or because the identity of the network has been replaced. When dealing with security aspects, it may prove limiting the ability to provide this level of transparent address autoconfiguration in some environments. However, the mechanics must be in available to support whatever level of automation in which the local environment is able to handle.

17.13. THE TRANSITION MECHANISM

The transition of the Internet from IPv4 to IPv6 has to meet two individual needs. There is a short-term requirement to designate particular technologies as well as methods to transition IPv4 networks. This includes the Internet and brings it into IPv6 networks and an IPv6 Internet. There is also a long-term requirement to execute broad-based operational planning for transition. This includes developing the means to:

- Allow decentralized migration schemes
- Accept the details of a long period of coexistence in which both protocols are a part of the basic infrastructure
- Create an understanding of the type of structural and interoperability testing which will be needed to make certain that a reliable and manageable Internet is possible in the long term.

Any IPng transition plan needs to involve the realities of the specific kinds of devices vendors will create and what network managers will deploy. The IPng transition plan needs to designate the procedures needed to correctly implement the functions which vendors will incorporate in their devices. When products do exist, it is far better to have them interoperate than not.

Objectives in Transition

It is important to designate the processes by which the Internet will make the transition from IPv4 to IPv6. To accomplish this fact, it is important to look into mechanisms that will be employed in the transition:

- How the transition will work
- Assumptions regarding infrastructure deployment elemental in the operation of these mechanisms
- Types of functionality which applications developers will be able to presume as the protocol mix alters over time.

The specifications that mandatory and optional mechanisms which vendors need to implement in hosts, routers, and other components of the Internet so that the transition can be carried out.

Defining the interaction between hosts that employ different combinations of these mechanisms.

People implementing these IPv6 systems will utilize the specifications detailed here. Network managers need to carefully look at their operational plan for the Internet so they can make the transition from IPv4 to IPv6 most effectively. The end result involves a transition plan for the Internet, which network operators and Internet subscribers can deploy.

Long-Term Transitional Effects

There are several transition related topics besides that which involves the definition of the particular IPv4 to IPv6 mechanisms as well as their deployment, operation, and interaction.

17.14. CONCLUSION

It is important to make the transition from a deployed protocol to a new protocol while obliging diversity and decentralized management. Due to the fact that it is often difficult to replace all legacy systems or software, it is important to understand the attributes and operation of a long aspect of coexistence between a new protocol and the existing protocol. The Internet is now believed to be a utility. There is significant structural and interoperability testing which needs to be a part of the pre-deployment aspect of your operation as well as any proposed software for the Internet. Testing the scaling up activities and power of a new protocol will usually provide specific hazards.

It is important to carefully look at the complete descriptions of problem areas that may occur in transition and coexistence. Network manager need to make significant recommendations with regards to testing procedures. In addition, it is important to look for coexistence operations procedures and working to simplify decentralized transition planning.

In terms of impacting standards, there are numerous IETF standards which are affected by IPv6. In some events, the operation of the protocol will be altered as a result of IPv6. One aspect is that which involves the security and source route mechanisms which are totally changed from IPv4 with IPv6. Both protocols and applications which had depended on the IPv4 functionality will have to be redesigned to have equivalent function in IPv6.

In terms of non-IETF standards, there are several products and user applications which depend on the size or structure of IPv4 addresses that will need to be modified to work with IPv6. While the IETF can simplify an investigation regarding the impact of IPv6 on non-IETF standards and products, the primary capability for this executes in the standards bodies and the vendors.

Some non-IETF standards which are effected by IPv6 include the POSIX standards, Open Software Foundation's DCE and DME, X-Open, Sun ONC, the Andrew File System, and MIT's Kerberos. The majority of products which yield specialized network security, including firewall types of devices which need to be extended to support IPv6.

The IETF does not work with APIs. This is primarily because there are too many environments in which:

- TCP/IP is used
- Too many operating systems
- Too many programming languages
- Too many platforms.

The security of the Internet has been a contentious point where there are many places where the level of possible security is far less than that judged necessary for the current and future uses of the Internet. In essence, there needs to be an overall improvement in the basic level of security in the Internet which is vital to its future success. Users need to be able to assume that their exchanges are safe from tampering, diversion, and exposure. Any company that wants to use the Internet to conduct business needs to be able to have a high level of confidence in the identity of their correspondents and in the security of their communications. The goal is then to yield strong protection as a matter of course throughout the Internet.

IPv6 Mobility

18

18.1. INTRODUCTION

CATNIP is an acronym for the Common Architecture for the Internet (CATNIP) which was set up as a convergence protocol. CATNIP incorporates CLNP, IP, and IPX. The CATNIP structure yields for any of the transport layer protocols in use such as TP4, CLTP, TCP, UDP, and SPX to operate over any of the network layer protocol formats such as:

- CLNP
- IPv4
- IPX
- CATNIP

When a high level of attention is given to details, it is possible for a transport layer protocol (e.g., TCP) to operate correctly with one end system employing one network layer such as IPv4 in addition to using another network protocol such as CLNP.

18.2. INTERNET ARCHITECTURE

The goal is to yield a common ground between the Internet, OSI, and Novell protocols. This also produces a fertile environment to advance the Internet technology to the point where performance of the next generation of internetwork technology grows exponentially.

CATNIP deals with OSI Network Service Access Point (NSAP) format addresses. A host and provider relationship is illustrated by Figure 18.1. Also, it uses a cache which has the ability to yield both quick identification of the next hop in high performance routing in addition to abbreviation of the network header by allowing the addresses to be eliminated when a valid cache handle is available. The fixed section of the network layer header then conveys the cache handles.

SIPP is an acronym for Simple Internet Protocol Plus which is a new version of IP that is designed to be indicative of expansion from IPv4. In fact, it is a progressive increase to IPv4, and it was not a structural design objective that takes such a fundamental step away from it. Features that operate in IPv4 remain in SIPP. However, functions that don't work were removed. It can be installed as a normal software upgrade in Internet devices and is interoperable with IPv4, and its deployment effort was intended to not have any flag days.

SIPP was created to operate well in terms of high performance networks such as ATM. In addition, it is still efficient for low bandwidth (e.g., wireless) networks. In addition, it yields a platform for new Internet features that will be needed in the near future.

SIPP expands the IP address size from 32 bits to 64 bits, in an effort to support more levels of addressing hierarchy as well as a much greater number of addressable nodes. SIPP addressing can be increased in units of 64 bits. This is achieved by a facility equivalent to IPv4's Loose Source and Record Route option. This happens in combination with a new address type referred to as cluster addresses which then identifies topological regions as opposed to individual nodes.

SIPP changes the method in which IP header options are encoded. This permits more efficient forwarding, less strict limits on the length of options, and increased flexibility for presenting new options in the longer term. A new capability is added to activate the labeling of packets that are property of specific traffic flows for which the sender asks for special handling, including non-default quality of service or real-time service.

TUBA is the acronym for TCP/UDP over CLNP Addressed Networks and is focused on decreasing the risk linked with migration to a new IP

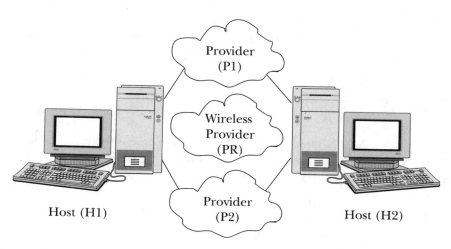

Figure 18.1. Host and Provider

address space. Furthermore, this proposal is encouraged by the need to permit the Internet to scale. The existing Internet transport and application protocols need to continue to operate unchanged. TUBA does not necessitate having to totally move over to OSI. It would indicate that only replacing IP with CLNP. TCP, UDP, and the standard TCP/IP applications would then run on top of CLNP.

TUBA effort increases the ability to route Internet packets via addresses that support more hierarchy as opposed to the current Internet Protocol (IP) address space. TUBA outlines the continued use of Internet transport protocols, specifically TCP and UDP. In addition, it also designates the encapsulation in CLNP packets. This effectively permits the continued use of Internet application protocols including FTP, SMTP, and TELNET. TUBA tries to upgrade the current system through a transition by using IPv4 to CLNP as well as the associated large Network Service Access Point (NSAP) address space.

TUBA utilizes a simple long-term migration proposal that is founded on a gradual update of Internet hosts in order to run Internet applications over CLNP, and DNS servers to return larger addresses. This proposal must have routers updated to handle the forwarding of CLNP besides that of IP. What is not required is encapsulation, translation of packets, or address mapping. IP addresses and NSAP addresses may be designated and used separately during migration, while routing and forwarding of IP and CLNP packets can be independently achieved.

CATNIP

CATNIP uses Network Service Attachment Point Addresses (NSAPs) and is well conceived, while the routing handles are creative. Its objective is to unite three major protocol families:

- IP
- ISO-CLNP
- Novell IPX

The objective fails in its rather cumbersome complexity of attempting to be the combination of several existing network protocols. Some reviewers feel that CATNIP fundamentally maps IPv4, IPX, and SIPP addresses into NSAPs, but doesn't work with the routing problems of both the current and future Internet.

However, CATNIP has poor support for multicasting and mobility. Furthermore, it does not strictly deal with such crucial topics including security and autoconfiguration.

SIPP

SIPP, on the surface, is a very elegant protocol well fitted to concisely meet current network requirements. The SIPP Working Group is the most powerful with regards to producing solutions which meet several aspects needed to produce a total protocol outline.

The biggest point of debate with regards to SIPP is to determine if it is adequate with regards to the SIPP 64-bit address size. Even though it is possible to count over a trillion end nodes in 64 bits, most users find it difficult regarding the overall capability real-world routing plans introduced. Most users believe that 64-bit addresses don't yield sufficient space for the hierarchy needed to meet the requirements of the Internet in the long term. Besides that, due to the fact that no one has any direct experience with extended addressing and routing concepts of the type proposed in SIPP, most users feel ill at ease with this mechanism. The greatest concern was the feeling that SIPP lacked some very important security issues.

Furthermore, SIPP was not able to address the routing problems in any meaningful way. Specifically, there is no dedicated attempt at developing methods to abstract topology information or to group information about areas of the network. There is also a serious doubt regarding the complexity in the SIPP autoconfiguration plans in addition to the general issues within SIPP besides that of its own header.

TUBA

TUBA most importantly provides features based on CLNP. Besides that there is a great deal of deployment regarding CLNP-capable routers across the Internet. In addition, there was a great deal of extensive deployment regarding CLNP-capable hosts or actual networks operating CLNP. Also, there is another feature with respect to TUBA which involves the possibility for convergence of ISO and IETF networking standards. If TUBA was founded on a changed CLNP, then the advantage of an existing deployed infrastructure would be missing and that the possibility of union would be decreased.

There are several aspects regarding CLNP which were problematic, including the decreased efficiency caused by the lack of any specific word alignment of the header fields, CLNP source route, the deficiency of a flow ID field, the deficiency of a protocol ID field, and the utilization of CLNP error messages within TUBA.

The CLNP packet format or operations would have to be altered in order to resolve several of these problems. However, the overall aspect to this is that there is a significant point of contention regarding the ability of the IETF to modify the CLNP standards.

The overall aspect of TUBA is therefore difficult with regards to SIPP or CATNIP. In fact, TUBA satisfies the requirements for several abilities regarding the power to:

- Scale to large numbers of hosts
- Support flexible topologies
- Media independance
- Datagram protocol.

All in all there are significant problems in all of the outlined protocols above. Both SIPP and TUBA would function in the Internet, but each demonstrates its own problems. Most of these problems will have to be corrected before either one would be ready to replace IPv4. The other problems can then be addressed over a period of time.

The New Protocol

In looking into IPv6, we see a many strengths and weaknesses of the several IPng proposals. SIPP was a big focus for concern in retrospect. Its main points included its complexity, manageability, and feasibility. But when looking into any protocol it is important to determine if it is adequate and correct. There are several limitations of SIPP's addressing and routing model, this is most true with regards to the use of loose source routing to achieve extended addressing.

These difficulties are handled by changing the address size from 8 bytes to 16 bytes in a fixed-length, and determining optional use of serverless autoconfiguration of the 16-byte address by employing IEEE 802 address as the low-order node ID sections. In addition, they apply for higher-layer protocols which employ Internet-layer addresses as a component of connection identifiers such as TCP and require that they utilize the entire 16-byte addresses.

Suggestions for the Future

All of these specification regarding IPv6 are further illustrated in the fact that the IPv6 criteria are representative of the reasonable set of requirements for an IPng. In addition, they apply for a specific recommendation that needs to be followed by the IETF with respect to a single IPng effort.

The most important level of this topic involves the need to create a distinct IPng mechanism. Most users felt that additional research would assist in the resolution of some of the problems. However, some people felt that for a single protocol to function, it would clear the way for users to focus the resources of the IETF on finalizing its details.

18.3. LENGTH OF THE ADDRESS

One of the biggest points of debate is the IPv6 design possibilities with regard to address size and format. During the IPv6 procedure there are different methods involved with dealing with this situation.

The first involves the view that 8 bytes of address are sufficient to meet both the current and future needs of the Internet. This figure is obtained by squaring the size of the IP address space. Any increases would waste bandwidth, advance inefficient assignment, and make problems in some networks including mobiles as well as other low speed links.

Second is the outlook that 16 bytes is correct. That length handles simple autoconfiguration in addition to companies with complex internal routing topologies in combination with the global routing topology that currently exists and will exist in the long term. Third is the aspect regarding the outlook that 20 byte OSI NSAPs need to be employed in the interests of global harmonization.

Finally is the outlook that variable length address that can be smaller or larger than 16 bytes need to be used to accept all the above options. Therefore, the size of the address may be modified to the needs of the specific environment. It also makes certain that the ability to meet any future networking requirements is present.

All in all, users believed that the 16 byte fixed length addresses designated the best trade-off between efficiency, functionality, flexibility, and global qualification.

18.4. IPNG FUTURE

It is important to look at aspects where IPv6 meets the requirements established within the IPng Criteria. There is a need for a complete specification due to the fact that the base specifications for IPng are complete, however transition and address autoconfiguration are key to the protocol's future. There is something to be said about structural simplicity since it needs to be easy to explain, and uses a well-established model. With respect to scale, an address size of 128 bits effortlessly meets the requirement to address over a billion networks even with respect to the intrinsic inefficient means of address allocation for efficient routing.

There is also the issue regarding topological flexibility such that the IPng design puts no limitations on network topology excluding the limit of 255 hops. In terms of performance the ease of processing is very important as is the alignment of the fields in the headers as well as the elimination of the header checksum which permits for high performance handling of IPng data streams. With respect to providing a powerful service, IPng incorporates no inhibitors to powerful service parameters as well as the addition of packet-level authentication that permits for the securing of control and routing protocols without the need to have individual procedures.

In terms of transition, the IPng transition plan is easy and effectively deals with the transition methods which will be available in the computing community. With regards to media independence, IPng maintains IPv4's media independence such that it may be possible to utilize IPng's Flow Label in some connection that is aligned with media such as ATM.

The datagram service is where IPng preserves a datagram service as its fundamental operational mode. Therefore, it is possible that the utilization of path MTU Discovery will add complexity for the use of datagrams in some events. In terms of ease of configuration, IPng will have easy and flexible address autoconfiguration that supports a large amount of environments that range from nodes on an isolated network to nodes deep in a complex Internet. In terms of security, IPng incorporates specific methods for authentication and encryption at the internetwork layer. In addition, the security features depend on the availability of a key management system. When dealing with unique names, IPng addresses can be employed as globally unique names even though they do have topological importance.

In terms of multicast support, IPng accurately integrates it into its main structure. In terms of extensibility, the utilization function permits for the introduction of new features into IPng when required in a method that decreases the disruption of your existing network. As this happens, it includes a Flow Label that may be used to draw a distinction for requested service classes. In terms of mobility, the proposed IPv4 mobility functions will function with IPng. With respect to the control protocol, IPng incorporates the familiar IPv4 control protocol features. While tunneling support involves the encapsulation of IPng or other protocols within it.

IPng is listed here as version 6 for the next generation. However, it is now crucial to take a look into IPv6 as well as its features. IPv6 is designed is the next step from IPv4. It yields the same functions that were known in IPv4 and are kept in IPv6. Functions that didn't work, however, or not used often were removed completely or only made optional. There are also a few new features which were added where the functionality was felt be needed.

IPv6 does yield an enhanced addressing and routing capability. In fact, the IP address size is expanded from 32 bits to 128 bits. This effectively yields support for:

- A far greater amount of addressable nodes
- Increased levels of addressing hierarchy
- Easier autoconfiguration of addresses.

Families of Addresses

There are several environments in which there is at least one network protocol that has been deployed or where an extensive amount of planning effort has been seized to establish an extensive network-addressing plan. In this type of case, there may be a lure to integrate IPv6 into the environment by utilizing existing addressing plans to designate all or a portion of the IPv6 addresses. The benefit is that it allows for unified management of address space across several protocol families. The utilization of common addresses can assist in expediting transition from other protocols to IPv6.

When the existing addresses are globally unique and assigned with respect to network topology this may be an equitable method. The IETF needs to work with other organizations to create algorithms that may be used to map addresses between IPv6 and other environments. The objective for this type of mapping needs to yield an unambiguous one to one map between separate addresses.

There are several methods considered for mapping algorithms for Novell IPX addresses, some types of OSI NSAPs, E164 addresses, and SNA addresses. Each of these candidates need to be carefully inspected to make certain that their use of this type of algorithm answers more problems than it creates. In some events it may be better to suggest either a native IPng addressing plan be employed, or an IPv6 address to be used within the non-IP environment. It is advantageous to use, in conjunction with other organizations, suggestions regarding the use of non-IPv6 addresses in IPv6 environments as well as IPv6 addresses in non-IPv6 environments.

OSI NSAPs

It is important to take the following into consideration when dealing with OSI NSAPs. First, the ES-IS/IS-IS model applies a routing hierarchy down to the Area level, however not all end systems in an Area must be in the same physical subnet. IS routers which exist on different links in a specified Area exchange information regarding the end systems they can each reach directly. However, the IPv6 routing model stretch out to the subnet level, as well as all hosts in the same subnet is believed to be on the same link. When mapping a CLNP addressing plan into IPv6 format, without altering the physical topology, it may be required to add an extra level of hierarchy to endure this clash. The Area number cannot blindly be mapped as a subnet number, unless the physical network topology compares to this mapping.

Second, it is preferable that subnet addresses can be consolidated for wide area routing purposes. This is effective in decreasing the size of routing tables. Therefore, network implementors need to make certain that the address prefix employed for all of their subnets is the same, despite whether a specific subnet is utilizing an absolute IPv6 addressing scheme or one taken from a CLNP scheme as above.

Finally, some hosts have greater than one physical network interface. In the ES-IS model, an end system may have greater than one NSAP address. Each of these determines the host as a whole. This type of an end system has more than one physical interface can be cited by any of the NSAPs, and reached through any one of the physical connections. In the IPv6 model, a host may have several IPv6 addresses per interface, however each of its physical interfaces needs to have its own unique addresses. This restriction needs to be applied when mapping an NSAP addressing plan into an IPv6 addressing plan for such hosts.

18.5. THE MECHANICS

There are four separate mechanisms that are considered to be elective mechanisms. Essentially, they are not mandatory components of an IPv6 implementation, however if these types of mechanisms are required they must be implemented as listed in this chapter.

This is accomplished first by the restricted NSAPA mapping into 16-byte IPv6 address. Second, it is a truncated NSAPA used for routing. Third, the normal IPv6 address, and finally the IPv6 address is conveyed as an OSI address.

When dealing with the restricted NSAPA in a 16-byte IPv6 address for International Code Designator (ICD) and Digital Country Code (DCC), it is useful to determine that many organizations may choose several reasons not to adhere to the suggestions here promoting the redesign of their addressing plan. In fact, they may choose to use their existing OSI NSAP addressing plan without any alterations for IPv6. It is important to note that this type of choice has definite concerns with regards to routing, because it indicates that routing between such organizations and the rest of the Internet is not likely to be optimized. An organization which employs both native IPv6 addresses and NSAP addresses for IPv6 will most probably have inefficient internal routing.

There is a discrepancy between the OSI or GOSIP routing model and the IPv6 routing model. The restricted NSAPAs can be routed hierarchically down to the Area level, however they must be flat-routed within an Area. Normal IPv6 addresses can be routed hierarchically down to physical subnet link level, but they only have to be flat-routed on the physical subnet.

Packets which have a destination address are essentially a restricted NSAPA which can be routed employing any standard IPv6 routing protocol, but only as far as the Area. When the Area is composed of greater than one physical subnet reached by greater than one router, no IPv6 routing protocol can route the packet to the proper final router. There is no answer to this problem within the current IPv6 methodology. Without any type of routing protocol, either the Area number must be hierarchically structured to compare to physical subnets, or each Area must be restricted to one physical subnet.

It is important within an IPv6 network which routes may be aggregated to decrease the size of routing tables. When a subscriber is employing both normal IPv6 addresses and restricted NSAPAs, these two types of address will not group with each other, because they differ from the second most significant bit on. This indicates that there may be an extensive operational penalty for employing both types of address with existing routing technology.

Truncated NSAPA

An NSAP address is composed of routing information such as the Routing Domain and area/subnet identifiers in the form of the Area. When it is used as a destination IPv6 address, the truncated NSAPA may be perceived as an IPv6 anycast address. An anycast address can be employed to designate either an IPv6 node, or possibly even an OSI End System or Intermediate System. It can be configured to determine the endpoints of a CLNP tunnel, or it may designate a specific OSI capable system in a distinct subnet.

When a truncated NSAPA is employed as a source address, it must be defined as a unicast address and it then uniquely assigned within the IPv6 address space. When a truncated NSAPA is employed as either the source or destination IPv6 address, either an NSAPA destination option or an encapsulated CLNP packet is required to be present. It is the responsibility of the destination system to take the correct action for each IPv6 packet received. This action may involve forwarding, decapsulating, or discardarding. It may even need to return to the initial host an appropriate ICMP error message.

When the truncated NSAPA is employed to designate a router, and an NSAPA destination option is available, then it is the responsibility of that router to forward the total IPv6 packet to the proper host with respect to the Destination NSAP field in the NSAPA option. This forwarding operation may be based upon static routing information such as a manual mapping of NSAPs to IPv6 unicast addresses, or it may be collected in an automated method that is similar to the ES-IS mechanism. It may even involve extensions to the Neighbor Discovery protocol.

Truncated NSAPAs are not significant within IPv6 routing headers, and there is no method of including full NSAPAs in routing headers. Should a packet whose source address is a truncated NSAPA cause an ICMP message to be returned for any given reason, the ICMP message may be dropped rather than being returned to the source of the packet.

This is a problematic area, because if a truncated NSAPA keeps a hierarchical structure, it can be routed similarly to a restricted NSAPA. This is a party to the same difficulty concerning the contrast between Areas and subnets. In the event of a GOSIP-like NSAPA, it needs to be truncated just after the Area number. In this event, the routing considerations will be analogous to those for restricted NSAPAs, except that final delivery of the packet will rely upon the last IPv6 router being able to interpret the NSAPA destination option or an encapsulated CLNP packet.

In a standard event, there is little which can be done since the NSAPA needs to have nearly any format and may possibly have very little hierarchical content succeeding truncation. There may be many events in which truncated NSAPAs are not able to be routed throughout large regions of the IPv6 network.

Full NSAPAs

In the event of a truncated NSAPA employed as an IPv6 address other than for a CLNP tunnel, the full NSAPA needs to be carried in a destination option. The NSAPA destination option is defined here, but has no alignment requirement.

The length fields are each one octet long and are indicated in octets. The destination node needs to check the uniformity of the length fields defined as:

Option Data Length = Source NSAP Length + Dest. NSAP Length +2

In case of discrepancy, the destination node will drop the packet and send an ICMP Parameter Problem, Code 2, message to the packet's source address, pointing to the Option Data Length field. The border between the source NSAP and the destination NSAP is easily aligned on an octet boundary. When using the standard 20 octet NSAPs the complete option length is 44 bytes and the Option Data Length is 42.

When this option is used, both end systems involved need to use NSAP addresses. There is an exception in that only one of the end systems utilizes NSAP addresses, the NSAP Length field of the other needs to be set to zero in the NSAP destination option.

This destination option is employed in two events.

- An IPv6 source node utilizing normal IPv6 addresses either as a unicast address or anycast address can yield a NSAP destination option header for interpretation by the IPv6 destination node.
- An IPv6 node can utilize a truncated NSAP address as a substitute for a normal IPv6 address.

IPv6 Addresses Within an NSAPA

Should this be needed for any given reason such as to embed an IPv6 address inside a 20-octet NSAP address — then the following format needs to be used:

A particular optional use of this embedding is to indicate an IP address within the ATM Forum address format. There is an alternate possible use that would be to permit CLNP packets which encapsulate IPv6 packets to be routed in a CLNP network via the IPv6 address structure. There are numerous leading bytes of the IPv6 address that can be used as a CLNP routing prefix.

IPv6 nodes are not needed to implement this option, except for nodes employing truncated NSAPAs besides that of CLNP tunnels. To shed light upon the relationship between the first three mechanisms, remember:

- When the first byte of an IPv6 address is hexadecimal 0x02 (binary 00000010), then the other 15 bytes will possess a restricted NSAPA mapped. The reference to restricted is employed to indicate that this format is currently limited to a subset of the ICD and DCC formats.
- When the first byte of an IPv6 address is hexadecimal 0x03 (binary 00000011), then the other 15 bytes are composed of a truncated NSAPA. Either a destination option which possesses the complete NSAPA of any format or an encapsulated CLNP packet needs to be present.
- When dealing with any other format of IPv6 address, a destination option that possesses a complete NSAPA can be available.

Security

Besides their use to retain an existing addressing plan, specific other uses of restricted NSAPAs may be conceived. They may be used as an intermediate addressing plan for a network that is performing a transition from CLNP to IPv6.

They may also be used in a header translation method for dynamic translation between IPv6 and CLNP. Finally, they could also be used to permit CLNP and IPv6 traffic to share the same routing architecture within an organization.

It is important to note that their use impacts several aspects. The most important of these involves the API and DNS. When applications need to function normally, everything which has to be modified to work with IPv6 addresses has to be modified more so for full NSAPAs. The methods designated in the present document are only a small segment of the total picture.

A destination option is selected to convey full NSAPAs, demonstrating partiality to a dedicated extension header. In the event of an extension header, all IPv6 nodes would have needed to understand its syntax just in order to ignore it. However, intermediate nodes can ignore the destination option without any knowledge of its syntax. Therefore, only nodes interested in NSAPAs are required to know knowledge regarding them.

Nodes

There are two classes of IPv6 nodes:

- The first involves nodes that know only about 16 byte addresses such as restricted NSAPAs which function very much like any other IPv6 address.
- The second involves nodes that know about 20 byte NSAPAs, either as an extension of the IPv6 address space or as the CLNP address space. In either event, regions of the network which contain such nodes are connected to each other by unicast or anycast tunnels through the 16 byte address space. Routing, system configuration, and neighbor discovery in the NSAPA regions are alternative IPv6 mechanisms.

18.6. CONCLUSION

This chapter has dealt largely with NSAP mapping and then branches into a discussion regarding the fundamental aspect of the Internet Protocol next generation. This format allows you to carefully look into the realm the Internet architecture and apply the protocols outlined here into the foundation of IPv6.

The goal is to produce a common ground between the Internet and IPv6. The Internet is growing, hence the need for IPv6. But the technology needs to expand as well, hence the need to look into various aspects of each protocol.

We then take this knowledge and apply it to the future of the Internet. In closely examining IPng criteria we can effectively resolve problems with this protocol so that overall functionality then details aspects regarding address length and its overall future requirements to meet the needs of the ever growing Internetwork.

IPv6 Packet Transmission

19

19.1. INTRODUCTION

In this chapter we will look at the specifications for the frame format for transmission of IPv6 packets. There is a discussion regarding the method of forming IPv6 link-local addresses on Ethernet networks as well as detailing the content of the Source/Target Link-Layer Address option employed in the Router Solicitation, Router Advertisement, Neighbor Solicitation, and Neighbor Advertisement messages. These occur at a point when those messages are transmitted on an Ethernet. Primarily we deal with the transmission of IPv6 packets over Ethernet, FDDI, Token Ring, ARCnet, and PPP networks. Transmission of packets (and routing information) on an Ethernet network is depicted in Figure 19.1).

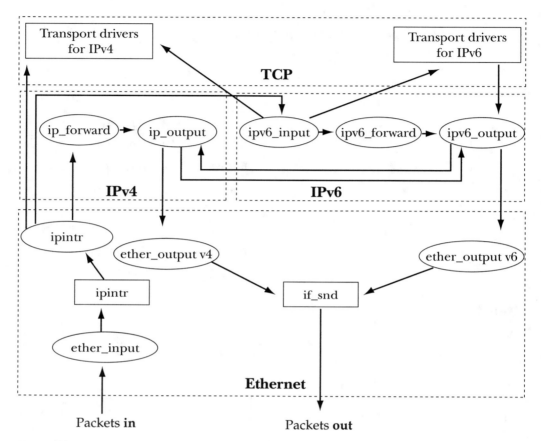

Figure 19.1. Transmission of
Packets on an Ethernet Network

19.2. FRAME FORMAT

In terms of an Ethernet, IPv6 packets are sent in standard frames. The Ethernet header is composed of the Destination and Source Ethernet addresses and the Ethernet type code, which must be composed of the value 86DD hexadecimal. The data field contains the IPv6 header, immediately succeeded by the payload, and possibly padding octets to meet the minimum frame size for Ethernet.

Maximum Transmission Unit

The default maximum transmission unit (MTU) size for IPv6 packets on an Ethernet is 1500 octets. This size may be decreased by a Router Advertisement that have an MTU option that designates a smaller MTU, or by manual configuration of each node. If a Router Advertisement is received with an MTU option designating an MTU larger than 1500, or larger than a manually configured value less than 1500, that MTU option must be disregarded.

In terms of stateless autoconfiguration and link-local addresses, it is important to look at the address token for an Ethernet interface. It is the interface's inherent 48-bit IEEE 802 address, in canonical bit order and with the octets in exact order in which they would appear in the header of an Ethernet frame. An IPv6 address prefix employed for stateless autoconfiguration of an Ethernet interface must be 80 bits in length.

Transmission on FDDI Networks

At this point we look at both the MTU and frame format for transmission of IPv6 packets on FDDI networks. This includes a method for MTU determination in the company of 802.1d bridges to other media. In addition, it also designates the method of forming IPv6 link-local addresses on FDDI networks as well as the content of the Source/Target Link-Layer Address option employed in Router Solicitation, Router Advertisement, Neighbor Solicitation, and Neighbor Advertisement messages when such messages are sent on an FDDI network.

Maximum Transmission Unit

The maximum transmission unit involved is when FDDI allows a frame length of 4500 octets (which includes a minimum of 22 octets) of datalink encapsulation when long-format addresses are employed. Deducting eight octets of LLC/SNAP header would theoretically allow the IPv6 packet in the Information field to be up to 4470 octets. Yet, it is far more preferable to permits both the variable sizes and possible future extensions to the MAC header and frame status fields. The default MTU size for IPv6 packets on an

FDDI network measures at 4352 octets. This size may be decreased by a Router Advertisement that is composed of an MTU option that determines a smaller MTU, or by manual configuration of a smaller measurement on each node. If a Router Advertisement is received with an MTU option determining an MTU bigger than the default or if the MTU is a manually configured value higher than that allowed, then the MTU option may be logged to system management. It must also then be disregarded.

Frame Format

FDDI yields both synchronous and asynchronous transmission, with the asynchronous class more segmented by the utilization of both restricted and unrestricted tokens. However, only asynchronous transmission with unrestricted tokens is needed for FDDI interoperability. As a result, IPv6 packets are transmitted in asynchronous frames employing unrestricted tokens. The power parameters impose that nodes need to be able to receive synchronous frames and asynchronous frames transmitted using restricted tokens.

IPv6 packets, in this case, are transmitted in LLC/SNAP frames via a long-format with 48 bit addresses. The data field is composed of the IPv6 header and the payload that is succeeded by the FDDI Frame Check Sequence, Ending Delimiter, and Frame Status symbols.

19.3. COMMUNICATION WITH BRIDGES

The MAC bridges that link to various media such as Ethernet and FDDI, have become very prevalent. The majority of them do IPv4 packet fragmentation as well as handle IPv4 Path MTU Discoveries while many others either do not do it, or do it wrong. The utilization of IPv6 in a bridged mixed media environment need not rely on support from MAC bridges.

To achieve proper operation when mixed media are bridged, the shortest MTU of all the media needs to be advertised by routers in an MTU option. Where there aren't any routers present, this MTU needs to be manually configured in each node that is linked to a medium with a bigger default

MTU. Multicast packets on this type of a bridged network need not be bigger than the shortest MTU of any of the bridged media. The majority of the time, the subnetwork topology will handle bigger unicast packets to be exchanged between specific pairs of nodes. To use this fact regarding high-MTU paths when available, nodes sending IPv6 on FDDI need to implement a simple means allowing for FDDI adjacency detection.

A node that implements FDDI adjacency detection (activated on an FDDI interface) must set a non-zero LLC priority in all Neighbor Advertisement, Neighbor Solicitation, and Router Advertisement for frames sent on that interface. Should FDDI adjacency detection be disabled on an FDDI interface, the priority fields of those frames need to be set to zero.

When an IPv6 frame was initially sent or traveled across Ethernet, prior to having been translated by a bridge and delivered to a node's FDDI interface, it will have a priority field zero. It is important to point out that a conforming bridge can yield a management defined Outbound User Priority parameter on each port.

Nodes that implement FDDI adjacency detection need to yield a configuration option to deactivate this facility. This option may be employed when a shorter MTU is preferred for reasons besides that which involves mixed media bridging. The default for FDDI adjacency detection therefore needs to be activated.

There is one possible use of the LLC priority field of the FC octet, and it involves the assistance of per-destination MTU determination. It would be enough for that purpose to require only those Router Advertisements, Neighbor Advertisements, and Neighbor Solicitations transmitted on FDDI to constantly have a priority value other than zero. Yet, it is far more useful to send all IPv6 packets on FDDI with a priority value other than zero.

Stateless Autoconfiguration

The address token for an FDDI interface is the interface's integrated 48-bit IEEE 802 address, in an official bit sequence that has the octet in the same sequence in which they would be shown in the header of an Ethernet frame. There is a different MAC address set manually or by software should not be used as the address token. An IPv6 address prefix employed for stateless autoconfiguration of an FDDI interface needs to be 80 bits in length.

Address Mapping

When dealing with an IPv6 packet with a DST (multicast destination address) that is sent to the FDDI multicast address whose first two octets are the value 3333 hexadecimal and whose last four octets are the last four octets of DST. They are sequences from most to least significant.

Transmission of IPv6 Packets Over ARCnet

This section deals with the particular frame format used for transmission of IPv6 packets as well as the method of forming IPv6 link-local addresses on ARCnet networks. It also specifies the content of the Source/Target Link-Layer Address option employed by the Router Solicitation, Router Advertisement, Neighbor Solicitation, and Neighbor Advertisement messages when those messages are sent on an ARCnet.

Frame Format

IPv6 packets are link-layer fragmented and then reassembled. The protocol id utilizes hex D4, which is the same that is used for IPv4. IPv6 packets are acknowledged by looking at the version number in the high half of the first octet of the data. This number is 4 for IPv4 and 6 for IPv6.

19.4. MAXIMUM TRANSMISSION UNIT

The maximum IPv6 packet length possible employing this encapsulation method is 60,480 octets. Due to the fact that this length is unrealistic, all ARCnet implementations on a designated ARCnet network will be required to agree on a shorter value. In the company of a router, this size should be decreased by a Router Advertisement that is composed of an MTU option, or by manual configuration of each node. Should a Router Advertisement be received with an MTU option determining an MTU larger than 60480, or bigger than a manually configured value that is smaller than 60480, that MTU option must be discarded.

Any implementation needs to be able to transmit and receive IPv6 datagrams as much as 576 octets in length. Furthermore, it is preferable to support IPv6 datagrams as much as 1500 octets in length.

Implementations may acquire arriving IPv6 datagrams which are bigger than their configured maximum transmission unit. In this case, it is not necessary to eliminate such datagrams.

Stateless Autoconfiguration

The address token regarding an ARCnet interface is the interface's configured 8-bit hardware address, in an official bit sequence. An IPv6 address prefix employed for stateless auto-configuration of an ARCnet interface then needs to be 120 bits in length.

Address Mapping

As ARCnet only yields one multicast address (hex 00), all IPv6 multicast packets are required to be mapped to this address.

19.5. IPV6 ACROSS PPP

Point-to-Point Protocol (PPP) yields a standard method of encapsulating Network Layer protocol information across point-to-point links. PPP also designates an extensible Link Control Protocol, and suggests a family of Network Control Protocols (NCPs) for the purpose of creating and configuring various network layer protocols.

This section designates the method for transmission of IPv6 packets over PPP links besides the Network Control Protocol (NCP) in order to set up and configure IPv6 over PPP. It also designates the method of creating IPv6 link-local addresses on PPP links.

19.6. PPP OVERVIEW

PPP has three primary components, the first involves a method for encapsulating datagrams over serial links. The second involves a Link Control Protocol (LCP) for creating, configuring, and testing the data-link connection. The final involves a family of Network Control Protocols (NCPs) for setting up and configuring various network-layer protocols.

To establish communications across a point-to-point link, each end of the PPP link needs to first transmit LCP packets to configure and test the data link. After the link has been created and alternative facilities have been negotiated as required by the LCP, PPP is required to transmit NCP packets to select and configure at least one network-layer protocol. When each of the selected network-layer protocols has been configured, datagrams from each network-layer protocol can be transmitted over the link.

The NCP for creating and configuring IPv6 over PPP is designated as the IPv6 Control Protocol or IPv6CP. The link will stay configured for communications until specific LCP or NCP packets close the link down, or until an external event happens such as a power failure, carrier drop, or something similar.

Transmitting IPv6 Datagrams

Prior to any IPv6 packets being transmitted, PPP needs to reach the Network-Layer Protocol phase, and the IPv6 Control Protocol needs to reach the Opened state. Only one IPv6 packet is encapsulated in the Information field of PPP data link-layer frames where the Protocol field designates type hex 0057, which is for IPv6.

The maximum length of an IPv6 packet sent over a PPP link is the same as the maximum length of the Information field of a PPP data link-layer frame. PPP links that handle IPv6 need to permit a minimum of 576 octets in the information field of a data link-layer frame.

19.7. PPP NETWORK CONTROL PROTOCOL

The IPv6 Control Protocol needs to support methods for configuring, enabling, and disabling the IPv6 protocol modules on both ends of the point-to-point link. IPv6CP employs the same packet exchange method as the Link Control Protocol (LCP). IPv6CP packets cannot be exchanged until PPP has reached the Network-Layer Protocol phase. In addition, IPv6CP packets received prior to this phase is reached need to be quietly eliminated.

The IPv6 Control Protocol is analogous to the Link Control Protocol except for the folowing:

- Data link-layer Protocol Field, where one IPv6CP packet is encapsulated in the Information field of PPP data link-layer frames and when the Protocol field designated type hex 8057 for IPv6 Control Protocol.
- Code field, where only Codes 1 through 7 Configure-Request, Configure-Ack, Configure-Nak, Configure-Reject, Terminate-Request, Terminate-Ack, and Code-Reject are employed. There are other codes that need to be treated as unrecognized and need to result in Code-Rejects.
- Timeouts are where IPv6CP packets cannot be exchanged until PPP has reached the Network-Layer Protocol phase. An implementation needs to be prepared to wait for Authentication and Link Quality Determination to complete before timing out waiting for a Configure-Ack or other response. It is implied that an implementation should only give up after user intervention, or a configurable amount of time.
- Configuration Option Types is when IPv6CP has a particular set of Configuration Options.

IPv6CP Configuration Options

IPv6CP Configuration Options permit the negotiation of advantageous IPv6 parameters. IPv6CP employs the same Configuration Option format designated for LCP, but has a separate set of options. When a Configuration Option is not incorporated in a Configure-Request packet, the default value for that Configuration Option is accepted.

19.8. THE INTERFACE TOKEN

This Configuration Option yields a means to negotiate a unique 32-bit interface token to be employed for the address autoconfiguration at the local end of the link. The interface token needs to be unique within the PPP link.

Prior to when this Configuration Option is requested, an implementation needs to select its tentative interface token. It is suggested that a value other than zero be selected in the most random method available. This makes certain that there is a high probability that an implementation will arrive at a unique token value. An excellent method of selecting a unique random number is to begin with a unique entity. A recommended source of singleness involves: machine serial numbers, other network hardware addresses, and system clocks.

It may not be enough to just employ a link-layer address alone as the entity. This is because it will not always be unique. Instead this entity needs to be calculated from a diverse amount of sources which are probably different even on identical systems where several sources can possibly be used at the same time.

Some excellent sources for unique or random entries are needed for the interface-token negotiation to be a success. If you are unable to find a good source of random entries it is suggested that a value of zero be employed for the interface-token sent in the Configure-Request. In this event, the PPP peer may yield a valid value other than zero interface-token in its reply. Remember, that if at least one of the PPP peer is able to create a unique random number, token negotiation will work.

Once a Configure-Request is received with the interface-token Configuration Option and the receiving peer implements this option, the received interface-token is contrasted with the interface-token of the last Configure-Request transmitted to the peer. With respect to the result of the comparison, an implementation needs to reply by one of these methods:

- Should the two interface-tokens be different, but the received interface-token measure zero, a Configure-Ack is transmitted with a interface-token value other than zero is recommended for use by the remote peer. This type of a suggested interface-token needs be of a different value from the interface-token of the last Configure-Request transmitted to the peer.
- Should the two interface-tokens be different, and the received interface-token not be a value of zero, the interface-token needs to be acknowledged. This is best illustrated when the Configure-Ack is transmitted with the requested interface-token. This indicates that the responding peer complies with the requested interface-token.

- Should the two interface-tokens be equal and not zero, a Configure-Nak is required to be sent which designates a different interface-token value other than zero recommended for use by the remote peer.
- Should these two interface-tokens be equal to zero, the interface-tokens negotiation needs to be eliminated by sending the Configure-Reject with the interface-token value set to zero. In this event a unique interface-token can not be negotiated.
- Should a Configure-Request be received with the interface-token Configuration Option and the receiving peer does not implement this option, Configure-Rej(ect) is transmitted.
- A fresh Configure-Request should not be transmitted to the peer until normal processing would allow it to be transmitted or until a Configure-Nak is received or the Restart timer runs out.
- A fresh Configure-Request should not be composed of the interface-token option if a valid interface-token Configure-Reject is received.

Receiving a Configure-Nak with a recommended interface-token that is not the same as that of the last Configure-Nak transmitted to the peer. This demonstrates a singular interface-token. In this event, a new Configure-Request must be transmitted with the token value recommended in the former Configure-Nak from the peer. However, if the received interface-token is the same as the one transmitted in the last Configure-Nak, a new interface-token needs to be selected.

In this event a new Configure-Request must be sent with the new tentative interface-token. This sequence involves the transmission of a Configure-Request, receive Configure-Request, transmit Configure-Nak, and receive Configure-Nak that can happen a few times. However, it is improbable that this will happen continuously. In fact, is it far more probable that the interface-tokens selected at either end will branch off quickly in order to complete the sequence.

If you need to institute negotiation regarding the interface-token when the peer didn't yield the option in its Configure-Request, then this option needs to be supplemented to yield a Configure-Nak. The tentative value of the interface-token provided needs to be satisfactory because the remote interface-token needs to be different from the token value chosen for the local end of the PPP link.

The subsequent Configure-Request from the peer may incorporate this option. Should the next Configure-Request not incorporate this option then the peer should not transmit another Configure-Nak with this option incorporated. Instead it needs to infer that the peer's implementation will not handle this specific option. The default, however, is that the implementation must try to negotiate the interface-token for its end of the PPP connection.

Interface-token Configurations

To best illustrate the interface-token Configuration Option format correctly it is important to detail several options at this point. The interface-token is the 32-bit interface-token that is most probably unique on the link or 0 should a good source of uniqueness not be located.

The Default Token Value is used if no valid interface token can be successfully negotiated. Instead, no default interface-token value can be assumed. The operation for recovering from such a case is not detailed. However, one alternative is to manually configure the interface token of the interface.

19.9. COMPRESSION PROTOCOL

This Configuration alternative yields a method of negotiating the utilization of a distinct IPv6 packet compression protocol. The IPv6 Compression Protocol Configuration Option is used to demonstrate the capability of receiving compressed packets. Each end of the link needs to individually request this option if bi-directional compression is preferred. The default, however, is that compression is not activated.

IPv6 compression negotiated with this option is distinct to IPv6 datagrams. However, this should not be mixed up with the compression following from negotiations through Compression Control Protocol (CCP), which possibly affects all datagrams.

The IPv6-Compression-Protocol field is two octets and demonstrates the compression protocol that is preferred. The values for this field are always equivalent to the PPP Data Link-Layer Protocol field values for that exact compression protocol. Data or the Data field is zero or more octets and is composed of additional data as designated by the specific compression protocol.

Limiting Role of IPv4 Compatible Addresses in IPv6

IPv4 compatible addresses are created to simplify the transition of IPv4 to IPv6, by using the available IPv4 address space and protocols to yield IPv6 connectivity. At the present time, they serve a function, relating to tunneling.

These functions permit isolated IPv6 nodes to emerge on the Internet and communicate with other IPv6 nodes through automatic tunneling, which needs a small amount of configuration. In addition, identifying an IPv6 router's next-hop interface address through a manually configured tunnel is also useful.

Yet, both of these tasks need implementations to consider an IPv4 tunnel as a fake (pseudo) Non-Broadcast Multiple Access (NBMA) link. In this form, all IPv4-compatible addresses are on-link to the tunnel interface and the IPv4 Internet creates one large link-layer, in which address resolution is a insignificant feature. Manually configured tunnels are employed with static routes to IPv6 prefixes. This is where the next-hop is an IPv4 compatible address on the link. Ideally, it can be viewed that IPv6 packets using IPv4 compatible addresses could be considered as using a specific type of link-local address, and the Hop Limit could be set to a value of one with no significant consequences.

The existing Transition Mechanism specification incorporates a condition to permit an IPv4 compatible address to be designated to an interface for native IPv6 communications, with all the specifications of Neighbor Discovery. It is this usage which needs to be limited because of reduced complexity and extended interoperability.

Neighbor Discovery

This designation illustrates the Neighbor Discovery (ND) protocol for IPv6. Nodes, hosts, and routers utilize Neighbor Discovery to conclude the link-layer addresses for neighbors that are known to exist on affiliated links and to instantly purge cached values that are invalid. In addition, hosts also use Neighbor Discovery to locate neighboring routers that wish to forward packets for them. In addition, nodes utilize the protocol to keep a record of which neighbors are reachable and which are not. Finally, they are there to observe changed link-layer addresses. When a router or the path to a router fails, a host then looks for functional option.

19.10. STRUCTURAL ISSUES

Even though IPv4 and IPv6 illustrate distinct network protocols, IPv4 addresses can be depicted as IPv6 addresses. However, they still designate an IPv4 endpoint that is an interface on a link connected to an IPv4 network and uses IPv4 protocols. It is possible to use them in several methods where both IPv4 and IPv6 packets on a specified interface (besides that of tunneling) can induce some interoperability difficulties. This dual type of usage also goes to unnecessary implementation complexity such as where the source address selection algorithm need not allow the usage of an IPv4-compatible address as source or destination with a global IPv6 address as either a destination or source.

Encapsulation of IPv6 packets in IPv4 packets basically uses the IPv4 network as a designated media type. There is a generic packet tunneling in IPv6, which provides the means by which one protocol may be utilized over another. In using the standard IP structure of an address that is affiliated with a specific interface it needs to be pointed out that the tunnel interface is not just an abstraction, but a genuine interface to a distinct media type that has its own rules and manners.

Finally, limiting the usage of IPv4 compatible addresses will clarify the definition, implementation, and use of this address form. In addition, it will pave the way for the IPv4 to IPv6 transition, by providing a clear designation that is easy to explain. If IPv6 is to be widely accepted and deployed, the training and educational aspects of the architecture must also be taken into account.

There are two definitions of the term Isolated Host which deal with IPv4-compatible address usage. Each is depicted in a clear manner in the following sections.

19.11. CLASS 1 ISOLATED NODES

The first explanation of an isolated host is a host which does not have an on-link IPv6 router, and which needs to encapsulate all packets to off-link destinations. However, this node is linked to an IPv6-capable Internet Service Provider (ISP) and has a provider based IPv6 address or PBA. This PBA is designated to the tunnel interface and is employed as the source address in outgoing packets. The node then has a manually configured tunnel to an ISP router. This PBA is based upon the ISP's prefix, while the IPv4 address of the IPv4 interface which has the encapsulated packets are forwarded to the ISP. Remember that the IPv4 compatible address is utilized as the link-local address in a routing protocol.

The isolated node has global IPv6 connectivity through the ISP. This isolated node has a default IPv6 route with the ISP router as next-hop. This may be designated by an IPv4-compatible address.

19.12. CLASS 2 ISOLATED NODES

Another type of isolated node is one that is not linked to an IPv6-capable ISP or does not have a PBA. However, they do possess an IPv4-compatible address and they talk with other IPv6 nodes that have IPv4 compatible addresses using end-to-end automatic tunneling. This indicates that the destination node also has an IPv4 compatible address. It also indicates that the packet will make a single hop whereas the IPv6 packet will not be forwarded.

For the nodes to communicate with other IPv6 nodes on the Internet, the remote IPv6 system needs to have automatic tunneling activated on every IPv6 node within the Internet. There is a point during the transition, however, when the IPv4 address space is all used up. At that point, the new IPv6 nodes will have the ability to achieve IPv4-compatible addresses that do automatic tunneling. These nodes will only have PBAs and will not be able to communicate with class 2 isolated nodes.

Therefore, while this class of system indicates a simple configuration, it is clear that from the initial stages that these nodes may only be able to communicate with a subset of the IPv6 network. Furthermore, the number of unreachable hosts will probably increase over time. In addition, the extended use of IPv4-compatible addresses for communications between IPv6 systems will use the IPv4 routing infrastructure, without announcing the use of IPv6 hierarchical routing. This effectively takes a toll on an already overworked service without any advantage in operational knowledge in the new technology.

It is also important to note that IPv4-compatible addresses need to be assigned to all physical interfaces that possess IPv4 addresses. There is also a problem regarding IPv4 compatible addresses that will have to be taken into special consideration with regards to name services such as DNS and DHCP. It will also deal with duplication of data and the possible resultant operational difficulties.

The Host

Hosts may have to work with several mechanisms for acquiring addresses, in addition to supporting dual address lifetime constructs. At a time when DHCP is widely used to acquire IPv4 addresses, DHCPv6 will not support the designation of IPv4 compatible addresses. Therefore, the server will not understand these types of addresses as being property of any specific client.

In addition, designating an IPv4 compatible address to the interface where IPv4 is operating may not be commonly available. When an IPv4 host utilizes SLIP, it can handle an IPv6 implementation via tunneling. However, it is not a native interface, therefore there may be other illustrations of media types that do support one protocol but not another.

The Router

There also needs to be consideration regarding the impact to IPv6 hosts. In fact, there are numerous concerns related to dual IPv6/IPv4 routers. At a time when encapsulation of IPv6 packets in IPv4 tunnels will be a an important feature of dual IPv4/IPv6 routers, it would be best to decrease the requirement for this function by having the initial host utilize automatic tunneling. The routers may then also have increased memory requirements too.

Link-Local Addresses

The interface token is used for creating IPv6 addresses of a PPP interface. They need to be negotiated in the IPv6CP section of the PPP connection setup. When there isn't any valid interface tokens that have been successfully negotiated, operations for recovering from this type of a case are not designated. One involves manually configuring the interface token of the interface. When there is an interface token that is negotiated in the IPv6CP phase of the PPP connection setup, it is repetitive to execute duplicate address detection as a segment of the IPv6 Stateless Autoconfiguration protocol.

19.13. CONCLUSION

The goal of this chapter is to acquaint you with methods of IPv6 packet transmission over Ethernet, FDDI, Token Ring, ARCnet, and PPP networks. In providing this broad overview it is helpful to gain a more global feel of the methods by which transmission occurs within IPv6.

Network Management Issues

20

20.1. INTRODUCTION

Standard IPv6 Neighbor Discovery and Address Autoconfiguration were designated for use over subnetworks where the fundamental media has a native broadcast capability. Non-Broadcast Multiple Access (NBMA) subnetworks don't have a native broadcast capability, however they are capable of concurrent connections to various nodes on an individual NBMA logical link.

The NBMA Next-Hop Resolution Protocol (NHRP) yields link-layer address resolution capability over NBMA logical links within a network-layer independent method. NHRP also provides a key function that dynamically discovers and resolves the address of the closest exit for the router of the node affiliated with a target address beyond the NBMA network section.

In this chapter we will look at the way in which IPv6 operates over NBMA media and how it depends on the use of NHRP to yield IPv6 Neighbor Discovery and IPv6 Address Autoconfiguration support. ICMPv6 messages are initially designated for standard IPv6 Neighbor Discovery, they are used for NBMA logical links. The standard IPv6 Neighbor Discovery operation is not used again because NBMA environments are beyond the area of the protocol.

The IPv6 interface token is utilized when auto-configuring an IPv6 address on a network interface. IPv6 addresses are constrained to logical network interfaces as opposed to being constrained to nodes.

20.2. DUPLICATE ADDRESS DETECTION

Duplicate Address Detection is executed with a small improvement to the NHRP protocol. The Next-Hop Resolution Protocol (NHRP) was created to provide link-layer address resolution capabilities across NBMA logical links in a network-layer independent manner. NHRP has an important discovery function by resolving the address of the closest egress router to the node linked with a target address beyond the NBMA portion of the network.

The NHRP client demonstrates whether the upper-layer destination address in the NHRP request is to be considered with a differentiator which is unique. To accomplish this goal, a bit is added to the Mandatory section of the proper NHRP messages. When this is set, this bit designates that a registration of this upper-layer to NBMA address binding is unique. This unique qualifier bit needs to be recorded in the (Next-Hop Client/Server) NHC/NHS cache for the specified entry.

Any effort to register a binding between the upper-layer address and an NBMA address when this bit is set needs to be rejected with a new NAK code of Internetworking Layer Address Already Registered. If this bit is set in an NHRP Resolution Request and several entries exist within the NHS cache, then only the Next-Hop Entry with this bit set will be returned. It is important to note that even if this bit was set at registration time, there can still be several Next-Hop Entries that might meet the NHRP Resolution Request due to the fact that an entire subnet can be registered through using of the Prefix Length extension.

20.3. NEIGHBOR ADDRESS RESOLUTION

The NBMA Next-Hop Resolution Protocol (NHRP) is used to find the lower-layer address for a specified IPv6 destination reached through an NBMA interface. This increases technology usability due to the fact that NHRP is an existing technology which is created to handle several upper-layer protocols via NBMA networks.

The operation for initial bootstrapping, neighbor discovery, and redirect handling are designated in the next section of this chapter in an effort to illustrate a clear relationship and sequencing between the IPv6 Discovery messages and the NHRP messages. When dealing with host bootstrap processing, the initial Virtual Circuit (VC) to the NHS can be established using information manually configured into the node or employing some type of media-specific group address.

At first, the host establishes link-local IPv6 addresses through the above procedures to create the local-identification token of the link-local address. The host records this link-local IPv6 address with its NHS by transmitting its link-local IPv6 address and its associated lower-layer NBMA address in an NHRP Registration Request message which is composed of a Responder Address Extension to the NHS. The NHS then operates on this message and transmits a proper NHRP Registration Reply that incorporates its unicast address in the extension. When the registration is successful, then the NHS reply will possess a NAK code of 0. In any other event, the NHS reply will demonstrate why the registration did not succeed.

It is at this point that the host has now registered its link-local IPv6 address with the NHS. The host then transmits an NHRP Resolution Request that is composed of the host's link-local address as the IPv6 Source Address as well as the link-local all-routers multicast address as the IPv6 Destination Address to the Next-Hop Server.

The NHS then replies with an NHRP Resolution Reply which has all of the cached bindings between the link-local all-routers multicast IPv6 address as well as all associated lower-layer NBMA addresses. At this point, the host now knows the lower-layer NBMA addresses for the IPv6 routers on its NBMA logical link.

When NHS is also the IPv6 router for the host's NBMA logical link, then the router needs to instantly transmit a unicast IPv6 Router Advertisement to the requesting host. When there isn't any IPv6 Router Advertisement received, the host needs to transmit an IPv6 Router Solicitation message to each known IPv6 router for its NBMA logical link. Those routers will then transmit a unicast IPv6 Router Advertisement back to the requesting host. The IPv6 Router Solicitation message needs to be transmitted as a unicast lower-layer message even though it can possess the link-local scope all-routers multicast address as the IPv6 Destination Address. Routers need to use the IP Authentication Header to authenticate IPv6 Router Advertisement messages at any point when the router has a proper IP Security Association with the destination node for the IPv6 Router Advertisement.

Now, the host knows the unicast IPv6 addresses of its routers, the lower-layer address of its routers, its routing prefixes, and if it must perform stateful IPv6 configuration. When stateless IPv6 autoconfiguration was designated by the received Router Advertisements, the host can then configure its global IPv6 addresses and uses the NHRP Registration Request to record its global IPv6 addresses with the NHS.

When stateful autoconfiguration is designated in the IPv6 Router Advertisement, then the host needs to adhere to the stateful configuration operation involved with DHCPv6. This effectively uses NHRP as needed to acquire lower-layer addresses for IPv6 addresses. When its global IPv6 addresses are configured, the node utilizes the NHRP Registration Request message to record those addresses with the NHS.

20.4. HOST PROCESSING

The NHRP client resolves anycast addresses utilizing the NHRP Resolution Request message to the NHS. This effectively deals with the target IPv6 address as an anycast address. When NHRP is used to resolve an IPv6 Anycast address, the NHRP Additional Next-Hop Entries Extension is incorporated with the NHRP Resolution Reply if greater than one IPv6 node has recorded that IPv6 Anycast address with the NHS.

The host can also set up and sustain connections with all routers for the goal of transmitting Router Solicits and receiving Router Advertisements if it so desires. When it goes this route, then the host needs to establish or remove connections every so often in an effort to support recurrent transmissions of IPv6 Router Solicit messages and reception of affiliated IPv6 Router Advertisement messages.

The time between IPv6 Router Solicit messages indicates how fast a host can respond to changes in the IPv6 routing prefix. In fact, the default interval between IPv6 Router Solicit messages can be no shorter than the minimum time between unsolicited IPv6 Router Advertisements.

Router Bootstrap Processing

At first, the router establishes link-local IPv6 addresses with the above operations to create the local-identification token of the link-local address. At this time, the router configures the globally routable IPv6 addresses on those interfaces that handle IPv6 routing. Thus due to the fact that it is a router, it already recognizes its global routing prefixes.

The router then utilizes the NHRP Registration Request messages to record each of its globally routable addresses with the NHS. When there isn't any available standards-track NHS synchronization method, the router needs to record its IPv6 addresses for a specified NBMA logical link with each known NHS for that NBMA logical link. The router cannot record an IPv6 address that is the property of one NBMA logical link with the NHS for a different NBMA logical link.

At this point, the router records each of the IPv6 interface's lower-layer NBMA address as well as the IPv6 link-local all-routers multicast address with each proper NHS. This effectively handles the unique qualifier bit that is not set in the NHRP Registration Request message. Also, the router cannot register an interface's lower-layer address, IPv6 link-local all-routers multicast address pair with an NHS which does not promote that interface's NBMA logical link.

Neighbor Address Discovery

When bootstrapped utilizing the procedure outlined above, the host is required to use the NHRP Resolution Request. The NHRP Resolution Response messages to acquire the lower-layer address that is associated with any IPv6 Unicast Adress (the IPv6 Unicast Address Format is illustrated in Figure 20.1) not already having a lower-layer address recognized by the host. In the event where the target IPv6 address is affiliated with a node that is not on the linked NBMA network, NHRP will reply with the lower-layer NBMA address of the nearest exit router to the node affiliated with the target IPv6 address. Therefore, short-cut routing is automatically yielded to IPv6 nodes connected through NBMA.

Neighbor Unreachability Detection

Even though the IPv6 Neighbor Solicit and Neighbor Advertisement messages are substituted by NHRP messages for the intention of designating the lower-layer address of neighbors, the Neighbor Solicit and Neighbor

Bits	3	5	n	56-n	64
	010	Registry ID	Provider ID	Subscriber ID	Intra-Subscriber

Figure 20.1. IPv6 Unicast Address Format

Advertisement messages are registered for use in Neighbor Unreachability Detection (NUD).

When the IPv6 Neighbor Solicit and Neighbor Advertisement exchanges illustrate that a remote node has become unreachable, then the other node needs to transmit a NHRP Resolution Request message to try to conclude the current reachability of the remote node.

Throughout NBMA networks, the Neighbor Solicit and Neighbor Advertisement messages are always unicast. In addition, they are only employed for the intention of Neighbor Unreachability Detection succeeding the reality of the neighbor that was set-up through NHRP. The Source Link-Layer Address Option can be used with Neighbor Solicit or Neighbor Advertisement messages via NBMA networks. NHRP needs to be utilized for the primary measurement of lower-layer addresses with the exception of a received ICMPv6 Redirect that is composed of a Target Link-Layer Address Option or for the event where manual configuration is provided. Neighbor Solicit and Neighbor Advertisement messages transmitted over NBMA networks can neither possess either the unspecified address nor a multicast address.

Security

As opposed to standard IPv6 Neighbor Discovery, NHRP is not created on the foundation of IP. This design determination was created so that NHRP can be used for multi-protocol networks. Furthermore, it is not restricted to IPv4 or IPv6 networks, even though this prevents the utilization of IP security mechanisms to authenticate NHRP. Finally, this is not a reduction in security relative to standard IPv6 Neighbor Discovery due to the fact that NHRP incorporates its own cryptographic authentication methods.

The reception of unauthenticated NHRP response messages can be forerunners of denial of service attacks. The utilization of the IP Authentication Header for IPv6 traffic can prevent an IP-layer host from faking attacks that would otherwise be possible if a node accepted unauthenticated NHRP response messages.

The acceptance of unauthenticated ICMPv6 Neighbor Discovery messages can also be forerunners to various attacks. The utilization of the IP Authentication Header can prevent or extensively curtail many of these attacks.

20.5. IPV4 COMPARISON

The IPv6 Neighbor Discovery protocol is associated with a combination of the IPv4 protocols ARP, ICMP Router Discovery, and Redirect. When dealing with IPv4 there is no standard method for Neighbor Unreachability Detection, even though Hosts Requirements designate some possible algorithms for Dead Gateway Detection that is a portion of the problems Neighbor Unreachability Detection tackles.

The Neighbor Discovery protocol yields several enhancements over the IPv4 set of protocols including Router Discovery. Router advertisements convey link-layer addresses. In addition, there is no extra packet exchange required to solve the router's link-layer address. Router advertisements also convey prefixes for a link.

Router advertisements activate Address Autoconfiguration. They may also advertise an MTU for hosts to utilize on the link. This makes certain that all nodes use the same MTU value on links that do not possess a clearly designated MTU. Address resolution multicasts are sent to over 4 billion multicast addresses. This significantly decreases address resolution that pertains to interrupts on nodes besides that of the target. Even more so, non-IPv6 machines need not be interrupted.

Redirects possess the link-layer address of the new first hop. Also, individual address resolution is not required upon receiving a redirect. Several prefixes can be affiliated with the same link. The default for hosts is to acquire all on-link prefixes from Router Advertisements. Yet, routers may be configured to eliminate some or all prefixes from Router Advertisements. In this type of event, hosts believe that destinations are off-link and transmit traffic to routers. At this point a router can then send redirects as needed.

As opposed to IPv4, the recipient of an IPv6 redirect believes that the new next-hop is on-link. In IPv4, a host ignores redirects designating a next-hop that is not on-link with respect to the link's network mask. It is believed to be important on non-broadcast and shared media links where it is not possible for nodes to understand all prefixes for on-link destinations.

Neighbor Unreachability Detection is a segment of the base code which extensively increases the robustness of packet delivery in the residence of failing routers, partially failing routers, or partitioned links and nodes which alter their link-layer addresses. Mobile nodes can move off-link without compromising any connectivity illustrated by stale ARP caches.

As opposed to ARP, Neighbor Discovery can observe half-link failures via Neighbor Unreachability Detection and effectively avert transmitting traffic to neighbors where there is no two-way connectivity. As opposed to IPv4 Router Discovery the Router Advertisement messages are not composed of a preference field. The preference field is not necessary to support routers of different stability. Instead, Neighbor Unreachability Detection will observe dead routers and change to a working unit. The utilization of link-local addresses to uniquely designate routers for the purpose of Router Advertisement and Redirect messages makes it feasible for hosts to sustain the router associations in the event of the site renumbering to use new global prefixes.

The Link-Local Address Change

The link-local address on a router may change rarely, if at all. Nodes that receive Neighbor Discovery messages use the source address to determine who the sender is. When several packets from the same router are composed of various source addresses, nodes will believe they come from various routers causing unwanted actions. This can best be illustrated by a node which will ignore Redirect messages that are thought to have been transmitted by a router besides that of the current first-hop router. Therefore, the source address employed in Router Advertisements transmitted by a specific router needs to be the same as the target address in a Redirect message when it redirects to that router.

When a router changes the link-local address for one of its interfaces, it needs to communicate this information to hosts regarding this change. The router must multicast a few Router Advertisements from the old link-local address with the Router Lifetime field set to 0. In addition, it also needs to multicast a few Router Advertisements from the new link-local address. The intended effect is the same as though one interface stops being an advertising interface, and another one begins to be an advertising interface.

Initializing the Interface

At a time when a multicast-capable interface is activated, the node needs to join the all-nodes multicast address on that interface in addition to the solicited-node multicast address that is affiliated with each of the IP addresses designated to the interface. The set of addresses assigned to an interface may change periodically.

Also, new addresses can be added and old addresses may be removed. In this event, the node needs to join and leave the solicited-node multicast address which is affiliated with the new and old addresses. Remember that several unicast addresses may map into the same solicited-node multicast address. However, a node cannot leave the solicited-node multicast group until all designated addresses affiliated with that multicast address has been removed.

Transmitting Neighbor Solicitations

At a point when a node has a unicast packet to transmit to a neighbor, yet doesn't know the neighbor's link-layer address — it executes what is called address resolution. In terms of multicast capable interfaces this involves establishing a Neighbor Cache entry in the *incomplete* state and sending a Neighbor Solicitation message targeted at the neighbor. The solicitation is transmitted to the solicited-node multicast address affiliated with the target address.

When the source address of the packet instigating the solicitation is the same as one of the addresses assigned to the outgoing interface - that address needs to be placed in the IP Source Address of the outgoing solicitation. In any other case, any one of the addresses designated to the interface needs to be used. The utilization of the prompting packet's source address makes certain that the recipient of the Neighbor Solicitation installs the IP address in its

Neighbor Cache so that it will probably be used in future return traffic belonging to the instigating the node.

If the solicitation is transmitted to a solicited-node multicast address, the sender needs to include its link-layer address as a Source Link-Layer Address option. In any other event, the sender needs to incorporate its link-layer address as a Source Link-Layer Address option. This includes the source link-layer address in a multicast solicitation that is required to provide the target with an address that it can send the Neighbor Advertisement.

Redirect

It is at this point that we look at the features that pertain to the sending and processing of Redirect messages. Redirect messages are transmitted by routers to redirect a host to a better first-hop router for a certain destination or to communicate with hosts whose destination is a neighbor.

A router needs to be able to designate the link-local address for each of its neighboring routers so as to make certain that the target address in a Redirect message designates the neighbor router by its link-local address. When dealing with static routing this needs to indicate that the next-hop router's address must be determined utilizing the link-local address of the router. When dealing with dynamic routing, this requirement indicates that all IPv6 routing protocols need to exchange the link-local addresses of neighboring routers.

Security

Neighbor Discovery is the target of attacks that make IP packets flow to unexpected places. These types of attacks can be used to cause denial of service, and they may also permit nodes to intercept and possibly modify packets destined for other nodes. IPv6 reduces the exposure to these types of threats when there isn't any authentication by ignoring Neighbor Discovery (ND) packets received from off-link senders.

The trust model for redirects is analogous to the one within IPv4. A redirect is accepted only if received from the same router which is currently being employed for that destination. Furthermore, it is normal to trust the routers on the link. When a host has been redirected to another node such as where the destination is on-link, there is no way to stop the target from sending another redirect to some other destination.

The protocol doesn't have a means by which to designate which neighbors are allowed to transmit a specific type of message. This type may include Router Advertisements such as any neighbor that can even be present during authentication. It can transmit Router Advertisement messages and effectively have the ability to cause denial of service. In addition, any neighbor can transmit proxy Neighbor Advertisements in addition to unsolicited Neighbor Advertisements as a possible denial of service attack.

Neighbor Discovery protocol packet exchanges can be authenticated via the IP Authentication Header. A node needs to include an Authentication Header when transmitting Neighbor Discovery packets if a security association for use with the IP Authentication Header exists for the destination address. The security associations may have been established through manual configuration or through the procedure of a key management protocol.

Received Authentication Headers in Neighbor Discovery packets must be verified as being correct. Furthermore, packets with incorrect authentication need to be ignored. It may be possible for the system administrator to configure a node to ignore any Neighbor Discovery messages which are not authenticated by either the Authentication Header or Encapsulating Security Payload. The IP Security Architecture and Encapsulating Security Payload handle confidentiality issues.

Multi-homed Hosts

There are a several mitigating issues that emerge when Neighbor Discovery is employed by hosts that possess several interfaces. If a multi-homed host receives Router Advertisements on all of its interfaces, it will have acquired information regarding on-link prefixes for the addresses existing on each link. When a packet needs to be transmitted through a router, choosing the incorrect router can cause a poorly functioning path. Some of the points to take into account include the fact that for the router to transmit a redirect, it needs to determine that the packet it is forwarding was initially from a neighbor.

One way of testing this is to contrast the source address of the packet to the list of on-link prefixes affiliated with the interface for which the packet was received. When the initial host is multi-homed the source address it employs may be the property of an interface besides that of the interface that is was transmitted from. In this event, the router will not transmit redirects, and poor routing performance is possible. The way this can be redirected is that the transmitting host needs to transmit packets out the interface affiliated with the outgoing packet's source address. Remember that this issue doesn't arise with non-multi-homed hosts as they only have an individual interface.

When the chosen first-hop router does not possess a route for the destination, it will not be able to deliver the packet. Yet, the destination may be reachable through a router on one of the other interfaces. Neighbor Discovery does not address this event, and in fact it does not emerge in the non-multi-homed events either. Even at the point in which the first-hop router does have a route for a destination, there may be a better route through another interface. There is no mechanism that exists for the multi-homed host to observe this event.

Should a multi-homed host not be able to receive Router Advertisements on one or more of its interfaces, it will not recognize which destinations are on-link on the affected interfaces. Some of the problems which can occur is that if no Router Advertisement is received on any interfaces, a multi-homed host will not have any method of recognizing which interface to transmit packets onto. This applies to on-link destinations as well. There are analogous conditions in the non-multi-homed host case, where a node considers all destinations as existing on-link, and communication then continues.

When dealing with the multi-homed case, more information is required in order to choose the correct outgoing interface. Optionally, a node needs to try to perform address resolution on all interfaces. This action involves extensive complexity that is not available in the non-multi-homed host case.

When Router Advertisements are received on some of the interfaces, a multi-homed host could decide to only transmit packets out on the interfaces for which it has received Router Advertisements. It is believed here that routers on those other interfaces will have the ability to route packets to their final destination. This is true even when those destinations exist on the subnet on which the sender connects, but doesn't have any on-link prefix information. If this is false, communication would not succeed, but even if true, packets will travel a less than perfect pathway.

IPv6 over ATM

This section deals with several models in the IP arena, and synthesizes a broad solution of IPv6 ND over ATM that supports cut-through routing without needing large scale multicasting of ND messages around an ATM network. In fact this section looks at how IPv6 over ATM interfaces use a MARS derived multicast server mechanism to distribute discovery messages throughout their Logical Link.

The IPv6 over ATM model designated in this chapter sustains the complete definition of the IPv6 protocols. There are no changes necessary for the IPv6 Network Layer. Due to the fact that the security association is not changed for ATM, this framework sustains all of the IPv6 security operations and features. This pertains to IPv6 nodes that choose their replies to solicitations based on security information in the same way as other data-links. This effectively sustains the operations of Neighbor Discovery because the solicited node chooses its reply to a given solicitation. Therefore, ATM is invisible to the network layer, except in an event where extra services are provided.

20.6. ADDRESS RESOLUTION

An IPv6 host executes address resolution by transmitting a Neighbor Solicitation to the solicited-node multicast address of the target host. The Neighbor Solicitation message is composed of a Source Link-Layer Address Option set to the soliciting node's ATM address on the Link-Layer (LL).

At least one node will receive the Neighbor Solicitation message. This is dependent on the type of Multicast Address Resolution Servers (MARS) (which is used with IP multicasting over ATM) and whether it is augmented or not. Should the receiving node be the target of the Neighbor Solicitation it will update its Neighbor Cache with the soliciting node's ATM address that is a part of the Neighbor Solicitation message's Source Link-Layer Address.

The solicited IPv6 host will reply to the Neighbor Solicitation with a Neighbor Advertisement message transmitted to the IPv6 unicast address of the soliciting node. The Neighbor Advertisement message will be composed of a Target Link-Layer Address Option set to the solicited node's ATM address on the LL.

The solicited node's IPv6/ATM driver will be sent to the Neighbor Advertisement and the soliciting node's link-layer address from the IPv6 network layer.

When dealing with destinations that are not currently considered to be Neighbors, a host transmits the packets to its default router. The egress router from a Logical Link needs to detecting the existence of an IP packet flow through it which can then take advantage of a cut-through connection. As it proceeds to forward the flow's packets in a standard manner, the router begins an NHRP query for the flow's destination IP address.

There are some very specific advantages outlined here which involve the IPv6 stacks on hosts which do not implement individual ND protocols for each link-layer technology. When the destination of a flow is solicited as a transient neighbor, the returned ATM address will be the one it selects when the flow was initially set up through hop-by-hop processing.

Logical Links

IPv6 is composed of a concept of on-link and off-link. Neighbors are those nodes which are determined as being on-link and whose link-layer addresses may be found using Neighbor Discovery.

Neighbor Solicitations transmitted for the goal of Neighbor Unreachability Detection are unicast to the specified Neighbor. Duplicate Address Detection is only needed within the link-local scope, which in this case is the Link-Local scope. Transient Neighbors are beyond the scope of the LL. No specific interaction is needed between the mechanism for creating a path through and the mechanism for detection of duplicate link local addresses.

20.7. TRANSMITTING DATA

When the IPv6 over ATM layer is provided with a packet from the local IPv6 Network Layer, it has to decide whether the packet that is being sent to either a unicast or multicast link-layer address. When a node is provided with an IPv6 Network Layer unicast packet to transmit, the node must first map the next hop address to a point-to-point virtual circuit (PtP VC) over which the packets are to be transmitted. At least, the mapping may be founded on the destination address. However, it may also incorporate the flow label information to promote handling quality of service based flows.

20.8. RECEIVING DATA

All IPv6 packets received on any unicast PtP VC are easily de-encapsulated and sent up to the IPv6 Network later. The IPv6 network layer then decides how the incoming packet is to be supported.

As opposed to IPv4 over ATM mechanisms such as Classical IP and NHRP which place calls from a transmitting node towards the receiving node, IPv6 will make receiving nodes place calls towards transmitting nodes in the most common case. This is a normal consequence of the way in which IPv6 resolves data-link addresses. In all cases, it is the transmission of a unicast packet by any node which will cause that node to call the destination or next hop node.

When one node in an LL has a packet to transmit to another node in the same LL, it will first execute a Neighbor Discovery on the destination address. This is executed to resolve the IPv6 destination address into a link-layer address which the transmitter can then use to send unicast packets. The Neighbor Discovery operation is executed by the transmitting node sending a Neighbor Solicitation packet to the proper solicited-node multicast address affiliated with the destination or next hop address for the outgoing packet. When the solicited node receives this packet it will reply with a Neighbor Advertisement packet which it will unicast to the soliciting node.

Due to the fact that the Neighbor Solicitation packet is composed of the data-link address of the soliciting node, the solicited node has all the information it needs to unicast the Neighbor Advertisement. Therefore, since the solicited node is usually the first to transmit a unicast packet in any exchange between two nodes, it will be the one which will start the setup of the PtP VC between the two.

20.9. CONCLUSION

It is fitting now that we have discussed several aspects which looks into the overall aspect of IPv6 to end with issues involving the most prevalent issue on many people's minds with regards to security. It is fair to say that all current IPv6 security mechanisms will work without modification for ATM. This deals with both authentication and encryption for both Neighbor Discovery protocols as well as the exchange of IPv6 data packets.

We have looked into the frame format for transmission of IPv6 packets as well as the method of creating IPv6 link local addresses over IPv4 networks. In addition, we see specifications regarding the content of the Source/Target Link-Layer Address option utilized in the Router Solicitation, Router Advertisement, Neighbor Solicitation, and Neighbor Advertisement messages as well as when those messages are transmitted on an IPv4 network.

The support for this method is to permit isolated IPv6 hosts, existing on a physical link which have no directly connected IPv6 router, to become completely functional IPv6 hosts by utilizing an IPv4 network as its virtual local link. Minimally, one IPv6 router utilizing the same method needs to be connected to the same IPv4 network if IPv6 routing to other links is required.

IPv6 hosts connected using this method neither need IPv4 compatible addresses nor configured tunnels. Using this method, IPv6 achieves a great deal of independence with regards to the structural links as it can step over many hops of IPv4 subnets.

While the majority of issues raised in this book do not present any new security risks. It is important to note that implementors need to be aware that besides possible attacks against IPv6, security attacks against IPv4 must also be taken into consideration.

Using IP security at both IPv4 and IPv6 levels must be avoided to promote an efficient operation. This is best illustrated by that fact that if IPv6 is running encrypted, encryption of IPv4 would be repetitive except if traffic analysis is perceived a threat. When IPv6 is running authenticated, then authentication of IPv4 will add hardly anything. On the contrary, IPv4 security will not protect IPv6 traffic when it leaves the IPv6-over-IPv4 domain. Therefore, implementing IPv6 security is necessary even if IPv4 security is obtainable.

Index

Stewart S. Miller is a well-renowned analyst, consultant, and author. His work with many Fortune 500 companies has placed him at the top of his field. He is President and CEO of Executive Information Services, a research and consulting firm that has consistently demonstrated the ability to increase its clients' investing power and provide a unique and fresh insight into all IT marketing trends. Mr. Miller's research and analysis strategy reports have become an invaluable resource for his clients. Best known as an "efficiency expert," Mr. Miller has ascertained success for his clients' endeavors and is an integral part of any mission-critical IT decision-making process.

Executive Information Services
1-800-IT-MAVEN
(1-800-486-2836)

Specializing in All IT Industry Sectors
Writing Computer Industry News and Analyses for Decision-Makers

• White Papers and Analyses	• Year 2000 Solutions	• Marketing Brochures
• Corporate Profiles	• INTERNET Trends	• Enterprise Solutions

Executive Information Services is a premier value-added information provider. Our specialty is in computer industry analysis. We cover a multitude of topics and write trade magazine articles, newsletters, journals, technical reports, and books.

For *analytical writing excellence* to create the "right" research and analysis for your information, technical, or marketing needs, contact:

Mr. Stewart S. Miller
President and CEO
Executive Information Services
Phone: 1-800-IT-MAVEN
Fax: 1-888-IT-MAVEN
E-mail: Miller@ITMaven.com

Other Books from Digital-Press

Microsoft Exchange Server V5.0: Planning, Design and Implementation
by Tony Redmond
1997 728pp pb 1-55558-189-7

Sendmail: Theory and Practice
by Frederick M. Avolio and Paul Vixie
1995 200pp pb 1-55558-127-7

Setting Up A Web Server
by Simon Collin
1997 200pp pb 1-55558-174-9

TCP/IP Explained
by Philip Miller
1997 450pp pb 1-55558-166-8

X.400 and SMTP: Battle of the E-mail Protocols
by John Rhoton
1997 207pp pb 1-55558-165-X

. . . .

Detailed information on these and all other Digital Press titles may be found in the Digital Press catalog(Item #400). To request a copy, call 1-800-366-2665. You can also visit our web site at: http://www.bh.com

These books are available from all good bookstores or in case of difficulty call: 1-800-366-2665 in the U.S. or +44-1865-310366 in Europe.

E-Mail Mailing List

An e-mail mailing list giving information on latest releases, special promotions, offers and other news relating to Digital Press titles is available. To subscribe, send an e-mail message to majordomo@world.std.com
Include in message body (not in subject line): subscribe digital-press